The Hegelian Aftermath

HENRY SUSSMAN is associate professor of comparative literature and associate dean of arts and letters at the State University of New York at Buffalo. He is editor of the *Glyph* volumes published by Johns Hopkins and author of *Franz Kafka: Geometrician of Metaphor* (also available from Johns Hopkins).

The Hegelian Aftermath

READINGS IN HEGEL, KIERKEGAARD, FREUD, PROUST, AND JAMES

Henry Sussman

THE JOHNS HOPKINS UNIVERSITY PRESS
Baltimore and London

The Johns Hopkins University Press, Baltimore, Maryland 21218
The Johns Hopkins Press Ltd., London

Library of Congress Cataloging in Publication Data

Sussman, Henry.
The Hegelian aftermath.

Includes bibliographical references and index.
1. Hegel, Georg Wilhelm Friedrich, 1770–1831.
Phaenomenologie des Geistes. 2. Spirit.
3. Conscience. 4. Truth. 5. Knowledge, Theory of.
6. Philosophy in literature. I. Title.
B2929.S95 1982   190   82–47971
ISBN 0–8018–2852–X   AACR2

For Tamara and Nadia Rebecca

CONTENTS

The Hegelian Aftermath

Introduction:
From Philosophy to Poetics

Outside or Inside?

No question is more decisive to the contemporary critical wars that rage around us than the one that plays on the border between the outside and the inside.[1] Is an "outside" to the conventions and practices of traditional philosophy possible? If so, what are its qualities and extent? How long and under what conditions does the "outside" of speculative philosophy remain detached and autonomous from the "inside"? Can the "outside" of Western metaphysics resist a relapse back within the system from which it separates? Does the "inside" in any sense preempt the radicality that the outside would claim? In some final sense, are the "outside" and "inside" situated on the same side of the border, or are they fated to a persistent relation of alterity?

Many of our most pressing concerns hang in the balance of this fundamental question regarding demarcation and its corollaries. The uses, motives, and procedures of literary criticism, for example, are at stake. A criticism confined to the interior of conceptual acceptability merely reiterates the known etiquettes of philosophy. It establishes the "truth," validity, derivation, representability, or formal esthetics of the artifact. The suggestion of an "outside" to systematic thought carries with it a deviation from these acceptable critical and scholarly functions. The critical text enters a collusion with that element of its esthetic occasion which is beyond the "inside." In this way, criticism passes from a reinforcement of scholarly propriety to a celebration of that for which scholarship is not equipped. Not merely the thrust of the critical vehicle but also its constitution is geared for the "outside." Gone are the reassuring measures of simplicity and verifiability. A criticism admitting and accommodating an "outside" to the system it once comprised is receptive to the inconsequentiality of the artifact— and assimilates within itself jokes, double meanings, and breaches of logic and derivation.

Yet if the notion of a distinct "outside" is merely a Fata Morgana, an heuristic device ultimately regressing to the interior, what does this imply for a reprobate criticism? Even if the foyer between the systematic outside and inside some day becomes open, free, and civil, criticism is unlikely ever to return to a purely subordinate function, to the service of derivation, authenticity, logic, or truth. Although in some senses a fictive construct, the "outside" has already reified itself in the new devices and games available to criticism, pleasures which once enjoyed, will not be relinquished. Wherever it situates itself, criticism is not again to be contained. If not a "real" divide, the border between the "outside" and the "inside" offers endless possibilities for play.

Enter Hegel

Let the noted and ponderous German philosopher Georg Friedrich Wilhelm Hegel (1770–1831) serve as an instance of the exasperation accompanying borders. In certain regards, no thinker could be more exemplary of a systematic "inside" to Western thought. By means of a comprehensive and striking *formal* expertise, Hegel manages to coordinate the technical achievements of occidental philosophy with its most sensitive topics of concern. Consistent with the ideology of organicism that he expounds, Hegel effects a continuity between the techniques of philosophical speculation and the fundaments of Western theology, idealism, and teleology. If a certain monumental quality attaches to the thought or name of Hegel, this is by virtue of the dual nature of his prodigy, the formal virtuosity that accompanies his cultural omniscience.

Yet even the pivotal works of this most central and consummating thinker are invaded and corrupted by the systematic "outside." As we will have occasion to observe in our discussion of Hegel's *Phenomenology of Spirit*, a very unsystematic arbitrariness creeps into the basic preconditions for abstraction. Hegel arrives at the hierarchical divide separating the sensible from the supersensible only by acts of considerable conceptual violence. In the *Phenomenology of Spirit*, Hegel may place his forced twists and leanings at the service of a smooth-running machine of logic and abstraction, but the blunt force involved in this application points in the direction of another, less domesticated realm, toward a world whose only principles are indeterminacy and linguistic copulation. Ironically, it is by virtue of operating so well and efficiently that the Hegelian thought machine discloses its underlying arbitrariness.

The "mainstream" Hegel, the Hegel at the very center of the institutional as well as conceptual *train* of Western civilization, is, then, never other than a divided or split Hegel, whose linguistic apprehensions belie the propriety of his hypothetical systems. And if the very paragon and consummator of Western civilization is hopelessly torn apart, what of his followers, for whom internal conflict and paralysis became explicit themes?

A dual cosmology, under the gravitational fields of both internal logic and the marginal arbitrariness of language, not only organizes Hegel's discourse but dominates the periods known as "the nineteenth century" and "modernism." This is a historical statement, one belonging to the necessities of the "inside" but also questioning the status of the innovations ascribed to the nineteenth and early twentieth centuries, whether "realism" or "vorticism."

The momentous theoretical and fictive works of the nineteenth and twentieth centuries *follow* Hegel in more senses than one. Not only are the Hegelian *themes* of destiny and sublimation important, but an entire battery of formal tropes, including bifurcation, inversion, reciprocity, and circularization, characterizes the workings of a wide range of major literary and theoretical texts. The influence of Hegel—direct or oblique, positive or negative—upon such writers as Kierkegaard, Nietzsche, Freud, Henry James, and Kafka is unmistakable. Whether we attribute to Hegel the power of originality or merely skill at gathering, this momentum is of great historical consequence. History might seem to squelch the agonizing problem of borders which Hegel broached by elevating this grand personage, in the spirit of *Aufhebung*, above the plane of indeterminacy.

There is, indeed, an historical dimension to my approach. I make no pretense of concealing the implicit veneration, resistance, or both maintained toward Hegel by those who followed in his aftermath. I dissimulate neither the historical thrust of my argument nor the assembly of formal operations that makes this history work.

But what is the history made possible by figures of speech and argumentation rather than personalities, eras, or influences?

This study takes Hegel as the central figure in a tropological history running continuously from Romanticism through modernism. The moving force in this history is not persons, authors, or cultures but rather the limits of discursive possibility. The basic outlines for a program of tropological historiography have been explored in the writings of Hayden White.[2] The compelling inference to be drawn from a set of readings encompassing Proust and Henry James as well as Hegel is that during the span from early Romanticism to well into the twentieth century, largely the *same* discursive and figural resources were available. Literary history, to the extent that it took place, did not *progress;* it did not *produce.* It resided within a common set of textual games and rules. There is an ineradicable historical bent to any study acknowledging the power of a thinker (Hegel) or the grammar of tropes that he assembled. But a tropological history is ahistorical in the sense that it posits neither an evolution nor an accretion of material in time. It will be suggested in chapter 4 that as a context for the particular conflicts that color and structure the Freudian enterprise, Goethe's writing may comprise as pertinent a background as Hegel's. To be sure, on the levels of both theme and structure, many of Hegel's most pressing concerns were shared with other writers, including Goethe. Yet it is in Hegel's works that the entire battery of conceptual tools comprising the horizon of discursive possibility for a vast range of Romantic and modern texts is combined with a unique concentration and comprehensiveness. It is on the basis of the intensity with which the discursive limits of an age are marshaled and deployed in Hegel's writing that the following essays revolve, although differently, around Hegel.

Philosophy Transfigured; Fiction Philosophical

If the history of the continuous Romantic-Modern age does not develop or increase, it does transfigure. The only movement during this period whose pursuit makes sense is a lateral shift in which the discursive procedures of philosophy become the property of fiction. Depending on the degree of irony that one ascribes to Hegel, the discursive tropes that he collected may or may not have been in the service of the revelation of a transcendental or absolute knowledge. But in the hands of a Kierkegaard, a Kafka, or a Yeats the same moves become the very stuff of literary radicality. During this period philosophy's point of orientation drops away. (The credibility ever attained by some hypothetical central truth remains questionable.) The leftover apparatus of philosophy becomes a legitimate literary concern and even focus.

The overall trajectory of this static evolution is a sideways hop, a lateral displacement. The battery of discursive gestures and tools available to philosophy becomes the subject and substance of poetics. No writer prefigures and embodies the overall shift from philosophy to poetics that takes place during the Romantic-Modern age more than Nietzsche. In Nietzsche's hands the watershed between philosophical etiquette and esthetic excess becomes a doubly permeable and insubstantial membrane. If the *Phenomenology of Spirit* is a metaphysical and teleological treatise in whose outlines the program of the *Bildungsroman* are to be discerned, *Also Sprach Zarathustra* is a philosophical novel whose systematic aspirations have been obliterated by fictionality. In Nietzsche's texts both the predicament and the agenda of the Hegelian aftermath are concentrated. Revulsion (*Ekel*) and suicide are the Nietzschean consequences of a certain literality (*Redlichkeit*). For Kierkegaard the ethics surrounding the matrix of marriage, and for Freud the pretensions of clinical objectivity, are similarly stultifying.

> As an aesthetic phenomenon existence is still *bearable* [*erträglich*] for us. . . . At times [*zeitweilig*] we need a rest from ourselves by touching upon, by looking *down* upon, ourselves and, from an artistic distance, laughing *over* ourselves or weeping *over* ourselves. We must discover the *hero* no less than the *fool* in our passion for knowledge; we must occasionally find pleasure in our folly, or we cannot continue to find pleasure in our wisdom. . . . Nothing does us as much good as a fool's cap [*Schelmenkappe*]: we need it in relation to ourselves—we need all exuberant [*übermütige*], floating [*schwebende*], dancing, mocking, childish, and blissful art lest we lose the *freedom above things* that our ideal demands of us.[3]

Art, in this passage from Nietzsche's *Gay Science,* functions not as a cultivated taste for the sublime but as a manifold of the possibilities excluded by the drives for truth, integrity, and objectivity. The hovering dance of art repudiates, in other words, the very terms upon which philosophy bases its reliability. The departure from extrinsic imperatives and necessity is *toward* poetry. The scenario of our looking down upon or floating above ourselves may not relieve us of contradiction. But the trajectory pursued in this sideways shift is from philosophy to poetics. Deprived, by internal conflict, of linear progress, this dislocation nonetheless signals the transvaluation of all values that describes the relation between Romanticism and modernism. It is in rehearsing the lateral dance of the crab and tarantula that Nietzsche provides an insignia for the Hegelian aftermath.

What of the history that does not move, that dances sideways instead of progressing, that yields no quantifiable increase? The history of the Romantic-Modern age is distinctly nonproductive. The epoch that transpires under the aegis of bifurcation, inversion, reciprocity, and circularity does not produce: it does not add materially to the limits of discursive possibility.

Or if it must produce, it produces precisely *nothing:* not the mystical and mystifying nothingness which is the obverse side of sublimation but the radical nothing which for Walter Benjamin is both the attraction and the upshot of children's games.[4] The Romantic-Modern age demands the notion of a nonproductive history, a history yielding this indifferent and unapologetic nothing. It is no accident that each of the followers of Hegel considered in this study reached toward a mode or economy of nonproduction. Kierkegaard opposed the mechanics of qualification and moral rationalization with a vacuousness that he located in Aristophanes' *Clouds*. The economies of the joke and homosexuality intimated for Freud and Proust, respectively, a domain alien to the imperative of increase, whether of conscious control or by human reproduction. And those Henry James characters fated to the compulsion of interpretation are invariably discomposed and maddened by an onus ultimately indistinguishable from nothing.

In much of his work over the past decade, the French critic Jean Baudrillard has advanced a notion of history based on the differential relations between signs rather than on the work ethic, which he finds as characteristic of Marxism as of bourgeois political economy. Baudrillard's critiques of the imperatives toward the notions of production, utility, and consumption that have infiltrated Marxist theory is double-edged: he is no more merciful toward the fundaments of capitalist metaphysics than he is toward their Marxist counterparts. Baudrillard eschews the "realm beyond political economy called play, non-work, or non-alienated labor"[5] in Marxist thought as an illusory release from the constraints of labor. Yet even as Baudrillard unmasks the ostensible whimsy corresponding to the esthetics of the revolutionary imagination,[6] the notion of a radical nothing, a repudiation of the necessity of production, is vital to his work. Baudrillard thus enunciates in terms of political and economic theory a resistance toward accretion in time articulated by virtually all of Hegel's aware followers.

> The culmination produced by Marxist analysis, in which it illuminates the demise of all contradictions, is *simply the emergence of history*, that is, a process in which everything is always said to be resolved at a later date by an accumulated truth, a determinant instance, an irreversible history. Thus, history can only be, at bottom, the equivalent of the ideal point of reference that, in the classical and rational perspective of the Renaissance, allows the spatial imposition of an arbitrary, unitary structure. And historical materialism could only be the Euclidean geometry of this history.
>
> It is only in the *mirror* of production and history, under the double principle of indefinite accumulation (production) and dialectical continuity (history), only by the arbitrariness of the *code*, that our Western culture can reflect itself in the universal as the privileged moment of truth (science) or of revolution (historical materialism). Without this simulation, without this gigantic reflexivity of the concave (or convex) concept of history or production, our era loses all privileges.[7]

What is decisive about this passage in terms of the concerns of the present study is its repeated appositional link between production and history. Both Marxist history and its capitalistic counterpart take off from a moment of reflexive illusion, one of whose primary instances, in the third chapter of Hegel's *Phenomenology of Spirit*, will be considered in detail below. In its retrospective stance, the historical perspective that rationalizes the facts of history reenacts the spiritual growth of the self-reflexive subject. Truth accumulates, subjective consciousness grows, and history produces. "The dialectic of production only intensifies the abstractness and separation of political economy," writes Baudrillard elsewhere.[8]

Baudrillard traces the illusions—the Appearance, if you will—as pervasive to Marxism as to bourgeois political economy to a scene of self-reflexivity common to both systems. In this regard he is not so far as he might surmise from the ironic Hegel who also plays within the pages of the *Phenomenology of Spirit*. Not only is self-reflection an optical illusion: so is the history that emanates from it. There can be no more compelling proof of this history's delusion than the discursive resources that reside at both ends of the Romantic-Modern age. Structurally and tropologically, they have not changed. From the perspective of the logical and rhetorical capabilities of discourse, history has not produced. The stasis that is Kierkegaard's rallying cry but which dominates the entire Hegelian aftermath gives the lie to the innovative claims of history on both sides of the ideological watershed.

History is the emperor who wears no clothes. To the extent that it produces, it yields precisely nothing. It was the labor of the Hegelian aftermath to dress, ornament, and embellish this nothing.

Another way of characterizing the nonproductive stasis that prevails throughout the Romantic-Modern period is by means of superimposition. While retaining the Appearance of historical and teleological evolution, Hegel's *Phenomenology of Spirit* yokes individual, collective, esthetic, and theological experiences in tandem. At any given moment it is difficult to ascertain whether the narrated process takes place within an individual, a thinking collectivity, or an extrinsic conceptual framework such as religion or esthetics.

Hegel's followers tended to find this perspectival uncertainty resulting from a superimposition of contexts a convenient esthetic device, even where fidelity to a predetermined teleological program was no longer possible. Superimposition as it is practiced by Proust, Walter Benjamin, and other modernists is a seamless welding of textual, psychological, sociological, and phenomenological levels. There is no definitive marker indicating where the psychological ends and the phenomenological analysis of time and space begins. There is no recourse to the fictive temporalizing devices operative in Hegel's *Phe-*

nomenology of Spirit or in *Bildungsromane* which assign different stages to, say, the life of the family and the life of the community. The superimposed contexts are synchronic. Any movement that occurs within such an arrangement does not extend in space but transpires between the strata of a contextual and perspectival overlay.

The Hegelian aftermath is concurrent with an age dominated by superimposition. The Kierkegaardian suspension between esthetic excess and ethical restraint is agonizing because the symmetrically disjunctive modes are capable of being experienced simultaneously by the same subject. As we shall have occasion to observe in detail, the external expanse encompassed in Proust's *Recherche* by Elstir's seascapes is a phenomenological correlative to the intrapsychic relations for which Vinteuil's music serves as an accompaniment. One of the key shocks that Walter Benjamin ascribes to the rise of modernity is precisely a collapse: of spatial articulation in the modern city, of ritual markers in the calendar. Not only does Benjamin, in his essay "On Some Motifs in Baudelaire," trace the emergence of this modernistic discombobulation in the nineteenth-century lyric and novel; he incorporates shock into his own text by collapsing, early on, its phenomenological (Bergsonian time), psychological (Freud), and literary contexts (*mémoire volontaire* and *involontaire* in Proust).[9] The superimposed cluttering that Benjamin infuses into his own writing is one according to which he reads and interprets the age running continuously from Baudelaire to Proust.

By the same token, modernist discourse, even within the phenomenological sphere, is organized by superimposition. The great Heideggerian project, to the extent that it was carried out, resulted in a dual articulation of space (*Sein*) and time. It is not far-fetched to assert that the organization of *Sein und Zeit* consists in a mutual superimposition of the spatial and temporal facets of experience. Superimposition enables both time and space to be articulated according to analogous linguistic operations.

The followers of Hegel may limit the range of their own locomotion and of development in general, but they do not proscribe the possibilities for movement altogether. They move not simply by extension but in involution, complexity, and the addition of superimposed planes.

Among the great later works of European Romanticism must surely be numbered Hugh Kenner's *The Pound Era*.[10] Even while incanting a paean to the innovations of modernism, this book incorporates those qualities that exemplify, for Philippe Lacoue-Labarthe and Jean-Luc Nancy in *L'Absolu littéraire*, Romanticism.[11] *The Pound Era* is woven of aphorisms and sharply drawn images. Its heroes, Pound and Lewis, are artificers in a sublime poetic substance sanctified by time and tradition. Promulgating awe of the great experiments and disfigurations that followed the turn of the century, *The Pound Era* nonetheless belongs to the liturgy of Poetry and Image.

Modernist distortion does not necessarily supersede Romantic sublimation, especially when Romanticism and modernism share the same horizon of discursive possibility. The bizarre juxtapositions and spatio-temporal distortions of a Kafka obscure the conceptual mechanics underlying his texts, a broken-down and obsolete machinery belonging to a prior age, like that used for executions in the "Penal Colony." Up until the past decade and a half, the breakthroughs of modernism, contributed by such authors as Kafka, Musil, Joyce, and Proust, have been synonymous with the radical capabilities of literarity. Modernism was the esthetic aegis under which the New Criticism flourished and which defined the nature of literature for generations of students and scholars in America.[12]

For all that modernism contributed to the style of twentieth-century life in the West, to the tangible domains of architecture and design as well as to the "pure" arts, equating it with the sum of all possibilities for innovation serves little productive purpose. In accordance with any historiographical or archaeological procedure, modernism configures a set of presuppositions and orientations as closed as those characterizing other moments or ages.

No writer has been more decisive to the detachment of current critical alternatives from the biases of modernism than Jacques Derrida. Particularly in his deconstructions of Husserl and Heidegger,[13] in whose work he discerns the traces of concepts of presence and representation with ancient histories in Western thought, Derrida forges a path leading away from rather than toward modernist attitudes. Heidegger, in his fascination with technology and his recourse to the etymological roots of concepts and words, is an exemplary modernist philosopher. In their style and effect, Heidegger's word plays are not far from those abounding in James Joyce's mature novels.

The border that divides Derrida from Heidegger is a highly intricate and complex one. But in locating "in a note on a note" in *Being and Time* an imperative toward presentation characteristic of the entire span of classical Western metaphysics,[14] Derrida opens a distance between contemporary criticism and the projects of modernism. No longer the implicit horizon of esthetic and critical possibility, modernism takes its place within the tradition that it prolongs, closely adjacent to Romanticism.

If the following study is reluctant to place Hegel definitively on the "outside" or "inside" of Western metaphysics, this is because of its intrinsic fascination with the machine-work of philosophy and its endurance in time. In refusing to locate Hegel squarely on the "outside" or "inside" of a reflexive tradition, my reading overlooks the *what* in favor of the *how* of the Hegelian discursive apparatus. Given my lack of any comprehensive overview of Western metaphysics, I take as my initial object the esthetic quality of the intricacy that Hegel managed to infuse into a discourse machine. The era not only of certain speculative conventions but of the machine itself may be over, replaced by the productions of cybernetics and artificial intelligence. Long before arriving at placement, the following essays stop at astonishment, the wonder at a complex and well-tuned machine.

Yet the success of such elaborate machines as Hegel's invariably requires the intervention of the arbitrary somewhere along the chain of determinations. Like the mail distribution for the officials who reside in the Herrenhof tavern in Kafka's *The Castle*, every precise coordination of functions requires an indiscrete kick or crumpling of a superfluous document. In Hegel's case, the variable Appearance is the wondrous but suspicious factor enabling the future successes of abstraction and cultivation. Appearance both panders to the desires of the machine and harbors the seeds of its inevitable breakdown. The suspect term is two-faced, collaborating with the machine but also dramatizing the linguistic indeterminancy on which the system founders.

By virtue of their orientation toward the *how* rather than the *what* of discourse, the following essays risk falling into a formalism of their own, a formalism inspired by the beauty of certain discursive gestures. If my writing has to some extent been struck blind by the beauty of a machine-work, this blindness is not to be justified, concealed, or ignored. My focus (or tunnel vision) has enabled me to formulate an account of the discursive tropes at play in Hegel and then to suggest their further repercussions as the conceptual limits of an era. The relations on which I have fixated have furnished me with a common ground on which to read a group of important but culturally remote writers: Hegel, Kierkegaard, Freud, Proust, and Henry James.

It is indicative of the extent to which Hegel served as the harbinger of an age that a dubious element informs the work of all of the writers following in this sequence. To varying degrees, all of the other authors considered in this book are system-builders, yet in each case a factor on one level capitulating to the systematic constraints becomes a hidden shoal that submarines the floating enterprise. In the works of the Hegelian followers as in Hegel's, there is an uncanny collusion between the totalizing and subversive factors. In light of the political developments of the past decade and a half, since the seminal works of contemporary critical theory appeared, an alternation between repressive and radical moments in reading may well furnish a more pertinent scenario than any decisive emergence beyond the systematic limits.

All of the Hegelian followers treated in this study vacillate, then, between the speculative system and the indeterminacy of the text. For Kierkegaard, the constraints of the ethical mode constitute a hopelessly belated attempt to erase esthetic excess. Yet even where the ethical is ironized, the Kierkegaardian speculations have relied upon internal division and symmetry for their form. Freud, while embarking in the best of faith upon a rhetorical lexicon of consciousness, reinscribes a metaphysical crisis within all but one of his major grammatical rubrics. For Proust, homosexuality not only is a matter of sexual preference but implies a countereconomy to the imperatives of reproduction and other-orientation in many of their ramifications. Yet the economy of homosexuality is unthinkable in isolation from the image of pregnancy. Alien to the ethos as well as the esthetics of heterosexual love, homosexuality emanates every bit as much from pregnancy, from the unique condition of fullness by involution. (Proustian pregnancy is yet another instance of modernist superimposition.) Finally, the works of Henry James devote considerable narrative resources to the generation of a certain enigmatic suspense, romantic as well as ghostly. Yet the moments of uncanniness in James's fiction are veritable catalogues of Hegelian operations. By means of a scenic construction conducive to a certain suspenseful stillness, James transfigures the normative operations of philosophy into a fictive phantasmagoria.

The Hegelian aftermath is thus relegated to an ambivalence, a schizophrenic uncertainty, already implicit in the system-building of Hegel. Hegel's major followers are informed and motivated by linguistic and textual apprehensions.

This does not imply, however, that they ever succeeded in resolving an impasse in some ways common to them and in some ways different to each—or that they definitively succeeded in severing their textual insights from the conventions of speculation.

Yet for all the force gathered by the Hegelian tropes examined in this volume—and it is no accident that Force became a central Hegelian metaphor—their impact and aftereffects can by no means be characterized as homogenous. The parodic gestures of

Kierkegaard in personalizing the "omniscient" narrative voice and in paralyzing the machinery of dialectics are of a vastly different order than the stylistic experiments of Proust or Joyce. Hegel grounded a *structural* horizon from which modernism found it extremely difficult to extricate itself. The modernist experiments, in their sidewards divergence from Romantic convention, were able to immerse themselves in the textual potential that Hegel had tangentially intimated and that his followers exploited in their resistance to the Hegelian formalism. The acknowledged "masterworks" of modernism find themselves in an anomalous position. While depending upon—literally hanging from—the scaffolding of such conventions as opposition and circularity, they are free to explore the very *stuff* of textuality, the tissue, the tone, and the resonances of language. The puns of Joyce, the seemingly endless phrases of Proust, and Kafka's dislocations of the time-honored conventions of the novel all continue, in different ways, a deconstruction of Hegelian conventions begun by Kierkegaard and Nietzsche. What these modernist experiments seem to have in common is their freedom from vertigo, their ability to hover in linguistic suspense without undue concern for the superstructure that supports them.

If the Hegelian aftermath demarcates a space, it is, then, an extremely variegated and diversified one. A close follower of Hegel, Kierkegaard limits his divergences from the machinery of speculation to minute—but profound—adjustments. The sabotage effected by the almost invisible revision becomes the model for Kierkegaardian irony. Freud's innovations, in proposing a lexicon of consciousness, are wider-ranging than Kierkegaard's, because they suggest how subjectivity itself may be structured by such linguistic processes as metaphor, metonymy, and synecdoche. Yet Freud's retreat from this apprehension, in the interests of clinical hygiene, politics, and posterity, is no less religious and in a sense frightened, than Kierkegaard's. In Proust, the operations and concerns of speculation are present as themes in an ever-deepening palimpsest whose ultimate *modus operandi* is the text. Opposition, discrimination, particularization, and repetition all enter the metaphoric economy of the work—but their systematic aspirations are effaced in the accretion of the novel's superimposed metaphoric strata. Henry James's *The Turn of the Screw* dramatizes the transposition from philosophy to poetics. The disjointed elements of a broken speculative machine enter the literary vocabulary of the story's uncanniness. This work is an instance of a text literally composed of philosophical fragments. The systematic heritage of its main events in no way detracts from their esthetic impact or horror.

Although highly differentiated, the Hegelian aftermath nonetheless comprises a space or scene. I would hope that the philosophical and rhetorical operations considered in the present study will exposit what Hegel (or Proust) would term the "laws" of this domain. The limits pertaining to all attempts at codification or classification thus apply to this enterprise. The categories involved in this attempt are closed and lead to more closure. Yet precisely in their finite quality, the processes of bifurcation, reciprocity, and inversion may be hopefully deployed, on a limited scale, in the illumination of specific texts.

In closing this introductory section, I return to the border between the outside and the inside as it is implicated in the current critical wars. As I write, it is November 6, 1981. An ostensibly monetary review of the American and world economies has resulted in an even further deflation of the skills and values of literacy. The academy is in a state of attack from the outside, although the most devastating weapon in this siege may well be indifference.

On the inside, however, a prodigious refinement takes place. The battle lines, drawn some ten to fifteen years ago, between "theory" and more traditional academic pursuits, have tightened. For at least a decade the pitch of the arguments has steadily increased to a level reminiscent of the tension that prevails on Mann's Magic Mountain at the outset of World War I. The armaments in this battle have included tropes and terms of marked subtlety, as well as accusations and other acts of personal and administrative aggression. Our graduate students are armed as well as taught; fitted out to attack the enemies of their mentors in a continuation of battles whose primal scenes they did not personally witness. Their rewards and scars are preordained.

As this development takes place, the outside of the academy diverges ever more sharply from the inside. By national policy, the public-at-large is consigned to ever lower levels of literacy, while the critical wars take ever more intricate and unexpected turns. The public-at-large, by virtue of conditioning by the electronic media, indifference, and perhaps despair, abandons the pursuit of general literacy in the acquisition of more pragmatic skills and experiences. The teachers of the literatures and languages of the land withdraw into intramural struggle.

In this book, I have written on some major authors and their texts. The sheer momentousness of such names as Hegel, Kierkegaard, and Freud betrays a certain craving for authority and accumulation on my part. I would hope that the burden of proof upon this study rests more on a vocabulary of tropes and a structural framework than on the volatile allegiances and disputes of the critical wars. Recent criticism has placed certain of the key terms in this study on the "inside" of a continuous Western metaphysical tradition; others are better situated in the foyer to the "outside." Whatever their placement, I would hope that these terms might assist those readers interested in pursuing them to elucidate some of the important writings of the Romantic-Modern age. These tropes, common to philosophy and literature, are neither exhaustive nor fixed. If they can add to the illumination of the texts that they address, they will have more than achieved their purpose.

The main part of this book was written during a fellowship from the National Endowment for the Humanities. Without the release from teaching and administrative duties that the fellowship allowed, in all likelihood the book would not yet be completed. I am deeply grateful for this assistance, and wish the Endowment every success in continuing to provide support to other students of the humanities and social sciences at critical moments in their work.

Two individuals in particular were instrumental in sustaining and furthering this project: Dr. Stuart L. Keill, for his attentive and creative reading of a history of a slightly different order; and, Cathleen A. Carter, whose superb typing not only first allowed me to read the various chapters but included a preliminary and indispensable editing.

In ways too numerous to mention (but which *could* be named) my family has given me every form of support. My lifelong friendships with Jeffrey Newman and Richard Netsky have helped me view this endeavor and all similar strivings with a measure of humor and detachment. The Lockwood Library at the State University of New York at Buffalo was most helpful in securing the materials that I needed in order to complete this book.

TWO

Five Hegelian Metaphors

[I]

The formalism of such a 'Philosophy of Nature' teaches, say, that
the Understanding is Electricity, or the Animal is Nitrogen, or
that they are the *equivalent* of the South or North Pole, etc., or
represent it . . . and confronted with such a power which brings
together things that appear to lie far apart, and with the violence
suffered by the passive things of sense through such
association . . . confronted with all this, the untutored mind may
be filled with admiration and astonishment, and may venerate in
it the profound work of genius.

Hegel, *Phenomenology of Spirit*

Hegel criticizes here a blunt literalism in the use of metaphor within the philosophical text. Underlying this criticism is a conception of
the *Phenomenology of Spirit* as an organic work whose process renders
fluid epistemological and grammatical oppositions between subject
and object[1] and whose temporal scheme is a continuous evolution of
stages.[2] The lengthy "Preface" to the *Phenomenology* may be read as a
multifaceted exposition of the ideology of the organic. The predominant components of this ideology are the necessities of mediation,[3]
interconnection,[4] and evolution within the philosophical discourse.
Organic process opposes the procedures of representation (*das
vorstellende Denken*)[5] and ratiocination (*das räsonierende Denken*),[6] which
are symmetrically opposed forms of induction and deduction. The
much briefer "Introduction" translates the polemical thrust of the
"Preface" into methodological terms. Twice Hegel demonstrates how
grammatical dualities are to be rendered fluid and continuous by
means of a third term that is not only the missing link within the
reductive formalism but also the remainder or leftover on which subsequent development will be based. In the first instance *erscheinendes
Wissen* (pp. 48–50), a knowledge that has incorporated its own appearance or illusoriness, presents itself as an alternative to a sequence
of postulations asserting the instrumental nature of knowledge. A

knowledge conceptualized as an instrument is based on epistemological and grammatical dualities opposing subject and object. *Erscheinendes Wissen* intervenes in these dualities by making them continuous, a gesture repeated at the end of the "Introduction," where Hegel introduces the perspectival dialectic that will be an ongoing component of his philosophical discourse. Here once again the new object (p. 56, *neuer Gegenstand*)* of knowledge, one not passively *in itself* or assertively *for itself* but *for us,* the thinking and discoursing collectivity, breaks a deadlock between indifference and purpose, mediating between them.

From the perspective of Hegel's ideology of organicism, the epigraph to this section comes as yet another broadside against the reductiveness of formal constructs and operations. Yet from a different point of view, in terms of the machinery that powers the *Phenomenology* on to its prodigious progress, Hegel's critique of metaphors that usurp control of the discourse is a forthright self-criticism, applicable to the *body* of the work that follows. The first four chapters of the *Phenomenology* are organized at least as much by the metaphors they entertain as by the formal procedures justified and schematized in the "Preface" and the "Introduction." Within these chapters, perception "is" salt and understanding "is" electricity. If understanding constitutes an advance beyond perception, it is to the extent that the metaphor of electricity affords certain conceptual capacities lacking (even if structurally potential) in the metaphor of salt. From the outset, then, the *Phenomenology*'s progress allows itself to be gauged on two scales that run parallel to each other: according to the formal operations that literally introduce the work and in a sequence of metaphors increasing in complexity. These metaphors are the following: the state of hypothetical temporal and spatial immediacy with which the *body* of the text begins, the thing of perception (*Wahrnehmung*), the electromagnetic force that emblematizes understanding, the interaction between master and slave, and the unhappy consciousness (*das unglückliche Bewußtsein*). The critical examination and historical assessment of the *Phenomenology* hinge on the selection and interaction of these doubled scales of progress, on the manner and extent to which they are invoked in reading this text.

Unlike the progress of the *Bildungsromane,* to which the *Phenomenology* has been compared,[7] the progress of this work is not even in the manner in which the experience of a central character might be. The text begins with a steep slope in conceptual complexity that culmi-

---

*Page references to the *Phenomenology of Spirit* refer to the English edition cited in note 1 to this chapter. German phrases derive from the German text cited in the same note.

nates in the transition from "consciousness" to "self-consciousness" at the end of "Force and the Understanding" ("Kraft und Verstand," chapter 3). In "Force and the Understanding" the text completes a sequence of detachments that finally enable the supersensible world (*das Übersinnliche*), an autonomous intellectual realm, to take off from the domain of physical and sensory experience from which, in *organic* fashion, it had to *evolve*. The emergence of a sphere that must no longer answer or refer to sensory experience is the sufficient condition for all higher conceptions, institutions, or confections of science, religion, and art.

As I have already suggested, Hegel instruments this sequence of detachments with a series of metaphors increasing in complexity. The salt that Hegel takes up as the thing of perception comprises an advance beyond the here and now of "Sense-Certainty" ("Sinnliche Gewißheit") in that the distinction between the property and the thing affords some rudimentary capacity for abstraction and generalization. The limit of the hypothetical stage whose certainty bases itself solely on sensory phenomena was an immediate slippage of particularity into universality, an inability to delineate *degrees* of generality. "This as well as That—such a thing we call a *universal*. So it is in fact the universal that is the true [content] of sense-certainty" (p. 60). The thing of perception, determined by a double process of inclusion and exclusion, contains at least a structural potential for the differentiation that is the basis for all abstraction. The thing of perception, as Hegel demonstrates, ultimately dissolves when the exclusionary moment by which the thing separated itself from other things attacks itself—that is, when the thing excludes itself. It is at this moment that electricity enters the discourse as a metaphor for understanding, precisely because it lifts this limitation. For if the fate of perception was to pursue the "whirling circle" (p. 74, *wirbelnde Kreis*) leading from the property to the thing and back again, a commonsensical process in which each thing is identified by a single property accorded the status of an essence (*Wesen*), the more complex structure of electricity eliminates this short circuit. The need to shuttle frenetically between the particular and the universal is held in check by the conception of a force that consists of two autonomous, reciprocally related counterforces. Electromagnetism is a metaphor for abstraction itself, for the activity of the particular charges does not compromise the existence of the total force, and vice versa. Electromagnetism, residing on both particular and general levels, sustains the oscillation between them, whereas in perception the middle ground could only be suggested, and in "Sense-Certainty" it did not exist at all. It is precisely this intermediary space—the scene of the play of forces, the inner world, and infinity—that is the generating matrix of abstraction.

The power, both narrative and conceptual, generated by a sequence of progressively complex metaphors invites us to disregard
the formal mechanics of the *Phenomenology* altogether. This work, we
could say, is a string of metaphors; the temporal dialectic incorporated by the term "sublation" (*Aufhebung*) and the spatial (perspectival)
dialectic joining *in itself, for itself,* and *for consciousness* are merely mechanical safeguards that Hegel offers us to save us from madness. We
could relegate the connective tissue of the *Phenomenology,* those passages asserting and assessing the progress of "consciousness," to a
level of importance lower than that of the metaphorical passages.
Correspondingly, we could elevate the metadiscursive passages that
problematize intentionality and signification *above* those moments
when Hegel laboriously bends his material to fit the dialectics of time
or history and space or perspective. Yet this strategy, involving the
separation of the formal out of the conceptual in the Hegelian discourse and the *elevation* of the speculative over the formal, was as
open to the nineteenth century as it is to our own,[8] and it is not our
purpose to repeat it. A far more fruitful enterprise would be to examine the location and the manner in which the Hegelian metaphor and
formal apparatus are joined in a common program: an account and
dramatization of the Hegelian text itself. Both the metaphors that
power the early *Phenomenology* and the formal devices that shape it
describe, albeit in a different manner, the necessities, gestures, and
developments within the text that they comprise.

The program of the following essay, then, is to read the *Phenomenology* in terms of its internal account of its own language, and to
include its formal operations within the lexicon of its own textuality.
Yet the Hegelian attitude toward language that may be extrapolated
from this text is far from unambiguous in itself. It is no accident that
the stages through which "consciousness" first passes in the *Phenomenology,* "Sense-Certainty," "Perception," and "Understanding,"
though organically linked, follow the stratification of the Kantian
system (as elaborated in the *Critique of Pure Reason* and the *Prolegomena to Any Future Metaphysics*). In these texts the locus of the
intuitions (*Anschauungen*),[9] appearances (*Erscheinungen*),[10] and representations (*Vorstellungen*)[11] is perception, the lowest common de-
nominator of cognition, a level cultivated by understanding and reason. On the one hand, when Hegel questions the certainty based on
sensory experience in the first chapter in terms of the problems attending the notions of meaning and intentionality, he conditions all
that follows in the *Phenomenology* by these linguistic concerns. But on
the other hand, since the higher crystallizations of cognition, culture,
and social organization increase primarily in the complexity of the
mediation they afford, Hegel's interest in problematizing language so

early in the *Phenomenology* could be as much to silence the question as to privilege it (just as Kant, despite a pre-Romantic insistence on subjectivity as the ultimate arbiter of experience,[12] makes his intuitions, appearances, and representations the *Bruchstücke* of the transcendental concept, the reduced fragments of the ideal filtering down to our level of apprehension).

Hegel's conditioning the *Phenomenology* with the problematization of language bespeaks an ambivalence toward language as much as it does an anticipation of current philosophical and literary interests. What may well emerge with greatest contemporary value from a reading of Hegel is not so much a repudiation of possibly mechanical formal operations as the schizoid break separating the counter-imperatives of the text: to read the *Phenomenology* both as a nonlinear, discontinuous metaphoric generator *and* in terms of the presuppositions enabling its formal apparatus to operate. The endurance of this schizoid structure may well constitute the ultimate impact of dialectical thought.

For indeed, Hegel establishes a formalism suited to phenomenological claims in the same gesture with which he attacks the (notably Kantian) formalism that preceded him. In his *Prolegomena* Kant paradoxically demonstrates that natural science proves the *necessity* of a priori synthetic judgments by delimiting the *possible* objects of experience. The *necessity* of the transcendental concept's infiltration into experience, in other words, becomes a function of understanding's capacity to abstract the total *possible* components of experience. In this case, the transcendental category of possibility enables understanding, in the form of natural science, to mediate between the randomness of experience and the ideal. Kant's formalism distinguishes itself precisely in the elevation of his philosophical discourse to the level of the conditions or presuppositions enabling given operations and levels of consciousness to be *possible:* "We cannot, therefore, study the nature of things *a priori* otherwise than by investigating the conditions and the universal (though subjective) laws, under which alone such a cognition as experience (as to mere form) is possible, and we determine accordingly the possibility of things as objects of experience."[13]

This levitation to the widest conditions of possibility endows the Kantian speculations with a distinctive breadth, but what Hegel finds in this atmosphere of expansion is death and emptiness. In a famous passage in the "Preface" to the *Phenomenology,* he compares this formalism to two forms of monotony, a two-tone painting unable to accommodate subtleties of color gradation and a whistling that does not deviate from its single tone (pp. 29–31). Hegel condemns the "dogmatism" (p. 23), "lifeless schema" (p. 29), and the external quality (p. 31) of such knowledge. Inner motivation and fluidity are the organic qualities that he privileges in reaction to the expansiveness of the Kantian formalism.

Yet for all of his invective against the stultifying effect of formalism, Hegel does designate those devices or figures that perform for his discourse the same function served by the Kantian rise toward the level of possibility. He specifies those figures, devices, or tropes on which, as on seamstresses' dummies, his material shapes itself in conformity with the *Phenomenology*'s ideological, historical, and anthropological aims.

> What, therefore, is important in the *study* of *Science*, is that one should take on oneself the strenuous effort of the Notion. This requires attention to the Notion as such, to the simple determinations, e.g., of Being-in-itself [*des Ansichseins*], Being-for-itself [*des Fürsichseins*], Self-identity [*der Sichselbstgleichheit*], etc.; for these are pure self-movements such as could be called souls if their Notion did not designate something higher than soul. (P. 35)

Not without self-irony, Hegel reflects on the privileged status attained by the figures or tropes instrumenting the perspectival dialectic that passes from simple assertion to critical disinterest in his discourse, almost the status of souls. Joining the exemplary instances in this passage of opposition and progress within a formal device would be the analogous figure within the dimension of time, the *Aufhebung*, as well as the notion (*Begriff*), the conceptual handle that, while ever evolving, always indicates the highest capability of a particular level of "consciousness."

Yet while Hegel suggests, implicitly or explicitly, some of the formal devices that precipitate out of the ideology of the organic, he leaves others *for us* to discern, for those of us extrapolating the impact of Hegelianism by means of terms whose derivation is more recent. The great formal laws of the Hegelian text are bifurcation, inversion, lateral displacement, the interiorization of the exterior, the exteriorization of the interior, reciprocity, the establishment of reciprocity out of difference, the introjection of difference into reciprocity, and the circularization of linear sequences. These tropes form the connective tissue of the Hegelian text and weave its diverse metaphors into a narrative functioning simultaneously as a novel, a logic, an anthropology, and a phenomenology. What these tropes, alongside the *Begriff* and the triadic structures of the *Aufhebung* and the *in itself, for itself,* and *for consciousness,* establish is the *possibility* for the text of the *Phenomenology*—the possibility for this complex work in which individual, collective, and philosophical subjects are superimposed onto each other and marshaled into a progress ostensibly leading from the primitive to the advanced crystallizations of cognition, science, social organization, and art. And if a fundamentally horizontal and aimless annexation of metaphors is spurred toward progress and destiny by a set of repetitive tropes whose application in some contexts becomes predictable, then this is a text demanding that its *possible* conditions be read, soliciting, in other words, a Kantian reading.

And it cannot come as a total surprise that the Kant of the first *Critique* and the *Prolegomena* anticipated a Kantian reading of the *Phenomenology*, even though there was as yet no *Phenomenology*. Kant, in elaborating the antinomies that accompany the apprehension of Pure Reason by the faculty and disciplines of understanding, outlines at least two movements that become stocks-in-trade of the *Phenomenology*'s *activity:* a collapse of contradiction into sameness and a complementary installation of contradiction within sameness.

> In the first (the mathematical) class of antinomies the falsehood of presupposition consists in representing in one concept something self-contradictory as if it were compatible (that is, an appearance as a thing in itself). But, as to the second (the dynamical) class of antinomies, the falsehood of the presupposition consists in representing as contradictory what is compatible.[14]

In this brief passage not only does Kant anticipate the direction that Hegel will take in response to the Kantian formalism but he predicts the outcome of (at least) two of the *Phenomenology*'s most notorious arguments. What is "represented as unified in a single concept"—let us interpolate the master and slave, who initially appear in a deadlock of reciprocal parity—erupts into deadly conflict when a factor of differentiation (in this case, life) is introduced. Conversely, the compulsive activity of Hegel's understanding, the proliferation of "differences which are not differences" (p. 95), results in the *withdrawal* of the curtain that *seems* to separate "consciousness" from what it observes.

If the crises and resolutions of the *Phenomenology* have already insinuated themselves within the margins of the Kantian speculations, then the appeal for a Kantian reading of Hegel may not be as patently absurd as it seems. Such an approach may enable us to resist amputating the formal Hegelian apparatus from the *Phenomenology*'s metaphoric tissue. If a reading of the early *Phenomenology* in terms of the Kantian category of possibility implies a certain historical regression, this regression, ironically, may enable us to do greatest justice to the historical legacy of this text. For precisely those formal operations introduced in the *Phenomenology* that were most vulnerable to the criticisms of the nineteenth century were destined to become the vibrant and shaping structures of twentieth-century art and theory—at play in arenas as diverse as the psychoanalytical subject, Kafka's paradoxes, and the interaction between the primary and the antithetical in Yeats's poetics. This chapter will first examine such operations as bifurcation, inversion, displacement, reciprocity, and circularization as they are generated in the early *Phenomenology* and as they interact with the text's metaphoric tissue. It will then pursue these formal tropes into the twentieth century, where they found a welcome home.

[II]

The *Phenomenology* functions simultaneously as a novel, an encyclopaedia, a history of ideas, a genealogy of symbolic forms, and a "logic" of its own operations.

As a novel, it records the development of a central character, "consciousness,"[15] which in turn breaks down into a group of subcharacters including "Sense-Certainty," "Perception," "Understanding," *Aufhebung*, and *in itself, for itself*, and *for consciousness*. It is the repeatability of these terms, their iterability[16] from context to context, that gives them the continuity of novelistic characters. The first three components of the above list, for example, initially appear as the basic *stages* of cognition. But Stoicism and Skepticism, the preliminary stages of The "Unhappy Consciousness," are negative examples of "Sense-Certainty" and "Perception," which prepared the way for the speculative breakthrough of "Understanding." And the narrative of the *Phenomenology* explicitly mentions all three substages of cognition as models for the substages of "Natural Religion," itself a preparation for esthetic and revealed religions.

Other characters of the *Phenomenology* are so by virtue of function rather than identity. Each stage of "consciousness" generates its own particular, universal, and *Begriff* (notion or conceptual horizon). The particular, the universal, and the *Begriff* change from stage to stage, are *relative* to their respective stages. Yet as *functions*, the particular, the universal, and the *Begriff* share in the continuing existence of characters. Infinity, a trope encompassing all of the stages of distinction-making and generalization involved in abstraction, constitutes the conceptual horizon of a not yet reflexive "consciousness." Yet beyond the threshold of "self-consciousness," on the inside of the reflexive sphere, the once formal fluctuations of infinity reappear, but under the organic rubric of life (*Leben*). Life is to "self-consciousness" what infinity was to "consciousness," a conceptual horizon. The function has continued while its filling has changed. The existence within the text of functional constants that attain the continuity of characters is in keeping with an ideology of the organic that has repeatedly stressed the importance of process over product and of development over rectitude.

The development of the philosophical characters in the *Phenomenology,* whether substantial or functional, is narrated by a narrator. But no sooner do we speak of a narrative voice in the *Phenomenology* than this construct bifurcates. There is a retrospective narrative voice that intervenes from the superior position of Absolute Knowing. This "omniscient narrator" often introduces sections and provides summations at their end but is also free to interrupt elsewhere:

> In so far as it ["self-consciousness which . . . knows itself to be *reality*"] has lifted itself out of the ethical Substance and the tranquil being of thought to its being-*for-self*, it has left behind the law of custom and existence, the knowledge acquired through observation, and theory, as a grey shadow which is in the act of passing out of sight. (P. 217)

The observations made by this rather sedate "self-consciousness" are behind it "as a gray shadow," yet the tone and point of view of this passage could apply to a character recently undergoing an experience in any novel with an "omniscient narrator." In the narrative of the *Phenomenology* this particular voice alternates with a blow-by-blow description of "consciousness"'s experience presumably as it is taking place. The narrative function providing the ostensibly immediate transcription of events has been designated by critics, at least with respect to the twentieth-century novel, as the *erlebte Rede,* or "narrated monologue":[17] "But sensuous being and *my* meaning themselves pass over into perception: I am thrown back to the beginning and drawn once again into the same cycle which supersedes itself in each moment and as a whole. Consciousness, therefore, necessarily runs through this cycle again . . ." (p. 71). *This* narrative voice confines itself to the endlessly extended present to which the phenomenological enterprise continually devolves, the present in which "consciousness" senses, perceives, and understands.

Not only does this philosophical novel pursue characters and narrate, if in different ways. As we have seen, *in itself, for itself,* and *for consciousness* are the text's perspectival constants. They are differentiated according to degrees of purpose and containment. *In itself* is a perspective of passive self-containment that can be positive or negative. It is negative in excluding otherness and the awareness that otherness might bring;[18] positive when the containment consummates a return to the self, the recuperation of a self-awareness that has been lost.[19] *For itself* is a perspective of assertion and purpose rather than passivity. The possibility of actualization that it affords is undercut by the general critique of action (as opposed to thought) formulated, for example, in the reading of Sophocles' *Antigone* in "The Ethical World." *For itself* enjoys the positivity of assertion,[20] but it suffers from the blindness of self-interest.[21] The perspective of being *for consciousness* is predicated by a reversal in which self-containment and self-assertion are seen from their *other* sides, that is, from the perspective of what they contribute to otherness, both to the overall development of "consciousness" and to the philosophical mind composing and reading the text. The pervasiveness of these three perspectival constants provides a trigonometric notation by which "consciousness" can often, if not always, sight its position and progress.

The *Phenomenology* is an encyclopaedia in the sense that it aspires to be a compendium of the landmarks of Western metaphysics, a retrospective alignment of its decisive moments and categories. While not a history of philosophy (that is, it does not provide successive readings of, say, Plato and Aristotle), it devotes considerable resources to setting the stage or elaborating the context in which key arguments in the history of philosophy arose—idealism and empiricism, for example. As the compendium of a tradition, the text performs the double function of aligning itself behind the privileged developments in the history of philosophy and aligning them behind it. The effect of this manipulation, like that of the attempt to provide an *immediate* transcription of experience, is to root the developments observed in the present, the present of writing.

Just as the *Phenomenology*'s narrative structure vacillates between immediate transcription and omniscient narration, its temporal perspective incorporates both diachronic and synchronic analyses. The text's diachronic purview encompasses the development from primitive hypotheses (for example, "the ancient Eleusinian Mysteries of Ceres and Bacchus" in "Sense-Certainty," p. 65) to the sophisticated rationality of modern science. This development is both conceptual and historical: it encompasses the evolution of the infrastructures (force, law, genus) making modern science possible but also situates certain particular crystallizations (phrenology, organic reason) within their wider intellectual contexts.

Closely related to this genealogy of scientific disciplines and symbolic forms is the text's anthropological stratum, accounting for the rise of more or less universal social institutions, most notably of a political and theological nature. It is within this strand of the text that the treatment of the dead preconditions and defines the ethical community. Sophocles' *Antigone* becomes an extended metaphor exemplifying a moment when the law of the natural community (the family) is at odds with that of the state. For Hegel, this moment is also the genesis of the unconscious. The predicament of an actor subjected to opposing but inescapable sets of laws implies that each action entails the repression of all other alternatives, alternatives fated to haunt the actor in a strikingly Freudian way. Thus an anthropological moment (the institutions regarding the treatment of the dead) and a psycho-historical event (the rise of the unconscious) join to form part of an historical progression. This moment is preceded by the organization of the city-state and succeeded by the concept of the nation. Similarly, Hegel's fundamentally ahistorical accounts of nature religion and sun worship will be marshaled in a progression culminating in the historical appearance of Judeo-Christianity.

It is, however, in its synchronic program that the text comes closest to its title, to being a *Phenomenology,* if we define this genre as a profile and dramatization of the structures of a "consciousness" that is continually asserting, negating, and surpassing itself. There seems to be little that argues against the conclusion drawn by Jacques Derrida in *Speech and Phenomena*[22] that the enterprise of phenomenology never passes beyond the perceptual field—this despite the fact that Hegel supplements his "Perception" with the elaborate scenario for abstraction in "Understanding." In its phenomenological dimension, the text observes "consciousness" as it in turn perceives—its own prior crystallizations and the limits that are the product of every stage. It is within the text's phenomenological dimension that there can be at least some reconciliation between its formal tropes and metaphors. As was suggested above, both of these components comprise a meta-language in which the text accounts for its own writing. The text's formal tropes tend to *formalize* its narrative necessities. The *Aufhebung* and the triad of *in itself, for itself,* and *for consciousness* implement the narrative functions allowing for progression in time and change of perspective. The text's metaphors, on the other hand, tend to emblematize *conceptual* developments, as electromagnetism embodies a particular type of abstraction. Both the formal and the metaphoric elements of the text's phenomenological program are descriptive of the development of "consciousness" and the constitution of the text. And if these formal and metaphoric components are ever at odds with each other, it is because they are descriptive of slightly different textual domains.

As a novel, an encyclopaedia, a history of ideas, a genealogy of symbolic forms, an anthropology, and a "logic" of its own operations, the *Phenomenology* is itself a germ, a microcosm of Hegel's writings. The synecdoche that enables this work, in reduced scale, to anticipate subsequent explorations also characterizes the interaction between the *Phenomenology*'s smallest and widest scales of activity. The movements of interiorization and exteriorization, which so often describe developments within the "immediate" transcription of events, also characterize the relations between the text's widest units. "Self-Consciousness" and "Spirit," for example, may be described as internalized or subjective emanations, respectively, of "Consciousness" and "Reason." This synecdoche, whose organic model is the seed, is one of Hegel's most successful, and for that reason most suspect, modes of coordination.[23]

For even more impressive than the array of generic expectations that Hegel awakens and the discursive functions that he isolates is the massive coordination of generic models and discursive functions that he effects. Perhaps more than any other single factor, it is the coordination within the Hegelian text that defines the *Phenomenology*'s unique power: the narrative force of the text's internal developments and the literary influence exerted by this work on other works and eras. Our discussion thus far has isolated four roughly defined discursive levels: (1) narrative, concerning the "events" that take place and divided, as discussed above, between retrospective and "immediate" narrations; (2) logical, enforcing the consistency of the argument and related to such procedures as opposition, negation, reversal, and inference; (3) formal, consisting of a battery of repetitive tropes that function independently of "consciousness"'s particular stage or position; and (4) metaphoric, those images whose function is, whether implicitly or explicitly, independent of the economies of the formal tropes or the logical operations.

The general coordination within the Hegelian text enables its narrative, logical, formal, and metaphoric strata to be mutually interchangeable. Where an argument reaches its logical termination—when, say, it becomes explicit that the increasingly abstract constructs of "Understanding" are based on *apparent* distinctions—the formal level is free to intercede—as when the stages of "Understanding" are collapsed and formalized into the trope of infinity. Infinity *circularizes* the steps of asserting and withdrawing differences that comprise "Understanding" within a single (organically) unified figure. Or when the limit of a stage becomes its formalization—again, "Understanding"—a metaphor can be summoned—in this case the theatrical curtain at the close of chapter 3—that "redeems" the formal flattening by reversing it into a self-reflexive moment. In emulation of the *Phenomenology*'s organic ideal, its discursive functions replace one another, complement one another, and compensate for each other's deficiencies.

[III]

If in "Sense-Certainty" and "Perception" Hegel outlines certain structures that will carry through for the rest of the work, it is in "Force and the Understanding" that he completes the battery of formal tools that not only allow for the speculative leap into the supersensible but provide for virtually all subsequent operations. Although understanding constitutes an intellectual stage against whose endless distinction-making and abstraction Hegel voices his skepticism, this chapter nonetheless consummates Hegel's program for the *Phenomenology*. In the wake of this chapter, additional substantive material from different scientific, socio-political, and esthetic contexts may be "fed into" this program, but the deep structures of the "readouts" will have been established. The master-slave conflict will comprise a meditation on the models of reciprocity and inequality completed in this chapter, while the "Unhappy Consciousness" will expand upon, in a self-conscious domain, the hierarchical configuration of metaphysical strata that the variable Appearance (*Erscheinung*) first allows.

And yet "Force and the Understanding" is merely the *completion* of a program elaborated fragmentarily in "Sense-Certainty" and "Perception," and the "accomplishments" of this third level rest heavily on precedents established in the two preceding chapters. The brevity of these chapters accentuates the manner in which they are templated on top of each other and follow analogous patterns.

In relation to the subsequent development of "consciousness," "Sense-Certainty" is a hypothetical zero point of mediation. As the "Preface" asserts at several points, such a position is untenable for a "consciousness" whose entire substance *is* its process and whose process consists of mediation and reflection. "Sense-Certainty" fails as a method for establishing philosophical certainty as soon as the attempt is made to verify it; the acid test to which Hegel submits the stage is a language examination. It is in the acts of uttering (p. 60, *aussprechen*), intending (p. 60, "meaning," *meinen*), and pointing out (p. 64, *aufzeigen*) that the immediacy promised by "Sense-Certainty" dissolves. Yet this failure is not entirely unintentional. The contradictions with which "Sense-Certainty" is *immediately* beset serve as an heuristic device whose purpose is to set the stage for the limited degree of mediation first afforded by "Perception." The *difference* between "Sense-Certainty" and "Perception" is an "unconditioned

absolute universality" (p. 77, *unbedingte absolute Allgemeinheit*), an unspecified modicum of abstraction that presupposes *some* autonomy
from the here and now. The "accomplishment" of the first two chapters becomes the generation of this difference, but the discernment of
the difference depends on the almost exaggerated parallelism of the
two chapters.

In both cases *we* can make the following statements: Introductory
and concluding segments are spoken by the "omniscìent" narrative
voice. The intervening argumentative nuclei are spoken from the
perspective of fictive immediacy, and both are divided into three
segments. The "consciousness" of which the chapters form part presumably has not yet been made aware of itself. The emphasis in these
chapters, then, is not upon the observing subject but upon the ostensibly exterior object, called an indifferent *This* (pp. 59, 67, *Dieses*).

In both cases the development of the argument follows the disintegration of this object of "consciousness." In "Sense-Certainty" the
indifferent object of "consciousness" immediately breaks down into a
here and a now. Opposing Kant, Hegel nonetheless falls back on
Kantian concepts of time and space when he prepares the fundamental task of modifying the object of the philosophical "consciousness."
The ultimate fate of this primordial division will be the fragmentation
of the initial here and now into a bewildering multiplicity of heres and
nows, each particular but also universal, there being no means at this
point for delineating greater and lesser degrees of generality. It is
appropriate to the nonabstraction of this stage that time and space
fragment into an indeterminate multiplicity of heres and nows, that
the extremes of the division should be the one and the many. The
typical model of division in the *Phenomenology* will be bifurcation, the
division of the one into two (usually opposing extremes). But this is
first possible only with the "unconditioned absolute universality" of
"Perception."

We could say of the tripartite argumentative nucleus of "Sense-
Certainty," then, that it begins and ends in moments of division, an
initial one and a final bewildering one. Between these instances of
division, a displacement and a reversal of roles take place, precisely in
the middle of the argument. If Hegel, acting as a *Regisseur,* began the
sequence insisting that the observing "consciousness" *play the role* of
nonessential (or particular) *to* the subject, posited as truth (*Wahre*) and
essence (p. 59, *Wesen*), then in the center of the argument he reverses
this priority. The division now takes place within the yet hypothetical
subject rather than the object. And predictably, if the here and now
upon which the stability of the *object* rested broke down, so does the I
(*ich*) that is the universal of selfhood harbor a bewildering plurality of

selves. The nucleus of the argument, then, links two progressive episodes of division or bifurcation with a lateral reversal displacing the
locus of the division from the subject to the object and back again.[24]

This argument is designed with a certain power in mind, and
Hegel apprises us of this power when he begins "Perception" by re-
casting the process of "Sense-Certainty" in only slightly new terms.
The identification of the thing by means of imputing truth and essentiality to one of its properties (pp. 70–71) recapitulates the slippage
between particular and universal that limited "Sense-Certainty." This
slippage will be contained only when "consciousness" repeats the cycle
in which Hegel arranges the inclusive and exclusive moments constituting the thing. The new level of abstraction afforded by a cyclical
arrangement of linear steps in this situation comprises the first such
move in the *Phenomenology*, one that will attain particular force in the
cycles of infinity (pp. 99–100) and life (pp. 106–7).

Despite the difference generated by the repetition of the cycle of
inclusion and exclusion, namely, the modicum of mediation between
the property (particular) and the thing (universal), the argumentative
structure of "Sense-Certainty" continues with great persistence. It
comes with little astonishment, then, in "Perception" when (1) the
indifferent *This* splits into complementary moments, in this case a
unity (*Eins*) and a multiplicity (*Auch*), the exclusive and inclusive moments constitutive of the thing; (2) the exclusive moment, soon re-
named the *In-so-far* (*Insofern*), itself bifurcates, and in such a fashion
that *its* moments are mutually contradictory; and (3) processes initially situated within the ostensibly exterior locus of the thing shift to
the "consciousness" observing the process and back again. "We are
thus the *universal medium* in which such moments are kept apart and
exist each on its own" (p. 72). "In other words, the Thing is the *Also*,
or the *universal medium* in which the many properties subsist apart
from one another" (p. 73). Once again, a progressive sequence of
bifurcations is interrupted by a lateral displacement.

In conformity with precedents already established, the insurmoun-
table constitutional crisis of the thing occurs when the *In-so-far,* its
exclusionary principle, divides against itself. "Accordingly, the Thing
is for itself and *also* for an other, a being that is *doubly* differentiated
[*das gedoppelte Insofern*)] but *also* a One" (p. 74). A new general notion
of the *In-so-far,* as that which separates a particular thing from others,
arises in conflict with the earlier notion of the *In-so-far* as that which
distinguishes particular properties within the thing. The bifurcation
of the *In-so-far* into lower and higher levels of generality sets the stage
for "Force and the Understanding," in which the second conception
of the force, the law, or the level of abstraction, is always higher than

the first, not only higher but more stable, flatter, and closer to death. Divided between the more and less general versions of its own exclusionary moment, the thing—aptly exemplified by salt—dissolves, having been excluded by itself.

While the bifurcation of the *In-so-far* constitutes the limit both of the thing and "Perception," this rudimentary, *unconditioned* self-reflection serves nonetheless as the basis for the great formal innovation of this stage of cognition. When the narrative translates the self-division of the thing into the terms of the ongoing perspectival dialectic, an interplay of symmetrical reciprocity emerges:

> With this, the last 'in so far' that separated being-for-self from being-for-another falls away; on the contrary, the object is *in one and the same respect the opposite of itself: it is for itself, so far as it is for another*, and *it is for another, so far as it is for itself*. It is for itself, reflected into itself, a One; but this 'for-itself', this reflection into itself, this being a One, is posited in a unity with its opposite, with its 'being for another'. . . . (P. 76)

Paradoxically, the measure of the thing's newly found stability and mediation is that it could be divided against itself. And the form of this internal division is a *reciprocal* interplay in which the degree of assertion (being-for-self) is equal to the degree of detachment (being-for-another). The preliminary, *unconditioned* abstraction or generalization, then, arises at a moment of self-division within the object of "consciousness." But no sooner does this division take place than it is measured, endowed with a form, contained. And the form assumed by this reflection necessary for all subsequent generalization is one of reciprocity: *mutual* activity on the part of opposites observing each other. These opposites are for themselves only to the extent that they are for the other, and vice versa. In reciprocity, in other words, the opposites are different only to the extent that they are the same; the same to the extent that they are different. Reciprocity, then, is a form of self-engendering sameness that produces difference, and a form of difference that can be converted into the same. While *accompanying* the most basic forms of division and reflection, reciprocity *determines* their form and extent. The form that reciprocity imposes on reflection is one of symmetry. Thus, while the mark of a potentially uncontrollable dissolution (of the heres and nows in "Sense-Certainty," for example), reciprocity is also a *control on* reflection. Reciprocal interplay is a control ensuring that any given division or reflection will terminate in a resolution. The equivalence of assertion and detachment in reciprocity is a program ensuring that opposition will always be resolvable into sameness, and that stalemates of parity will always be convertible into differences. From this point on, the narrative and the speculative sequence that the narrative powers will be assured of *momentum*. Inertia will never break the sequence, because resolutions of sameness and difference are preprogramed, by the structure of reciprocity, to metamorphose into their opposites. As we have seen, it is in the midst of reciprocal relations that the space is opened for an unconditioned abstraction. And this space will produce the factor that opens up the supersensible world, a horizontal shifter of value that will, when turned on its end, form a vertically superior domain no longer answerable to sense-experience.

If we pause here at the first notable instance of reciprocity in the *Phenomenology*, it is by virtue of both the resilience and the duplicity of this trope. Reciprocity is both the central mechanical principle of reflection and the release clause that disqualifies the determinations upon which mechanics and reflection are based. Reciprocity originates in a symmetry of cause and effect, but it engenders an endlessly hovering indeterminacy in which the forces and lines of causality and objectivity are hopelessly blurred. Within the Hegelian system, reciprocity serves as the foyer that departs from the engine room of philosophical disputation, leading to a vertiginous uncertainty between the cause and the effect, the self and the other, and domination and subjection. In the *Phenomenology*, abstraction and its implications arise precisely from the midst of a reciprocal interchange; Appearance, with all the metaphysical nuances that it causes, emerges as a savior or messiah that literally redeems reciprocal uncertainty.

It is precisely this sustained, teetering imbalance, announced in the exchange of Hegelian forces, that becomes a decisive factor in the modernist poetics. Although elusive, Hegelian reciprocity is far from fragile. By virtue of its adaptability, we will confront it in a wide variety of contexts. Kierkegaard incorporates this shifter into his scenarios of seduction, making it unclear whether the exotic designs are in the hands of the prowlers or the prey. Reciprocity describes as well the involution of Freudian narcissism. It also qualifies much of the uncanniness of Henry James's prose, in both the events that it stages and the interpretative quandaries that it poses.

In terms of the already complex coordination of discursive levels that Hegel initiates in these chapters, the following statements can be made: On the level of the narrative, he establishes an alternation between a transcription of phenomena ostensibly taking place in a temporal and spatial present *and* a cumulative retrospective and prospective assessment of progress. Paradoxically, it is the second, *most* teleological of these voices that is freest to expand the range of metaphoric association and is most self-critical of both the stage at hand and the text in general. In both chapters it is at the moment just

before the new level of "consciousness" is introduced that the narrative makes its most radical comparisons. The narrative designates the
Eleusinian mysteries of Ceres and Bacchus and the eucharist as the
forebears of "Sense-Certainty." And it presents the animals, who relate to the sensible world by eating it up yet manage *not* to attach a
metaphysics of certainty to this devouring, as more discerning than
orthodox believers in "Sense-Certainty" and its corollaries. In a similar fashion the narrative, at the end of "Perception," compares the
circular process by which the thing is identified by a property and a
property is taken for the thing to sophistry (and, implicitly, to Plato's
Sophist).[25] Schizophrenically, then, the narrative voice supplying the
greatest teleological thrust and closure is the one that is metaphorically most promiscuous. Or, the metaphoric liberties taken by
the voice make it inherently ironic, all the more so in regard to the
calm progress that is the performative intent of this voice. The voice
of immediate transcription is also metaphoric. The running commentary on the breakdown of the thing is predicted by the use of salt as an
exemplification of the thing. Both voices, then, the "immediate" as
well as the "omniscient," are fundamentally figural. Even if the voice
of consummation is the one that takes the widest associative liberties,
both narrative voices are ironic in their metaphoricity.[26]

On the level of logic, in both chapters Hegel orchestrates the *negation* of the substantive hypotheses on which the stages are based. Both
stages posit a subject-object distinction that is undermined in two
ways: (1) the ostensible singularity of the subject or object breaks
down into a multiplicity, and (2) the subject-object designation proves
reversible, as does that between the entire process and its hypothetical
audience, whether regarded as the philosopher or the philosophizing
collectivity.

The formal manifestations of these logical moves are wide-reaching. Bifurcation becomes a primal thrust of movement in the
Hegelian text. A given crystallization will be superseded for no other
reason than because it will bifurcate. Because of the logical reversibility of the pairs formed by the subject-object distinction, bifurcation implies an ongoing displacement of the interior to the exterior,
and vice versa. The interiority of the exterior and the exteriority of
the interior are formal extensions of the reversibility of the subject-
object distinction. Once the operations of bifurcation and reversal
have expanded into the ironic exchange by which the interior and the
exterior are always already transformable into each other, the sufficient conditions for reciprocity have been attained. Reciprocity, the
other-sided (*gegenseitig*) observation of the activities of the self in an
other or of another in the self, is the basic model for reflection, self-

consciousness, and criticism in the Hegelian text. Establishing a space, if not a finished model, for reciprocity is the highest formal crystallization of the first two chapters.

The coordination established in the first two chapters of the *Phenomenology* is, then, prodigious. Narrative, logical, formal, and metaphoric functions combine in rehearsing "consciousness"'s break from the sensible world. Yet this rupture is prefigured in a split narrative voice whose countertemporalities and orientations are radically different, and in formal operations that expand to constitute self-bracketing and self-externalizing spatial and conceptual fields.

[IV]

The "achievement" of "Understanding" that completes "consciousness"'s detachment from sensation and literally breaks the gravitational field of the empirical world is a conception of force in which the existence of *particular,* reciprocally related counterforces does not compromise the existence of the force as a (*general*) whole. The metaphor of a conceptual force on a higher level of generality than the particular subforces that make it up, a conceptual force somehow above the activities of expression (*Äußerung*) and repression (*zurückdrängen*) to which the subforces are relegated, is a model for abstraction itself. The general, conceptual force derives its structure and motion from the subforces yet is not subject to their limitations (their particularities of valence or direction). The primary metaphor that Hegel selects for the conceptual stage of "Understanding" is from the referential sphere of physics. An electromagnetism that incorporates, assimilates, and supersedes its positive and negative charges yet nonetheless remains structured by them is an apt example for the abstraction bonding two different planes of generality.

Spatially conceived, a bond between lower and higher levels of generality or particularity is vertical. Yet the highest conceptual crystallization suggested in the first two chapters of the *Phenomenology* was a reciprocity whose spatial extension was horizontal. A passage from "Perception" cited above (from p. 76 of the text) demonstrates a self-assertiveness to the extent of being for another (and vice versa) that takes place in the plane of a reflection before a mirror. Hegel's formal task in "Force and the Understanding" is to turn a horizontal reciprocity on its end so that it becomes a vertical mutual interrelation between the particular and the universal. This gesture of literal upending constitutes the configuration of superior and inferior horizontal strata basic to all scientific and theological speculation, and registered with particular persistence in the ontology underlying much of Romantic literature. The emergence of a vertical stratification in the *Phenomenology,* however much this event conforms to the internal requirement for evolutionary development, reinstates the limits of the Kantian hierarchy within the Hegelian scheme. As will be discussed in fuller detail below, the shifter of valence that will facilitate the conversion of horizontal reciprocity into vertical hierarchy and of the data of sense-experience into the immobility of law is the variable Appearance (*Erscheinung*). The capabilities of Appearance overlap with those of metaphor itself: imputation and transference. Appearance is able to *impute* actuality or semblance (*Schein*) to phenomena and to *transfer* the status of actuality to semblance, and vice versa. In this manner, Appearance converts the almost physical movement of reversal in models of reciprocal action into conceptual terms (semblance and actuality) that harbor metaphysical valences within them. Once the semblance or actuality of a phenomenon is at stake, a vertical configuration has been summoned, with all the hierarchical and judgmental valences that may be attached to the distinctions between truth and appearance, seeming and being. It is the semblance or show in Appearance that makes possible the subtle translation of physical motion into metaphysical evaluation and that forges the bond between the empirical world and something above and beyond it. All subsequent crystallizations of theology, culture, politics, and art will be predicated and structured by this bond. Yet Appearance, the converter of actuality into semblance, is itself pure shift, pure transference, pure variation. Paradoxically, then, the ontological strata and system that sublimate themselves *above* the level of the sensible rest upon a factor of pure difference.

We have already seen how "Perception" began with a double gesture of recapitulation and deformation; the first phase of "Perception" was a repetition of the stages of "Sense-Certainty," but translated into new and slightly different terms. It is not surprising, then, that "Force and the Understanding" begins with the vacillation between unity and multiplicity that occupied "Perception" (p. 81). But in "Force and Understanding" the mutually negating moments of inclusion and exclusion are incorporated into a single figure, a term figuring their transformation into each other. This is the figure of force.

> But this movement is what is called *Force.* One of its moments, the dispersal of the independent 'matters' in their [immediate] being, is the *expression* of Force; but Force, taken as that in which they have disappeared, is Force *proper,* Force which has been *driven back* into itself from its expression. First, however, the Force which is driven back into itself

must express itself; and, secondly, it is still Force remaining *within itself* in the expression, just as much as it is expression in this self-contained-ness. (P. 81)

If inclusion and exclusion were the complementary moments that constituted the thing or object of perception, expression (*Äußerung*) and repression (or withdrawal, *züruckdrängen*) constitute the notion of force that is the object of understanding. Expression and repression—not only is the substantial rhetoric of thinghood (*Materien*) translated into the dynamic interaction of forces but the linguistic problems touched upon in the commentary at the end of "Sense-Certainty" now occupy the center of the stage. *Expression* constitutes the force that is understanding's emblem and its notion (*Begriff*). While the properties of the thing were themselves *substance*, the activities making up the language-object that is force are *functions* or *relations*. Hence they are free to disappear into each other.

The metaphor of force thus lifts the *substantive* limitations of the thing of perception. Force is a dynamic rather than a static entity, composed of functional rather than substantial elements. Force transcends the thing in yet another way. In its dynamic quality it is no longer subject to the division that finally sunders the thing. The motion, relativity, and now unity of the force make it, despite its metaphoric grounding in the world of physics, the organic *answer* to the thing's substantiality.

> Force as such, or as driven back into itself, thus exists on its own account as an *exclusive One*, for which the unfolding of the [different] 'matters' is *another* subsisting essence; and thus two distinct independent aspects are set up. But Force is also the whole, i.e. it remains what it is according to its Notion; that is to say, these *differences* remain pure forms, superficial *vanishing* moments. (P. 82)

As opposed to the thing, force does not allow itself to be sundered, discomposed by the conflict between the different levels of generality that it encompasses. The force's relatively lower level of generality consists of the complementary subforces, analogous to positive and negative charges of electricity, that express, repress, incite, repel, and disappear into each other. Yet force demonstrates the hitherto unprecedented capability, in either "consciousness" or its objects, to bond this particular level of functioning to its general existence as a whole. Ironically, the transition to the "more" organic metaphor of force from the thing brings about an *increase* in the unity that is a compositional requirement of substances.

The metaphoric displacement from the thing to the force effects a shift from the static to the organic, from substantive to functional components, and from irreconcilable duality to unity. Yet even in the wake of such dramatic changes, the formal physics that we have begun to explore, a physics whose movements already include bifurcation, lateral displacement, and reciprocal relations, continues to operate. It is *predetermined,* in light of this physics, that the force, even a force reconciling its greater and lesser degrees of generality, should bifurcate and be opposed by an *other.*

> What appears as an 'other' and solicits Force, both to expression and to a return into itself, directly proves to be *itself Force.* . . . There are at the same time two Forces present; the Notion of both is no doubt the same, but it has gone forth from its unity into a duality. Instead of the antithesis remaining entirely and essentially only a moment, it seems, by its self-diremption into two wholly *independent* forces, to have withdrawn from the controlling unity. (Pp. 83–84)

Predictably, Hegel's basic definition of force is in accordance with a double logic. Force sustains both a double movement (expression and repression) and an ontological status that is double (particular *and* general). Consistent with this logic, the two forces emerging from the bifurcation taking place in the above passage represent *both* two particular counterforces (say, positive and negative electricity) *and* the irreducibly different particular and general levels encompassed by the figure of force.

Yet the formal program fragmentarily formulated in the text's initial chapters not only provides for this multidimensional doubling but also predicates the nature of the interaction between doubles, whether regarded as entire forces or subforces. And the form of this interaction is the reciprocity introduced in "Perception," but achieving its fullest physical (as opposed to metaphysical) elaboration in "Understanding." This reciprocity was already intimated in the passage cited above (p. 81), in which an internal necessity dictated that the expression and repression constitutive of the force imply each other ("the Force which is driven back into itself *must* express itself"). This rhetoric of reciprocal interaction reaches its fullest physical or mechanical expression in the following passage:

> From this we see that the Notion of Force becomes *actual* through its duplication into two Forces, and how it comes to be so. These two Forces exist as independent essences; but their existence is a movement of each towards the other, such that their being is rather a pure *positedness* or a being that is *posited by an other,* i.e., their being has really the significance of a sheer *vanishing.* . . . Consequently, these moments are not divided into two independent extremes offering each other only an opposite extreme: their essence rather consists simply and solely in this,

that each *is* solely through the other, and what each thus is it immediately no longer is, since it *is* the other. They have thus, in fact, no substances of their own which might support and maintain them. . . . Force, as *actual*, exists simply and solely in its *expression*. . . . This *actual* Force, when thought of as free from its expression and as being for itself, is force driven back into itself. . . . Thus the realization of Force is at the same time the loss of reality; in that realization it has really become something quite different, viz. this *universality*, which the Understanding knows at the outset. . . . (Pp. 85–86)

The reciprocity that describes the interaction both within and between forces is indeed multidimensional. First of all, the general existence of the force, its existence as an abstraction or concept, and its actualization in a particular form are mutually dependent. In order to be actualized, force as an abstraction must be divided into concrete subforces, but in order to be conceptualized, the concrete subforces must be collapsed and unified into an abstraction. In terms of this passage, the real (particular) existence of the force disappears into the thought (*Gedanke*) of a generalization (*Allgemeinheit*), and the notion (*Begriff*) of force divides into mutually opposed particulars. Not only do the general and particular levels of the force relate reciprocally to each other but the opposing particular forces into which the abstraction divides in order to be actualized exist "solely through the other."

The reciprocally related counterforces into which the force divides exist purely in relation to each other. They are expressive and relative rather than substantial. In a sense, it is the physical and mechanical nature of the counterforces that enables them to disappear into each other without a trace. The pure relativity and functional nature of the counterforces is an effect of the physical and mechanical metaphor of force. Yet it is only a brief step from this reciprocal mechanics to the operating principles of Hegelian intersubjectivity. Purely functional vectors may disappear into each other, but this self-consuming physics lays the groundwork for the recognition of the self in an other, and the complementary identification of the other through the self. This scenario for recognition not only will condition all subsequent Hegelian interactions but will reverberate well beyond Hegel.

As dynamic, complex, and intricate as the interplay of forces in "Understanding" may be, a current of discontent with the purely relative nature of the game and the distinctions that it produces runs throughout the chapter. The expression and repression constitutive of the thing, for example, were described, in a passage cited above, as "superficial, vanishing moments" (p. 82, *oberflächliche verschwindende Momente*). The potential to make *something more* of the reciprocal play of forces, to give it purpose and destiny, arises, as it were, between

them, or more accurately, between the two forms of abstraction required to account for a force that is both particular and general. By
virtue of the logic of bifurcation which dominates this chapter, not
only does the force itself split but so does its abstraction or generalization (*Allgemeinheit*)—between two equally speculatively unattainable
extremes. The "first generalization" (*erste Allgemeinheit*) is an immediate (*unmittelbar*) presentation of force as an actual object (p. 86,
wirklicher Gegenstand). The generalization arising in opposition to the
first one is the negative of the ostensibly objective force, a pure, and
by implication self-contained, conceptual interiority.

In the space between these mirror images of speculative impossibility (reminiscent of the opposition between ratiocination and representation in the "Preface"), Hegel places the potential for elevation
and purpose. This between-space is the ground for the play of forces.
It is also home to the variable Appearance (*Erscheinung*), which provides the teleological direction and delineates vertically superior and
inferior realms. Appearance converts the basically horizontal picture
that Hegel sketches of a space *between* two serially successive generalizations into a vertical configuration, with all the relations of priority,
superiority, and determination that such a configuration implies:

> This true essence of Things has now the character of not being immedi-
> ately for consciousness; on the contrary, consciousness has a mediated
> relation to the inner being and, as the Understanding, *looks through this
> mediating play of Forces into the true background of Things*. The middle term
> which unites the two extremes, the Understanding and the inner world,
> is the developed *being* of Force which, for the Understanding itself, is
> henceforth only a vanishing. This 'being' is therefore called *appearance;*
> for we call *being* that is directly and in its own self a *non-being* a surface
> show. But it is not merely a surface show; it is appearance, a *totality* of
> show. This *totality*, as totality or as a *universal*, is what constitutes the
> inner [of Things], the play of Forces as a reflection of the inner into
> itself. In it, the Things of perception are expressly present for con-
> sciousness as they are in themselves, viz. as moments which immediately
> and without rest or stay turn into their opposite, the One immediately
> into the universal, the essential immediately into the unessential, and
> vice versa. This play of Forces is consequently the developed negative;
> but its truth is the positive, viz. the *universal*, the object that, *in itself*,
> possesses being. (Pp. 86–87)

The elevation from the sensible to the supersensible depends on
the establishment of a continuity between the purely sensible existence represented by the "first generalization" of force and the purely
intellectual existence of the "second generalization." The phrase "es-

tablish a continuity" in fact falls short of the immediacy with which sensible and supersensible, particular and universal, must give rise to each other. This immediate conversion is effected by the semblance or show (*Schein*) at the etymological heart of Appearance (*Erscheinung*). *Schein* is an immediate bond between being and nonbeing: "*being* that is directly and in its own a non-being." It is on the basis of this bond that Appearance, as a totalization of self-consuming play, fosters an endless and restless conversion between particularity and generalization, "the One immediately into the universal, the essential immediately into the unessential." Already, then, the conversion *to* a superior ontological realm must embody the immediacy and immanence that will define the realm itself. The superiority of the elevated realm will consist in a hypothetical immunity from mediation and differentiation.

"Appearance" (*Erscheinung*) is a general rubric for the substitution effected by show (*Schein*), a generic term, even though Hegel has not yet taken up his discussion of biological taxonomy: "appearance, a totality of show." Arising in the between-space of the horizontally aligned reciprocal play of forces, Appearance is the sum total of the bond that facilitates a wide-reaching set of substitutions: general for particular, inner for outer, negative for positive. The superior realm that precipitates out of Appearance is, not a mystical otherworldliness whose principles are inherently arbitrary and inscrutable, but a transformation of relations that have been painstakingly anticipated in this organic text. The relations modified in the course of the overall or systematic conversion that the term "Appearance" both facilitates and emblematizes are ones of particularity and generality, interiority and exteriority, and positivity and negativity.

So it is in the above passage, then, that as a totalization of the physical and therefore external play of forces, Appearance opens up a reflexive *interior;* in its particularity and self-consumption, the play of forces is relegated to a negative status, but this merely particular negative will harbor the operating principles, the positivity, of the superior domain. As the multifaceted converter within the Hegelian enterprise, Appearance also claims the privilege of determining the usefulness of the now-superseded stages of "consciousness." In re-evaluating the progress of "consciousness" in "Sense-Certainty" and "Perception," Appearance retracts this experience and assigns it a metaphoric or figurative status. What provided the positivity or certainty of sense-experience now becomes metaphoric for a reflection taking place in an inner world. Appearance thus performs upon the entire two preceding stages of "consciousness" what was rehearsed during both of their intermediate stages: Appearance interiorizes within "consciousness" processes that ostensibly took place in an exterior sensible actuality:

> The *being* of this object for consciousness is mediated by the movement of *appearance*, in which the *being of perception* and the sensuously objective in general has a merely negative significance. Consciousness, therefore, reflects itself out of this movement back into itself as the True; but, *qua* consciousness, converts this truth again into an objective *inner*, and distinguishes this reflection of Things from its own reflection into itself: just as the movement of mediation is likewise still objective for it. (P. 87)

There is yet another conversion performed by the variable Appearance. Paradoxically, in its context, this substitution of a vertical for a horizontal spatialization is the most radical of Appearance's many shifts; yet it is precisely this conversion that carries the heaviest teleological and metaphysical weight. *Appearance opens up* the supersensible (as Matthew Perry may be said to have opened up Japan) by *projecting* a reflection that occurs in a horizontal plane into a vertically superior space that functions as a heaven.

> Within this *inner truth*, as the *absolute universal* which has been purged of the *antithesis* between the universal and the individual and has become the object of the *Understanding*, there now opens up above the *sensuous* world, which is the world of *appearance*, a *supersensible* world which henceforth is the *true* world, above the vanishing *present* world there opens up a permanent *beyond*; an it-self which is the first, and therefore imperfect, appearance of Reason, or only the pure element in which the truth has its *essence*. (Pp. 87–88)

This passage dramatizes the shift from an *inner* truth to an *over* truth. In Hegel's first image of the *rise* of the supersensible, the superior domain constituted by Appearance (*erscheinende Welt*) literally imposes or superimposes itself over ("schließt sich . . . über") the sensible world as its truth. There is a truth value attached to the vertically superior stratum, and this judgment is all the weightier in its descent from a permanent beyond (*bleibende Jenseits*). So momentous is this rise, this projection upwards, that it heralds the appearance of "reason," which is an objectification and externalization of the knowledge gained in "self-consciousness," even though the text has not yet attained "self-consciousness."

In a passage that commemorates the triumphant rise of the transcendental world, the replaceability of vertical for horizontal spatialization reasserts itself in full force:

The inner world, or supersensible beyond, has, however, *come into being* (*entstanden*): it *comes from* the world of appearance which has mediated it; in other words, appearance is its essence and, in fact, its filling. The supersensible is the sensuous and the perceived posited as it is in *truth*; but the *truth* of the sensuous and the perceived is to be *appearance*. The super-sensible is therefore *appearance qua appearance*. We completely misunderstand this if we think that the supersensible world is *therefore* the sensuous world, or the world as it exists for immediate sense-certainty and perception; for the world of appearance is, on the contrary, *not* the world of sense-knowledge and perception as a world that positively *is*, but this world posited as superseded, or as in truth an *inner world*. (P. 89)

In this passage the verb *entstehen* describes the emergence of the "inner world, *or* supersensible beyond" (my emphasis). The beyond has come into being quite literally by standing up. It is in this passage that Hegel most fully elaborates the mediatory function of Appearance. Paradoxically, the activity of this term, at whose center stands an *immediate* bond between being and nonbeing, concentrates itself preponderantly in *mediation,* between both opposites and ontological strata. Hegel elaborates this mediation by exploring the resonances of the terms for filling (*Erfüllung*) and mediation itself (*Vermittlung*). Appearance constitutes both the *filling* (that is, the contents) of the supersensible world and its *fulfillment*. If the beyond emerges from the intermediate position of Appearance (between the sensible and the supersensible), Appearance is both the *medium* of the beyond and its *broker* (*Vermittlung*). The supersensible is the negated or transformed data of sense-experience placed (*gesetzt*) or taken for truth. (Hegel's term for *perception, Wahr-nehmung,* is a taking of the sensible for truth.)

In relation to the beyond, sense-experience is a figuration of "consciousness" emptied of any substantive truth or value it might have *appeared* to have. In relation to a sense-experience that never completes this elevation, the beyond can only appear as an elusive, pure appearance (*appearance qua appearance*). Appearance, the almost biological medium out of which the supersensible and transcendental grows, sells sense-experience to transcendence, monopolizing a metaphysical commerce.

Once the initial but by no means whimsical foothold in the supersensible has been secured by means of the complex variable Appearance, the fate of understanding will be to repeat its operations on increasingly higher levels of abstraction. This repetition-compulsion toward generality will spell both the contribution and limit of "Understanding." The law of force will be to force what the supersensible is to the sensible: an abstraction of force's particularity, a totalization of what in the force is negative by virtue of particularity. Yet the law, and the levels of abstraction that succeed it (kingdoms of laws and supersensible worlds), will repeat the processes undergone by force. The initial entity, whether the force, the law, or the supersensible world, will bifurcate into subentities. But then the horizontal division will be turned on its end, and the second subentity will be elevated to a higher level of abstraction than the first. In conformity with the model of mediation or brokerage provided by Appearance, the relation between the relatively higher and lower levels of abstraction will be one of inversion or perversion.

The notion of the law, for example, will institutionalize the relation of the supersensible to sense-experience. In the train of ratios or elective affinities that are a unique intellectual by-product of "Understanding," the notion of the law is to force what the transcendental beyond is to the here: negativity (or difference) made positive; relativity (or change) stabilized; process sublimated into permanence:

> . . . the distinction between the Forces, along with both those distinctions, likewise collapses into only one. . . . what there is in this absolute flux is only *difference* as a *universal* difference, or as a difference into which the many antitheses have been resolved. This difference, as a *universal* difference, is consequently the *simple element in the play of Force itself* and what is true in it. It is the *law of Force*. (P. 90)

> Consequently, the *supersensible* world is an inert *realm of laws* which, though beyond the perceived world—for this exhibits law only through incessant change—is equally *present* in it and is its direct tranquil image.
>
> This realm of laws is indeed the truth for the Understanding. . . . (Pp. 90–91)

In the physical field of force, the opposed counterforces simply vanish into each other. In the deterministic representations that comprise laws, expressions or assertions leave a trace. The form of this legal script is such that the same-named pushes off from itself; the same becomes different; the different becomes same ("das *Gleichnamige* sich von sich selbst abstößt"; "das *Ungleichwerden des Gleichen*"; "das *Gleichwerden des Ungleichen*"). Or identity, to use terms employed in this century, produces difference; difference underlies the hypothesis of identity. This notation represents the highest development of the logic and mechanics of reciprocity evolved through the first two chapters of the *Phenomenology*.

The attraction of opposites and the repulsion of the selfsame comprises the most extreme formal crystallization of the Hegelian reciprocity. This formula arises from the combination of an ongoing structure of *binary opposition* with a relation of *reversal* between successive stages of abstraction. The attraction of opposites and the repulsion of the selfsame is an instance of reversal (or inversion) being permanently implanted within a matrix of binary opposition. The examples that Hegel selects for this chapter all demonstrate, in different spheres, this concurrence of bifurcation, abstraction, and reversal. The magnet, polarized yet whole, self-repulsive and opposite-attractive, embodies most concretely the reversal produced by abstraction. This reversal applies both to the relation between opposites and to that between successive levels of abstraction. As a codified writing, the law metamorphoses the traceless and therefore blameless force into an enduring statute of reversal.

The highest level of abstraction accommodated by "Understanding" occurs when law is applied to law, when the supersensible is defined as the stabilized image (*stilles Abbild*) of legal activity. Yet in accordance with the principle of magnetism, even the supersensible turns on itself. Typically, the relation between the divided elements of the supersensible world is one of reversal.

> *This second supersensible world* is in this way the *inverted* world and moreover, since one aspect is already present in the first supersensible world, the inversion of the first. With this, the inner world is completed as appearance. For the first supersensible world was only the *immediate* raising of the perceived world into the universal element; it had its necessary counterpart in this perceived world which still retained *for itself the principle of change and alteration*. The first kingdom of laws lacked that principle, but obtains it as an inverted world. (Pp. 96–97)

Just as the law engenders its own opposite, one supersensible produces the inversion or perversion (*verkehrt*) of itself. The adjective *verkehrt* sustains translation both as "inverted" and "perverted," and shares with its English and French counterparts the placement of the verbal stem for turning at its center. Extended to the end, abstraction reaches a cul-de-sac where elevation literally turns into degeneration, where exchange (*Wechsel*) and alteration (*Veränderung*) become self-justifying principles (*Prinzip*). At the horizon where a no longer possible elevation merges into aimless repetition, the movements of bifurcation, displacement, and reversal coinciding in the figure of Appearance rebound in the form of automatic negativity.

As the examples selected for the chapter demonstrate, not only does the inverted world metamorphose sweet into sour, positive electricity into negative, or social deviance into rehabilitation. Automated, left to their own devices, the structures of "Understanding" open the space for negativity in itself. They form the frames surrounding

Bosch's apocalyptic paintings and set the stage for the "Wal-purgisnacht" scenes in Goethe's *Faust*. The possibility of recuperating or rehabilitating this automatic negativity is questionable, as is the finality of the resolution provided by the lifting of the curtain at the end of the chapter. This latter act is a *performance* of resolution, but the laborious effort with which "Self-Consciousness" begins in the wake of the compulsive repetition of "Understanding" undermines the decisiveness of this gesture.

Given the transcendental aspirations of "Understanding," the de-volution of dynamic processes into inert representations is convertible into advancement. This does not, however, make "Understanding" immune to its internal failures. Limit, relative to each stage, is as necessary a product of "consciousness"'s development as are the con-ceptual horizon and advancement itself. The repetitive operations of "Understanding," which become, if anything, more effortless as the horizon of abstraction widens, harbor the seeds of understanding's decline while constituting its uniqueness. Just as "Perception" faltered when its exclusive principle opposed fundamentally unrelated prop-erties to each other, so "Understanding," in the momentum of its operations, imposes the status of essentiality on what is basically indifferent.

Hegel cites motion as a phenomenon whose elements are not *neces-sarily* interrelated. The law of motion, not motion itself, is what retro-spectively imposes the necessity of the division and opposition of the components of motion.

> In the law of motion, e.g., it is necessary that motion be split up into time and space, or again, into distance and velocity. Thus, since motion is only the relation of these factors, it—the universal—is certainly divid-ed *in its own self*. But now these parts, time and space, or distance and velocity, do not in themselves express this origin in a One; they are indifferent to one another, space is thought of as able to be without time, time without space, and distance at least without velocity—just as their magnitudes are indifferent to one another. . . . The necessity of the *division* is thus certainly present here, but not the necessity of the *parts* as such for one another. But it is just for this reason that that first necessity, too, is itself only a sham, false necessity. (Pp. 93–94)

In this passage, the law passes from being the institutionalization of order and stability to being the culprit, the written code that betrays the indifference of the phenomena *in themselves*. The transgression consists in imposing *apparent* differences where there were none, in manipulating the phenomena according to the internal requirements of abstraction. The generation of *apparent* differences is the dark side of the variable Appearance, without which those differences, as well as abstraction in general, would be impossible.

Once the law usurps the privilege of determining, by virtue of its internal economy, where the fissures in nature lie, understanding is vulnerable to a systematic loss of control. The necessities discovered by laws are formal and logical necessities intrinsic to expression, not within the represented phenomena themselves. From the *apparent* differences generated by an Appearance capable of substituting non-being for being it is only a short step to an interpretative process gone mad, dominated to such an extent by its internal compulsions that it becomes a machine.

> This necessity, which is merely verbal, is thus a recital of the moments constituting the cycle of the necessity. The moments are indeed distinguished, but, at the same time, their difference is expressly said to be *not* a difference of the thing itself, and consequently is itself immediately cancelled again. This process is called *'explanation'*. A *law* is enunciated; from this, its implicitly universal element or ground is distinguished as *Force;* but it is said that this difference is no difference, rather that the ground is constituted exactly the same as the law. . . . *Force is constituted exactly the same as law.* . . . (Pp. 94–95)

The supersensible world, as well as the law that is one of its sub-categories, could not have been opened up without Appearance, which, as we have seen, owed its capabilities to formal operations of bifurcation, displacement, and substitution developed in the first two chapters. With this goal attained, however, with the opening of the heavens that sustain transcendental projection, the time has come to contain, close the lid on, and deny those very formal operations. Operations that on the underside of the beyond were necessary to give "consciousness" any movement at all have now become a mechanistic threat to the transcendental. Hegel's containment of "Understanding" by applying to it a critique of formalism is thus a cover-up, a concealment of the operations that make "Understanding" possible. The necessity of the law is spurious, because it is "merely verbal" (*nur im Worte liegt*). The law is a narrative or recital (*Hererzählung*) of its moments. The law has been kidnapped out of the service of the phenomenon itself (*der Sache selbst*) and forcefully impressed into the misrepresentations of language. This corruption can be identified with a name, "explanation" (*Erklären*), and the most ominous aspect of this language disorder is its mechanical operation. Its moments form the cycle of a machine: "It is an explanation that not only explains nothing, but is so plain that, while it pretends to say something different from what has already been said, really says nothing at all but only repeats the same thing" (p. 95).

Even in the Hegelian text, then, formal operations serve as a convenient whipping boy for the profound ambiguities toward language that occasionally surface. In certain moments of confusion, even Hegel unleashes the general Romantic frustration with the *Ding an sich* against the formal operations that he himself had synthesized and that constitute the enduring contribution of the *Phenomenology*.[27] In this text Hegel assumes the double task of accounting, in formal and logical terms, for the movements of philosophical language *and* of legitimizing the thrust of Western civilization in many of its theaters. This ambivalence toward the operations of bifurcation, displacement, and reversal is a sore spot where the irreconcilability of these enterprises is felt most acutely.

"Explanation," in the above passage, is a pejorative term, a rubric for the mechanistic processes of abstraction. Yet it merely repeats a gesture that was essential to understanding; just as Appearance totalized semblance (*Schein*), relativizing the status of being, explanation totalizes the internal operation of laws. The initial description of explanation as a cycle reflects a mistrust of the linguistic processes involved in the formulation of laws. But at the end of "Understanding," infinity (*Unendlichkeit*) totalizes understanding's activities, becoming a trope for the entire process. And the form that this trope assumes is precisely that of a cycle. Life itself, in "The Truth of Self-Certainty," not only will borrow this cyclical structure but will appropriate, in *very* slightly different terms, the steps of infinity.

Thus, at a particular moment when the legitimizing function of his program is threatened, Hegel invokes Romantic truisms *against* the structures of his own text. But in other contexts these structures will emerge with renewed force. The unique resilience of these formal tropes is evident both in the rich variety of the operations that Hegel has developed in the course of "Understanding" and in the complex but by no means arbitrary manner in which he has been able to interrelate them in a narrative. A summary of these formal developments would read as follows:

(1) The abstraction implicit within the notion of force has for the first time opened a space for mediation that was totally absent in "Sense-Certainty" and present only rudimentarily in "Perception" (there in the "unconditioned absolute universality"). A space between two reciprocally related counterforces is the setting for this mediation.

(2) The variable Appearance, situated in this intermediary space, shifts the horizontal interplay of forces into a vertical configuration of

strata. Appearance imputes the status of nonbeing to being and transforms the certainty of sense-experience into the uncertainty or negativity of speculation. Appearance thus allows sense-experience to be *projected* into a superior transcendental domain, where it functions as a negative basis for speculation.

(3) The vertical projection first allowed by Appearance, when combined with the bifurcation that is the basic operation of the Hegelian logic, produces a model for abstraction in general. According to this model, an abstract entity will always be bifurcated, and the second subentity will exist on a higher plane of abstraction than the first. The relation between successive levels of abstraction is one of *inversion.* The higher level of abstraction embodies the *form* of the lower level without the content. But since the higher level depends on the lower level for its *form,* the only change that the abstraction can produce is a transfiguration of values.

(4) The principle of inversion, when introduced into reciprocal relations, initiates an automatic reversal of values whose magnetic model is the attraction of opposites and the repulsion of the selfsame. This generation of difference out of identity and intimation of identity in difference may assume either a horizontal or a vertical spatialization. "Understanding" tropologizes the stages of abstraction by collapsing them into a single figure. This collapse of multiple operations into a single figure performs the same totalization by means of which sense-experience is projected into the transcendental domain under the single rubric of Appearance. Hegel calls the initial totalizing trope, describing the relation between laws and the phenomena they modify, explanation. On a thematic level, explanation is presented as a negative instance of empty formalistic reasoning. But Hegel does not summarily dismiss the value of codifying formal operations of "consciousness" or language as figures or tropes. In the trope that he identifies as infinity (*Unendlichkeit*) Hegel encapsulates the major procedures of "Understanding." The magnetic principle of the attraction of opposites and the repulsion of the selfsame, when applied to the sequence of steps in abstraction, touches off an endless rhythm of ebb and flow, which Hegel terms infinity.

> We see that through infinity, law completes itself into an immanent necessity, and all the moments of [the world of] appearance are taken up into the inner world. That the simple character of law is infinity means, according to what we have found, (a) that it is self-*identical,* but is also in itself *different;* or it is the selfsame which repels itself from itself or sunders itself into two. What was called *simple Force duplicates* itself and through its infinity is law. (b) What is thus dirempted [*das Entzweite*], which constitutes the parts thought of as in the *law,* exhibits itself

as a stable existence; and if the parts are considered without the Notion of the inner difference, then space and time, or distance and velocity, which appear as moments of gravity, are just as indifferent and without a necessary relation to one another as to gravity itself, or, as this simple gravity is indifferent to them, or, again as simple electricity is indifferent to positive or negative electricity. But (c) through the Notion of inner difference, these unlike and indifferent moments, space and time, etc. are a *difference* which is no *difference*, or only a difference of what is *selfsame*, and its essence is unity. As positive and negative they stimulate each other into activity, and their being is rather to posit themselves as not-being and to suspend themselves in the unity. The two distinguished moments both subsist; they are *implicit* and are *opposites in themselves*, i.e., each is the opposite of itself; each has its 'other' within it and they are only one unity.

This simple infinity, or the absolute Notion, may be called the simple essence of life, the soul of the world, the universal blood. . . . (Pp. 99–100)

This definitive, in the sense of ultimate, recapitulation of the processes of "Understanding" arranges a formal model of reciprocity and a logic of reversal that derives from the physics of electromagnetism into a *sequence* of steps. Yet this sequence turns around on itself to form a cycle and a trope, a trope encompassing the multiplicity of operations within a single figure. Paradoxically, in consummating, or *topping off*, processes of considerable intricacy with a single figure, Hegel outlines a process that is by nature endless. This is the highest formal and conceptual crystallization in the first three chapters. The movements of first force, then law, and finally codes of law have achieved their most abstract formulation—in terms of the categories of identity and difference. Disparate and seemingly arbitrary descriptions from all of the first three chapters, involving not only electromagnetism but also criminal justice, the thing, and animals, have been drawn together by means of a trope, whose formal principles Hegel here enunciates. Under the rubric of the term "infinity," Hegel has formulated the *possible* conditions of his own discourse, the conditions accounting for the operations that he has thus far deployed. The moment of infinity, or endlessness, then, is a moment of formal awareness. Even while railing at the *Ding an sich* in his critique of explanation, Hegel has written Kant into his own text as the possibility whose contours have the shape of infinity.

Throughout the chapter on "Understanding," Hegel's examples and metaphors, like abstraction itself, have demonstrated the dual capacity both to bond the particular and the universal and to absorb the reversal between successive stages of abstraction. Electricity itself, like the magnet and the rehabilitative, as opposed to the punitive, system of criminal justice, bridges different levels of generality while sustaining opposition. There is, however, a metaphoric fabric in this text that while less explicit than such examples is no less decisive to its internal accounts of its thematic, formal, and textual programs. An undercurrent of theatrical imagery, for example, runs throughout the chapter. Even the ostensibly physical forces *play roles* in relation to each other ("In the first place, the second Force appears as the one that solicits," p. 84), and the roles these forces play, soliciting almost in the sexual sense and withdrawing, are manifestly theatrical.

The climax of this subliminal drama within abstraction and speculation occurs, of course, with the lifting of the curtain at the end of the chapter. This theatrical curtain lies between the observer and the drama. It has made the operations of "Understanding" *appear* to be elsewhere and other than the observer, who is the implicit subject of the Hegelian *Phenomenology*. A process of abstraction that by Hegel's specification became trapped in mechanical repetition is thus *resolved*. The resolution consists in a massive change of stage scenery, a shift from an exterior to an internal theater.

As a resolution or sublation of "Understanding," the lifting of the curtain is problematical. The act is more a *deus ex machina* than a summation.[28] Yet in terms of the preceding reading, the emergence of the theater within the text is a function of the enunciative process by which the text's formal procedures have been made explicit. The internalization enacted by the lifting of the curtain is itself one of these operations.

To be sure, not all of the formal operations by which the Hegelian text constitutes itself share the same status. The inference of a vertical stratification from a horizontal reflection performed by Appearance, for example, is far weightier in its metaphysical and teleological presuppositions and implications than some of the prevalent Hegelian displacements and reversals. Yet despite the differing degrees of metaphysical orientation effected by the various Hegelian formal tropes, they all contribute to an ongoing and explicit vocabulary of the text's operations. The *Phenomenology's* unique integrity comprises the explicitness of the operations both enunciated and fashioned into a narrative in this chapter.

[V]

We cast the *Phenomenology*, then, in a well-known literary role. It is the venerable source of assurance and integrity in the community that is also suspect, the standard of value based on a cultural currency that is counterfeit. This ambiguity arises, as I have suggested, from the *Phenomenology*'s twin birth and twin destiny. Divided at birth, this text is *both* the consummation of a civilization, a diachronic account of a panoply of learned disciplines placed in tandem, *and* a metaphoric generator, producing the metacritical structures and terms that describe its own operation as a text.

This doubling of aims and functions is *almost* schizophrenic. And indeed, a schizophrenic text, such as Kierkegaard's *Either/Or*, would be one way of *pronouncing* this tendency while avoiding the sometimes arbitrary resolutions to which Hegel occasionally reverts in order to assure narrative continuity. Many of the accounts and terms in the *Phenomenology* are easily placed on one side of its functional divide or another—on the side of history and teleology or on the side of textual self-dramatization. In the most general of terms, we can say that the primary contribution of the first four chapters is to generate the logical terms and formal tropes that will structure the subsequent discourse, and that the accounts of religion, art, and politics in the latter sections of the text presuppose these structures and belong to a history of cultural forms.

Yet in a typically Hegelian manner, there are constructs that cross these lines, that function within both counterprograms, and save the text from the stark termination in schizophrenia that becomes Kierkegaard's response to the Hegelian formalism. Among these double constructs we would have to number Appearance, whose translation of the movements of reflection into a hierarchical configuration is also a translation of *formal* structures into historical and teleological progressions. The notion (*Begriff*) and sublation (*Aufhebung*) also fall into this intermediary category, playing both structural and metaphysical roles. The *Begriff* is both a structural and a metaphysical horizon, while the *Aufhebung* translates the mechanics of negation into the teleology of history.

The existence of these double functions which accommodate both of the counterprograms of the *Phenomenology* is symptomatic of a wider coordination within the Hegelian text. The suspicion lurking behind the text's irreproachable aims is, not that it should have provided a successive account of the major crystallizations of Western culture or that it should have generated a formal lexicon of its own functioning, but that these radically different programs could have been marshaled with such precision and *seamlessness* in support of each other.

The model of abstraction elaborated in "Understanding" contains the lineaments of this coordination. Each time a process is *totalized* to a new level of abstraction, it is lubricated in the sense that tensions and frictions involved at the lower level of generality are diminished. In "Understanding," Appearance figures and totalizes sense-experience, the law of force totalizes the operations of force, the kingdom of laws totalizes the operations of law, and the cycles of explanation and necessity totalize the operations of "Understanding" itself. The tropologizing of a process, the subsumption of a sequence of steps under a single figure, drastically reduces, in subsequent stages, the irregularities initially at play in that operation.

According to the omniscient narrator of the *Phenomenology*, the limit of "Understanding" is precisely the absence of friction made possible by tropologization. The mechanical circularity involved in the assertion, withdrawal, and elevation of distinctions constitutes the limit of "Understanding," but the resolution of this impasse is precisely the smooth circularity afforded by tropes. Both the crisis and the outcome of "Understanding" are defined by circularity, and the nature of circularity is infinity (*Unendlichkeit*).

If circularity is the outcome of "Understanding," the *Phenomenology* has reached a premature dead end. The impetus that the text as a whole *needs* in order to continue consists in the breaking, or at least the bypassing, of this circularity. In terms of the impasse at the end of "Understanding," we may say that when the infrastructure of tropologization becomes locked into an unresolved circular motion, the superstructure consisting of the interior/exterior relations between the largest units of the *Phenomenology* creaks into motion. Or again, we may say that the coexistence of circular and lateral models of movement in the text enables an involuted circle to be broken by a lateral thrust that was from the outset held in reserve.

What is most suspicious about the Hegelian coordination is the endlessness of such possible resolutions. The different models of motion and logical relation sustained by the text are so great in number and variety that each impasse generates its own resolution. The solutions arise after the fact, with the retrospective confirmation of rationalization.[29] The "Lordship and Bondage" section, for example, is so conditioned by an inequality and reversal of positions emerging from equilibrium that it needs no resolution. Upheaval is so deeply implanted in this scenario as an ongoing potential that for once the text can afford to allow the conceptual and narrative outcomes of an episode to dangle. Yet this apparent indirection is more than answered by the "Unhappy Consciousness." If "Lordship and Bondage" establishes an infinite imbalance in an intersubjective relationship projected vertically, the figure of the servant, or priest, in the "Unhappy Consciousness" sets this eccentricity aright by means of the self-denying but also self-elevating gesture of sacrifice.

"Lordship and Bondage" and "The Unhappy Consciousness" are transitional episodes, in which the formal structures of the first four chapters are provisionally translated into intersubjective[30] and historical terms. They are distinctive both in their steadfastness to the text's formal program and in their metaphysical resonances. Both episodes are extensions of moments of "Understanding." "Lordship and Bondage" returns to the reciprocal interplay of forces and explores its intersubjective implications. A hypothetical condition of perfect intersubjective symmetry produces inequality in two forms: the fight to the death and labor, the sublimated product of this conflict. In formal terms, the episode describes the generation of social and historical difference out of a hypothetical state of perfect sameness.

The "Unhappy Consciousness" repeats the projection upward performed by Appearance in "Understanding," but once again, this takes place within an intersubjective sphere. If "Lordship and Bondage" grew out of the reciprocity of forces, the "Unhappy Consciousness" again turns reciprocity on its end and bonds the mutable to the unchangeable (pp. 127 ff., *das Unwandelbare*). The middle term is no longer the mystifying variable, *Erscheinung*, but the priest, or servant (p. 136, *Diener*), whose acts of renunciation and self-sacrifice bond the higher and lower domains by emulating the former and redeeming the latter. Renunciation and sacrifice translate the withdrawal of a physical force into terms of social utility and historical destiny. Henceforth, in conformity with the inversion of value that defines the relationship between successive stages of abstraction, the highest moral values will always accrue to self-restraint, which is the intersubjective and social correlative to being-for-another (as opposed to being-forself).

These two episodes, then, comprise particularly striking instances of one of the most vibrant forms of the Hegelian coordination: translation. Translation, for Hegel, is a substitution of terms that takes place in conjunction with a structural continuity. "Lordship and Bondage" and the "Unhappy Consciousness" *translate* the dynamics of the physical world into intersubjective relations and the history initiated by them while sustaining the operations that define the text's possibility.

The section immediately preceding "Lordship and Bondage," "The Truth of Self-Certainty," has, for example, provisionally translated the terms of "Understanding" into (1) ego or *ich* (the newly uncovered subject); (2) desire (the *force* of intersubjective relations); and (3) life (an organic embodiment of infinity). With these transpositions behind it, "Lordship and Bondage" is free to unfold. This development consists in a breaking of equilibrium and a double cross, the shattering of a hypothetical state of balance between two subjects and the ironic reversal of the initial inequality between them.

The extreme sparseness of the details that would provide the famous confrontation in this episode with a specific context, as well as the abstract equilibrium of the subjects at the beginning, has tended to be overlooked by readers who have invested this passage with a social significance. Yet there is little question that the imbalance for which the passage is famous emerges only from an intricate and painstakingly established equipoise:

> Self-consciousness is faced by another self-consciousness; it has come *out of itself*. This has a twofold significance: first, it has lost itself, for it finds itself as an *other* being; secondly, in doing so it has superseded the other, for it does not see the other as an essential being, but in the other sees its own self.
>
> It must supersede this otherness of itself. This is the supersession of the first ambiguity, and is therefore itself a second ambiguity. First, it must proceed to supersede the *other* independent being in order thereby to become certain of *itself* as the essential being; secondly, in so doing it proceeds to supersede its *own* self, for this other is itself.
>
> This ambiguous supersession of its ambiguous otherness is equally an ambiguous return *into itself*. (P. 111)

In the above passage Hegel demonstrates stylistically as well as thematically the exaggerated state of balance and duplication with which the confrontation between master and slave begins. In their sequence the first two paragraphs of this passage virtually duplicate each other; in their substance they describe a self-discovery by means of an other that depends on a virtual duplication of subjects. Translated within an intersubjective sphere, the physical principle of the magnet, the attraction of opposites and repulsion of the selfsame, structures an interpersonal dynamic whose principles include the following: recognition of self in another; recognition of another in the self; self-confirmation through another. The ongoing potential for the reversal of valences in abstraction will transform this fundamentally affirmative link between self and other into something quite different by the end of the "Lordship and Bondage" section. The mutual affirmation of the self by the other, and vice versa, will extend itself, by reversal, into a confirmation of the self through the *obliteration* of the other.

The above passage is situated at the outbreak of the doubleness that surrounds undifferentiated self-other relations. Since there is no way to distinguish between the countersubjects, they relate to each other as simple doubles. This doubleness pervades the rhetoric of the passage, as well as its style, and the relations that it describes ("This has a twofold [*gedoppelte*] significance . . . and is therefore itself a second ambiguity [*zweiter Doppelsinn*]"). The master-slave conflict begins in this state of hopeless double vision. The *force* of the argument will derive from the introduction of factors of inequality within a state of balanced symmetry.

The initial factor of inequality leading to the denouement of this story is life itself (p. 106), which is an organic figuration of the formal procedures combined by infinity. Death, as the negation of life, confirms by contrast the existence of both reciprocally related countersubjects. The master claims his superiority because he risks his life, that is, acknowledges death. His superiority consists in a certain autonomy that he gains from his ability to dispense with life, and this is precisely the privilege that eludes the slave, who is limited to relations of dependency. The master's autonomy keeps the slave in thrall; the slave's reliance on his work defines his servitude. The master consumes the thing whose production defines the slave's existence. In a new wrinkle added to "Sense-Certainty," the master derives self-certainty by devouring not sense-objects but the *thing* of perception, which is the product of the slave's labor.

Yet it is only in keeping with the double logic with which this episode begins that the initial imbalance should be doubled. The second imbalance owes its constitution to the relation between kingdoms of laws and supersensible worlds in "Understanding." It is the *inverse* of the master's domination. The dramatic climax of the episode consists in the systematic undoing of the master's superiority. If life, and by implication death, was the *first* factor of inequality introduced into a hypothetical condition of perfect reciprocity, the work initially appearing as bondage becomes the imbalance that reverses the first imbalance. Reliance on the slave has made the master's relation to life dependent, not autonomous. Conversely, work has made the slave independent. The fear that initially held the slave in thrall is a form of the self-consciousness that is a precondition for all subsequent cultural productions. Taken previously as a sign of subjection, work embodies the restraint (or repression) of desire that constitutes the slave's ultimate mastery. The slave triumphs in his self-consciousness and surrender. The negativity of reflection and submission comprise a negativity that is superior to death or its risk. The slave's realization in work is a more self-aware and hence higher form of positivity than the master's.

If "Lordship and Bondage" gives the physics of "Understanding" a detailed intersubjective treatment, it remains for the "Unhappy Consciousness" to reinstate in human terms the hierarchical configuration opened up by Appearance. In a predictably Hegelian fashion, no sooner does "consciousness" become aware of itself than its danger becomes *excessive* interiority, imprisonment within a hopelessly involuted, self-contained world. Hegel's misgivings regarding the self-containment of which "self-consciousness" is capable constitute yet another indication of his suspicion toward the self-referentiality of language. Unhappy "consciousness" is the discontented child of a *freed* "self-consciousness," one not constrained to confront an external objectivity. Unhappy "consciousness" is an *internalized* form of the reciprocity that takes place, in "Lordship and Bondage," between two ostensibly external subjects: "The duplication of self-consciousness within itself, which is essential in the Notion of Spirit, is thus here before us, but not yet in its unity: the *Unhappy Consciousness* is the consciousness of self as a dual-natured, merely contradictory being" (p. 126). The resolution to this unbearable state of internal division will arise from the capacities for surrender and repression demonstrated by the slave in relation to the master.

The answer to the paralyzing internal bifurcation that is the condition of unhappy "consciousness" is provided by the figure of the servant (*Diener*), who is the slave expressed positively and projected into the heavens of speculation. Yet it is a long step from the intersubjective exploration of identity and difference in "Lordship and Bondage" to the theological self-renunciation consummated by the servant. This explains why the chapter on the "Unhappy Consciousness" is so schematic. Stoicism and Skepticism are invoked as stages of "free self-consciousness" preliminary to the unhappy "consciousness." Stoicism and Skepticism occupy in relation to the unhappy "consciousness" a position analogous to that of "Sense-Certainty" and "Perception" in relation to "Understanding." If "Sense-Certainty" comprised a hypothetically unmediated absorption in sense-experience, Stoicism is a hypothetically equal absorption into pure thought, thought without substance. In Skepticism, as in the thing of perception, a crude balance is reached: the oscillation between inclusion and exclusion in the thing becomes a falling in and out of conceptual unity in Skepticism. The unhappy "consciousness" totalizes and tropologizes these movements, just as Appearance totalizes the sensible. If the torment of the unhappy "consciousness" is an infinite vacillation within a bifurcated subject, the poles of the vacillation are defined by the stages of Stoicism and Skepticism.

The degree of the tropologization in the unhappy "consciousness" is equal to the degree of repression involved in passing from the potentially infinite reversal between master and slave to theological self-sacrifice.[31] The structure of this tropologization is complex. Unhappy "consciousness" is a trope of processes in "Stoicism" and

"Skepticism," which are in turn tropes of the processes of the physical world. The splendid exploration of formal operations *in themselves* in "Lordship and Bondage" is, then, "answered" or retracted by the schematization that resolves the division in the unhappy "consciousness" with the figure of the servant.

Thus, at the same time that "Lordship and Bondage" and the "Unhappy Consciousness" effect a decisive translation of the physical world into the intersubjective terms of history, psychology, and culture, they are also compelling examples of Hegelian coordination. The former episode effects the initial *translation* of the dynamics of *reciprocity* into intersubjective terms. The "Unhappy Consciousness" *internalizes* this conflict and subsumes its stages into a single trope. The trope, "Unhappy Consciousness," fashions a doubly involuted *circle* of totalization, encompassing both the stages of "consciousness" and the prior stages of "self-consciousness." It will be a notable and perhaps enduring contribution of recent critical theory to have fostered and promulgated a healthy suspicion toward the speculative system in which the servant's self-sacrifice at the end of the "Unhappy Consciousness" implies a universal truth and destiny. This organic *inference* of the transcendental from the empirical recapitulates and expands upon the dawn of the beyond out of Appearance. Such moments typify the capacity of the Hegelian formal apparatus to be manipulated, to be marshaled into a not thoroughly warranted progress, to *force* resolutions in the interest of an ulterior and encompassing goal. Yet even with orientations and acts that are and must be so suspect, in its wider composition the Hegelian formal apparatus exerts a profound historical and conceptual influence, one not worthy of underestimation.

[VI]

To attempt, at the end of so technical an elaboration of the formal tropes of the early *Phenomenology*, to suggest their wider historical and theoretical implications is a self-defeating task that can itself only produce spurious resolutions. Yet the particular affinity between the crystallizations of Romantic literature and the twentieth-century problematics of shock, mechanical reproduction,[32] the esthetics of adultery,[33] the repetition-compulsion, and psychoanalysis in general arises at least in part from the concern shared by both epochs for the formal operations synthesized and elaborated by Hegel. A vast swath of Romantic literature occupies the space of the unhappy "consciousness," the setting of an internal, reciprocal division suspended between transcendent and mutable worlds. Even such notable texts as the Keatsian odes and Shelley's "Triumph of Life," which question this configuration, arise within the tragically paradoxical condition that defines unhappy "consciousness." The Romantic performative gestures of blessing and curse, desire and complaint, and the fascination with intermediary characters such as Prometheus all arise in an attempt to assimilate the differences that the unhappy "consciousness" both fixes and unfolds.

The "beaded bubbles winking at the brim" of the beaker that the speaker in Keat's "Ode to a Nightingale" contemplates as a vehicle of escape stare the perceiver back in the eye, lending the wish an aura of uncanniness.[34] In this manner the sublime elevation inspired by the bird's song dissolves into a haunting alternation between desire and complaint. And this alternation emerges from the reciprocal reflection in which certainty of self is secured only by certainty of another, a formulation that, as we have seen, is an intersubjective version of a configuration first possible in "Understanding": the attraction of opposites and repulsion of the selfsame. Wordsworth's attack, in his "Preface to the 'Lyrical Ballads,'" against the rhetorical and technical conventions of the Poetic Diction is an esthetic arena for the types of attacks against formalism made by Hegel. Yet just as Hegel privileges certain structures (circularity, for example) in the act of rejecting others (such as the form/content duality), Wordsworth accommodates certain idealist structures while he clears away the rubble of the deterministic Diction. The poet's superiority over other people in "sensibility," "enthusiasm," and "tenderness," as well as the desirability of "immediate" knowledge and the "immortality" of poetry, serve Wordsworth as points of conceptual fixity analogous to those that he finds oppressive in the Poetic Diction.[35] In its internal division between the changing and unchangeable, the "Unhappy Consciousness" sets the stage for Romantic literature. Yet this vertical configuration of realms, although justifiably suspect, is possible only by virtue of formal moves rehearsed in "Understanding." And some of these moves do not lend themselves easily to resolution, reduction, or neat historical categorization.

The relation between the two parts of Goethe's *Faust*[36] is defined by the Kantian antinomy that makes the workings of the transcendental concept appear to human understanding in the form of paradox. What is paradoxical in *Faust I*, an existential drama describing the impact of the negativity of language on human reason and morality, is no longer paradoxical in *Faust II*, which takes place on the other side of the mirror of reflection (1. 2430), beyond life. *Faust II* dramatizes positively the Mephistophelean functions of subversion, negation (1.

1338), and paradox (1. 4030), which could only wreak havoc on the
lives of Faust and Gretchen. The primary positive models for the
negativity of language dramatized in *Faust II* are the following: (1) an
economy based on paper money rather than precious metal, with a
value system that is arbitrary rather than "representational"; (2) the
volcanic eruptions and seismographic tremors situated at the "source"
of Western culture, Greece; and (3) the figure of the feminine not as
a static and permanent embodiment of the ideal but as pure self-
reflection, or as Hegel would have it in his reading of Sophocles'
Antigone, "the everlasting irony [in the life] of the community" (*Phenomenology,* p. 288). In *Faust II* Faust is not the adversary of Mephistopheles but a fellow witness to the fundamental linguistic upheaval
in reaction to which social order, theology, and the pantheons of
culture and esthetics are belated and cosmetic attempts at containment. The scenario of the Emperor and his wars translates the arbitrary values accruing from paper money into social and political
terms. Anticipating the uncertainty that Heidegger discovers under
the ground of Being, Faust's journey to the geological bedrock of
Western culture unearths a violent language of quaking that anticipates all subsequent cultural refinements. Helena's irony with regard
to her status as a mythological character and the temporal paradoxes
implicit in her existence as a trans-temporal inciter of desire extends
the negativity witnessed by Faust to the esthetic sphere.

   If the farthest point of Faust's removal from the existential contradictions of *Faust I* is the confrontation with Helena, the denouement
of *Faust II* consists in the reinstatement of "consciousness" and the
cares of life. Faust dies in old age, aware of the paradox that the
wisdom necessary for the fullest sensual gratification emerges only
too late. *Faust,* and *Faust II* in particular, thus harbors the seeds of the
Yeatsian poetics. On the most concrete level, figures from *Faust* such
as waterfowl (11. 7296–7306, 8808–9), the dolphin (11. 8316–20),
the smithy (1. 10744), and the Emperor (1. 5951) are transported into
Yeats's poetry, where they appear in such poems as "The Wild Swans
at Coole," "Leda and the Swan," and the two "Byzantium" poems.[37]
The paradox bemoaned by Faust, that sensuous gratification is hopelessly lost to the educated "consciousness" which has learned to perfect it (11. 11251–58), colors the "Crazy Jane" poems[38] as well as
"Sailing to Byzantium." *Faust I* describes the condition of what Yeats
terms the primary man. *Faust II* dramatizes the separation from and
return to the primary; in great detail it extends and refines the lineaments of antithetical existence or art. The model of tinctures and
phases of the moon formulated in Yeats's *A Vision*[39] is a compendium
of Hegelian formal operations. The primary and antithetical tinc-

tures, related by mutual negation, are themselves gyres. The figure of the gyre combines opposition, repetition, and expansion: in spiraling outward, it vacillates between its internal poles, turns upon itself, and expands toward an opposite. Upon two mutually opposed gyres that, like the reciprocally related counterforces of "Understanding," disappear into each other, Yeats superimposes the circuit of the moon, the totalizing circumference of the circle. For Yeats as well as Hegel, the circle tropologizes the operations of dialectics. The phases of the moon encompass all gradations of light and darkness appearing on the lunar surface, including total light and total darkness. Yeats superimposes this figure of all possible proportions of mixture between the two extremes upon the trajectory of the artist. He thus synthesizes a movement between life and art that is both continuous and contradictory, extending toward completion yet exploding under its internal tensions: "Things fall apart; the centre cannot hold" ("The Second Coming," 1. 3).[40]

In the almost inevitable slippage from Hegel and Goethe to Yeats we have moved from the Romantic concern with the formal operations of dialectics well into the twentieth century. In connection with Yeats it would be difficult to avoid noting the "primary-antithetical" relation joining, respectively, Leopold Bloom and Stephen Dedalus in James Joyce's *Ulysses,* or the Proustian *reprise,*[41] which finds its progression only in recollection, or the "fairy tales for dialecticians"[42] that Kafka wrote, at least according to Walter Benjamin. But perhaps the most substantial legacy of the formal operations synthesized by Hegel in the chapters that we have discussed consists in the foundation of the psychoanalytical subject, the subject of psychoanalysis, in the phenomenological subject, the subject implied by the Hegelian *Phenomenology.* This discussion, introduced here briefly, will be taken up in greater detail in the chapter on Freud. In general, the operations that provide dialectical relations in the Hegelian text with success, with progress and resolution, are for Freud symptoms of repression (*Verdrängung*). As we have seen, it is precisely at moments of immanent crisis that the implicit subject of the *Phenomenology* performs its greatest feats of resilience and recovery. In this regard two such moments have been particularly striking: One is when understanding, caught in a tautological circuit of explanation that is by nature endless, is summarily and in toto shifted inside the subject, where its processes begin on a new threshold. A similar recovery breaks the inertia of the unhappy "consciousness," with its hopeless internal division. The servant is precisely the factor that *breaks through* the ceiling of containment. He pays for this privilege with his abstinence.

In both of these situations, Hegel's talent consists in his ability to break a deadlock while remaining in conformity with the already established operations of bifurcation and lateral displacement and with the perspectival shift between *in itself, for itself,* and *for consciousness.* Yet it is precisely Hegel's referral and regression *back* to formal givens at moments of crisis that constitutes the restraint at the basis both of civilization and neurosis.

The psychoanalytical subject is the subject of the *Phenomenology* projected within a personal field or space. The pathology of the psychoanalytical subject consists of the standard operations of the Hegelian subject. Psychoanalytical *disorders* are isolated instances of the formal operations at play within the Hegelian subject. Formal operations are convertible into *pathological* manifestations because of the internal necessity within the Freudian enterprise to construct *positive* models for psycho-neurological *disturbances.*

Laws of symmetry prevail within the phenomenological unconscious as it is elaborated by Hegel in his analysis of Sophocles' *Antigone,*[43] and these laws are suspended within the Freudian dream or joke. Yet it is significant that both Hegel and Freud appeal to Greek tragedy, with its unresolvable double binds, in synthesizing models of an unconscious that is held in check by repression. For Hegel, action is inescapably reductive. The unconscious consists of the actions and principles that the tragic character, in reaching a decision, is no longer free to follow. The alternatives that were excluded by action literally pursue the character until they achieve their retribution, attacking from the back, from the blind side of unconsciousness. For Freud too, repression defends the borders of "consciousness": *"the essence of repression lies simply in turning something away [Abweisen], and keeping it at a distance [Fernhaltung], from the conscious."*[44] A dominant form of repression involved in paranoia is projection, which is defined in terms of the lateral shifts within the Hegelian subject.

> The most striking characteristic of symptom-formation in paranoia is the process which deserves the name of *projection.* An internal perception is suppressed, and, instead, its content, after undergoing a kind of distortion, enters consciousness in the form of an external perception. In delusions of persecution the distortion consists in a transformation of affect; what should have been felt internally as love is perceived externally as hate.[45]

Freud links paranoid manifestations closely to homosexual desire, and homosexuality proceeds from the dialectics of sameness and difference and self and other. Rather than making an *other* his object-choice, the homosexual "begins by taking himself, his own body, as his love object, and only subsequently proceeds from this to the choice of some person other than himself as his object."[46] The homosexual *takes* the same when a logic of opposition and the repulsion of the selfsame demands that he take an *other*. The disorders of paranoia, then, both the active manifestations and their psychosexual underpinnings, are defined in relation to a philosophical "consciousness" whose operations, largely with Hegel's assistance, may be presupposed.

The configuration linking the id, the ego, and the superego is manifestly mediational. "The ego seeks to bring the influence of the external world to bear on the id and its tendencies, and endeavors to substitute the reality principle for the pleasure principle which reigns unrestrictedly in the id. The ego represents what may be called reason and common sense, in contrast to the id, which contains the passions."[47] Here, prefiguring the strictures of the superego, the ego mediates between the instincts and reason, effecting a substitution of the reality principle for the pleasure principle. Such a relatively late Freudian construct as the repetition-compulsion undermines the neatness of such a structure and challenges the subject-object relation that had been previously postulated between the patient (or analyst) and the unconscious. *Beyond the Pleasure Principle* (1920)[48] gives the unconscious an indomitable life of its own, even if death, as the restoration of stasis, is the repetitive message of this life. Repetition, whether it is a "source of pleasure [*Lustquelle*]"[49] as in this text, or whether it produces the discomfiture of uncanniness, is a function of the tropologization and circularization within certain of the formal operations that we have observed. In *Beyond the Pleasure Principle*, the repetition-compulsion is the sign of a restorative psychic economy that functions alongside an acquisitive and productive one. This text, then, whose point of departure is an automatic psychic repetition ultimately deriving from the cycles that form within the Hegelian subject, is a major factor in restoring a dualism seemingly lost from the psychoanalytical enterprise. Predictably enough, the structure of this dualism is antithetical. "*Protection against* stimuli is an almost more important function for the living organism than *reception of* stimuli."[50] The parity between the reception of stimuli and the defenses against them goes a long way in explaining the curious balance that the death and life instincts achieve in this Freudian text.

Beyond the Pleasure Principle restores the parity of death, defense, and regression within a psychoanalytical system that might have otherwise reached too high a degree of completion and development. This text permanently installs the indirection of dualism within the Freudian corpus. Yet the metaphors that Freud selects in order to describe both his earliest efforts and this final indecision are inevitably dialectical, derived from the formal operations that take place within the space of the subject implied by the *Phenomenology*.

Ironically, then, the greatest vulnerability of the formal tropes of the Hegelian test has consisted in their success, the resilience of their internal structures and the power of their historical and theoretical impact. Profound suspicion is an inevitable by-product of any speculative system making claims as wide-reaching as the Hegelian claims of progression and resolution. The Hegelian system's elevation and the vertical strata that it forms are the primary justifications for this doubt. That the formal tropes of the early *Phenomenology* verge upon a speculative horizon does not deny them their force and suggestiveness in tracing the generation and structuration of philosophical and literary language.

THREE

Søren Kierkegaard and the Allure of Paralysis

[I]

THE INTIMATE APPROACH

The trajectory that we are plotted to follow in examining Kierkegaard's relation to Hegel is one filled with hidden curves and sudden reversals. On the one hand, it is possible to argue that the resources of Kierkegaard's entire philosophical discourse, the stylistic and narrative elements as well as the substantive assertions, arise in reaction against the progress, resolution, and consummation claimed by the Hegelian enterprise. Yet in order to mount this multifaceted resistance to Hegel, Kierkegaard had to be a Hegelian of the first order. It will emerge from the following discussion that Kierkegaard's rejection of certain Hegelian tropes does not preclude their operation—indeed their decisiveness—within the dynamics of his own discourse. In relation to Hegel, Kierkegaard will occupy a position that we have observed is already contained within the Hegelian text itself. In the last chapter we witnessed an unresolvable divergence between the claims of completion and continuity made by the omniscient narrative voice in the Hegelian text, and a fragmentation toward which certain of the oppositional and circular tropes, left to their own devices, inevitably lead. In a similar fashion, Kierkegaard unleashes a battery of discursive weapons against the pronouncements of the omniscient Hegelian narrative voice—yet the indebtedness of the attack itself to Hegelian operations is massive, although its precise nature warrants detailed consideration.

The exploration of Kierkegaard's relation to Hegel is fated, then, to dialectical intricacy and uncertainty, to a certain abruptness in changes of orientation characteristic of Kierkegaard's conflicts and impasses themselves. And yet, at the beginning of such an inquest at least, there is much to recommend the most concrete, even tactile appreciation

possible of Kierkegaard's transformation of the Hegelian discourse. At
a point before the pronounced complexities of this instance of philosophical influence have emerged,[1] it may be instructive literally to feel
(or *hear,* as Kierkegaard would say) those superficial but nonetheless
decisive innovations that his discourse announces, for all philosophy as
well as for itself.

In light of the announcements that Kierkegaard has to make before the symposium of philosophy, which for him functions as a theatrical or operatic stage, it is not by accident that the beginning sentences of the 1843 *Either/Or* run as follows:

PREFACE

[by Victor Eremita]

Dear reader: I wonder if you may not sometimes have felt inclined to
doubt a little the correctness of the familiar philosophic maxim that the
external is the internal, and the internal the external. Perhaps you have
cherished in your heart a secret which you felt in all its joy or pain was
too precious for you to share with another. Perhaps your life has
brought you in contact with some person of whom you suspected something of the kind was true, although you were never able to wrest his
secret from him either by force or cunning. Perhaps neither of these
presuppositions applies to you and your life, and yet you are not a
stranger to this doubt; it flits across your mind now and then like a
passing shadow. Such a doubt comes and goes, and no one knows
whence it comes, nor whither it goes. For my part I have always been
heretically-minded on this point in philosophy. . . .

Gradually the sense of hearing came to be my favorite sense; for just
as the voice is the revelation of an inwardness incommensurable with
the outer, so the ear is the instrument by which this inwardness is
apprehended, hearing the sense by which it is appropriated. . . . *(E,* 3)[2]

This passage combines the themes of secrecy and uncertainty that
are crucial to the compendium of figural operations known as irony
with the musical motif in which the principles of the Kierkegaardian
esthetics are concentrated. Ironically, the passage begins with a philosophical problem that is both rigorous and central to Hegel's writing:
the relation between interiority and exteriority. But although Eremita
begins with a classical philosophical problem, the dimensions of which
define the epistemological field out of which irony arises, his gestures
and pictures are hardly characteristic of philosophical rigor. Eremita's
pursuit of the problem of interiority versus exteriority assumes the
form of a series of questions posed directly, in a bleeding-heart voice,
to the reader. Not only does Eremita presuppose sympathy and intimacy with the reader but he even presumes familiarity with the reader's personal experiences. "Perhaps you have cherished in your heart

a secret. . . . Perhaps your life has brought you in contact with some person. . . ."

On the basis of his claim to privileged knowledge, Eremita violates several honored discursive conventions. He abandons philosophical and scholarly pretenses of objectivity and detachment (intimately bound up with the notion of exteriority). In his posture Eremita throws to the winds the neat separation, in less "personal" texts, between the writer and reader. Even though his suggestion that "perhaps neither of these presuppositions applies to you" introduces the logic of Either/Or and brings us back to the heart of dialectical process, the narrator's *personal approach* abolishes decisively the possibility of a neutral philosophical discourse.

In no more than the two simple words "Dear reader," Kierkegaard launches a formidable attack against the Hegelian textual function that would assess past accomplishments and prognosticate future developments. In place of the void separating the reader and the consummating voice that emerges from and disappears into objectivity, there is now a sympathy, an intimacy, almost a conspiracy uniting the narrator and the audience. It is appropriate that this overtly personal voice should address the epistemological opposition between the outside and the inside, for what has been born in these lines is an *internal philosophical voice,* a voice of rigorous articulation nonetheless detached from philosophical pretensions to objectivity or truth. The personal nature of the voice limits the degree of veracity that may be invested in it; correspondingly, the target of the articulation, the audience, is also a person or persona rather than a judge.

Another way of formulating the operations that have been performed upon the neutral philosophizing voice is to say that both the author and the reader have become *fictional characters.*[3] For in accordance with Kierkegaard's subtle encouragements, we have almost too quickly glossed over the implications of the fact that the above sentences emanate not from "Søren Kierkegaard" but from "Victor Eremita." "Eremita" is in turn the fictive editor of the counter esthetic and moral texts comprising *Either/Or,* "written" by "Esthete A" and "Judge William." The personal approach and conspiracy performed by Eremita's voice thus go hand in hand with a general fictionalization, a metamorphosis from philosophical rigor to fiction.

The involution afforded by the use of pseudonyms and surrogate authors and editors in Kierkegaard's work is the narrative correlative to the unreliable intimacy of "personal address." Throughout Kierkegaard's works philosophical discourse proceeds along an involuted sequence of fictive characters and author-surrogates acting as readers, writers, or both.[4] Such texts as *Either/Or* and *Repetition* include not only fictive characters but characters who act out or parody the production and reception of the very texts in which they figure. The sequence of internalized fictive readers and writers along which the Kierkegaardian text moves is thus as sure an indicator of movement as is the substantive development from point to point. The effect of the simultaneity of the internalized theater of reading and writing in the text with the reader's assimilation of Kierkegaard's arguments is farce, a sustained subcategory of Kierkegaardian irony.

The fictional complexity of the situation in which "Victor Eremita" presents the writings of "Esthete A" and "Judge William" to an equally fictional audience qualifies in a crucial way the "subjectivity" that the above citation announces to philosophy. To be sure, the narrator assumes in relation to the reader a confidential role. In a tone of almost maternal consolation, his voice hypothesizes the readers' sorrows and secrets, the conditions under which they may have experienced the uncanny confusion between the internal and the external. Yet the trust invested in the role of confidant and the personal interaction orchestrated by the direct address do not legitimate a subjectivity of self-expression or intention. The product of the intimate voice that we hear in these lines and the complex narrative structure of which they are a part is not personal self-expression raised to the level of philosophical objectivity but self-expression undermined by a complex fictive narrative structure. For Kierkegaard to strive for a "more personal" philosophical discourse would merely repeat such earlier reactions as Hegel's refutation of the Kantian *Ding an sich* and Wordsworth's repudiation of the Poetic Diction. The "direct address" made by various Kierkegaardian personae cannot be detached from the wider fictional framework in which the discourse is encompassed. To introduce with great fanfare a "personal touch" into philosophical discourse only to retract this intimacy through layers of narrative involution is an inherently paradoxical gesture. The subjectivization of philosophical discourse so audibly and tangibly evident throughout Kierkegaard's writings thus occurs not for its own sake but as a means of producing—and performing—irony.

Yet if in the above passage Kierkegaard imposes the unreliability of fiction upon the ground rules of philosophy, another of the innovations for which we are in his debt is his allowing literary criticism to play within and even form the discourse of philosophy. As important as Kierkegaard's "editors" and surrogates, whether esthetic or ethical, are the literary, dramatic, and musical works that he imports and carefully reads within the frameworks of his arguments. Whereas in Hegel a literary work such as Sophocles' *Antigone* is primarily *illustra-*

tive of the conflicts between nature and culture, family and state, female and male, and thought and action,[5] in Kierkegaard works of art shape the dynamics and conclusions of his various texts. Kierkegaard was among the first to give an uncannily modern form of literary criticism, one presuming to pursue lines of association running counter to the surface meanings of the works in question, a determining role in philosophical inquiry. *Either/Or* and *The Concept of Irony* are as much "about" *Don Giovanni,* Scribe's *The First Love,* and the Platonic dialogues as about any thematic concerns, whether love, morality, or even such literary categories as narrative. With Kierkegaard, then, criticism acquires a new intonation for philosophy. No longer a moral directive, it becomes a procedural function. If Kierkegaard's personal approach reveals a fictive machinery encompassing the philosophical stage, the procedural correlative of this fictionalization is the literary-critical operations that now shape the argumentation.

Kierkegaard's overall reaction to the Hegelian program's claims of consummation and resolution was to fictionalize the objectives, narrative functions, gestures, and cultural sources of philosophy. Both Kierkegaard's arguments and his models, which are invariably works of art, revert to fiction. Closely related to this grounding of philosophical precedents and aims in fiction is the repeated insistence on a figural as opposed to an ontological constitution and basis of reality.[6] Instead of reaching conclusions or defining imperatives, Kierkegaard's arguments characterize figures of speech and rhetorical terms, such as irony. Even such pivotal Kierkegaardian terms as "despair" and "dread" indicate linguistic procedures and textual strategies far more than they define substantial and fixed metaphysical categories.[7] As will be observed below, Kierkegaardian irony is a composite lexicon of rhetorical tropes including metaphor, oxymoron, and parabasis. The opera *Don Giovanni* and the farcical Berlin theater visited by the narrator of *Repetition* do not stage empirical performances so much as the linguistic distortions involved in displacement and repetition. Kierkegaard extensively refers to so venerable a historical personage as Socrates with regard not to his tangible impact on human affairs but to his role as an *eiron,* a demystifier, a shadow of the state, in terms of his rhetorical and critical functions.

Even the passionate interactions of love staged in the "Diary of the Seducer" are far more linguistic in nature than interpersonal or even physical. The interaction between the seducer and the object of love is that between a writer and reader; both lovers exist to each other as projections or literary images. It is because Johannes's beloved yet thoroughly unreliable Cordelia exists to him only as a sign whose significance he must project or fill in that she appears to him as a picture:

> The image I now have of her shifts uncertainly between being her actual and her ideal form. This picture I now summon before me; but precisely because it either is reality, or the reality is the occasion, it has a peculiar fascination. I am not impatient, for she certainly lives in the town, and that is enough for me at present. This possibility is the condition of her image appearing so clearly—everything should be savored in slow draughts. And should I not be content, I who regard myself as a favorite of the gods, I who had the rare good fortune to fall in love again? (*E*, 330)

In these words Johannes, "author" of the "Diary of the Seducer" and a subcharacter of "Esthete A" (in turn a surrogate of "editor" "Eremita," who is in turn a surrogate of "Søren Kierkegaard"), describes the preliminary appearance of the object of his love. This is no woman of flesh and blood but an image that hovers between substantiality and ideality. The dancing image of the yet-to-materialize Cordelia is implanted in both theaters of a doubled scene of writing. As Cordelia, the quarry of the seducer's quest, this image is the fictive internal audience within the text, to be addressed and possibly moved by Johannes's writing. And yet this not necessarily so innocent Cordelia also functions within a more general economy. As the unfinalized projection of her "author," Cordelia is not merely the audience to some writing or rhetoric but that writing itself. She shares the indeterminancy and unreliability of all the questions that her author, whether "Johannes" or "Kierkegaard," raises. Is she an empirical other or merely a projection? Is she merely the "reader" of the seducer's presentations, or as an imagistic or fictive entity does she also constitute a text, one also demanding interpretation and reading by the seducer and the external reader? Cordelia is thus both an element within the "Diary"'s exchange of reading and writing and an image for the widest implications of that transaction. A figure herself, she exemplifies how any reality (or other ontological category) extrapolated from Kierkegaard's writing has a figural and rhetorical basis rather than a substantial or essential one.

What I have thus far termed Kierkegaard's fictionalization of philosophical discourse and his insistence on a figural constitution of reality arise within the intricate context of his reading and interpretation of Hegel. While the Hegel we examined in the preceding chapter himself may not have been so adverse to certain forms of indeterminacy and groundless infinite activity, the Hegel that Kierkegaard required as a contrast to his own unpredictable irony was condemned to the promotion of a neutral and endless general progress. Kierkegaard's response to Hegel was a multifaceted attempt to halt or paralyze that progress. Ironically, the attempt to paralyze those traditional philosophical movements that were concentrated in the Hegelian discourse became a program or counterprogram encompassing much of Kierkegaard's work.[8] Kierkegaard's systematic attempt to block Hegelian progress explains disparate, even contrary tendencies in his writing. Both the esthetic excesses that Kierkegaard attributes to Don Giovanni and Socrates and the explicit limits of the ethical life arise out of a desire for broken progress. Even the unresolvable deadlock between excess and measure often reached or asserted in Kierkegaard's work is itself an expression of a willed stasis. The dialectical logic of Either/Or is the logical embodiment of a paralysis assuming other dramatic, narrative, and thematic forms in Kierkegaard's writing.

Although in thematic and tonal terms Kierkegaard's individual works maintain their own integrity, his multifaceted project of undermining Hegelian progress constitutes a set of repetitive gestures that operate across his corpus. These operations become the tropes, or figures, defining the uniqueness of the Kierkegaardian text; they occupy a position analogous to that of the definitive tropes within the Hegelian discourse. In many respects these Kierkegaardian figures are adaptations of the characteristic Hegelian operations, bearing close similarities to them. Perhaps the primary element that they share is an ability to disrupt comprehensive and teleological schemes of progress.

The remainder of this discussion of Kierkegaard will assume the following form: Before proceeding to a discussion of *The Concept of Irony* as a general compendium of Kierkegaardian tropes and of *Either/Or* as a dramatization or performance of these disruptive textual activities, I will outline these figures and furnish examples of them from a range of Kierkegaardian texts. As a means of summarizing Kierkegaard's *general* disruption or paralysis of the Hegelian pretensions to consummation and continuity, I propose the following terms: aphorism, displacement, repetition, and logical deadlock. While in no way exhaustive, these categories characterize a multitude of occasions, occurring in a wide variety of Kierkegaardian texts, in which the possibilities of conceptual unity, narrative and argumentative completion, and logical development are placed into question, challenged, and even parodied. To include this general but in some senses inevitable introduction to the transition from Hegel to Kierkegaard, I will

attempt to delimit and characterize these Kierkegaardian strategies
one by one.

Aphorism

> When the child must be weaned, the mother blackens her breast, it
> would indeed be a shame that the breast should look delicious when the
> child must not have it. So the child believes that the breast has changed,
> but the mother is the same, her glance is as loving and tender as ever.
> Happy the person who had no need of more dreadful expedients for
> weaning the child. (*F&T*, 28)

Thus reads the first of the aphoristic refrains that conclude each of
the four sections comprising "Johannes de Silentio"'s prelude to *Fear
and Trembling*. Each section of the prelude recounts or amplifies a
different moment in the story of Abraham's aborted sacrifice of Isaac
at the command of God in Genesis. Just as each segment explores a
different interpretative narration afforded by the Biblical narrative,
each concluding aphorism considers a different logical possibility arising from the situation of weaning. "De Silento"'s gloss on the Bible is
thus interspersed with aphorisms that are themselves metatextual
glosses on "de Silentio"'s reading.

The sacrifice of Isaac is the first fully articulated test of faith in the
Old Testament. Although literally the text suggests a happy ending
magnanimously bestowed by God in gratitude for Abraham's agonizing renunciation, "de Silentio" seizes on the situation as a matrix for
unexplored logical possibilities, many emerging from the Hegelian
configuration of the master and the slave. Perhaps Abraham sensed
that God's demand was a hoax, and went along with the scheme as a
means of manipulating God. Perhaps God's role in the story is irrele-
vant, for the dread inherent in Abraham's decision—whether to kill
Isaac or not—is a structural ambiguity underlying all choices and
actions. In subsequent glosses, "de Silentio" considers these and other
possibilities, but more important than any single one is the fact that
Kierkegaard transforms the Bible's first major testimonial to absolute
faith into a black box of logical uncertainty.

In exploring the theme of weaning, the aphorisms interspersed
with the story, such as the one cited above, also take cognizance of a
transformation from certainty to open-ended possibility. In the above
passage, the mother disfigures herself, wearing the black of death and
negativity on the very corporeal site of maternal nurturing in order to
effect a fundamental separation. While the Biblical text stages a separation or weaning of the Israelites from an absolute intimacy with
God the father, the metatextual aphorism instruments a critical wean-

ing from ideality by means of a negativity that blackens the very breast of life.

Since aphorism is the mode of utterance that Kierkegaard synthesized in an attempt to extend a philosophical weaning from ideality to the very technique of writing, certain of the qualities of the above example apply to his aphorisms in general. Of the above instance we would note the *obliqueness* of its commentary. Its focus on the theme of weaning comments on a Biblical text and a philosophical problem, the status of the ideal, in a way that would be most difficult to anticipate. Yet within this oblique commentary there is a *focus* on one particular tangent to the problem. The mother's act of disguise initiates a brief discussion of the problem of continuity and change. Although the mother loves the child as always, the latter can perceive the breast only as different. In its fragmentariness the aphorism limits the area of its concern, which it then invades with the suddenness of guerrilla warfare. The *closing* of the aphorism is just as abrupt and constitutes yet another characteristic Kierkegaardian gesture. While itself only the most cursory treatment of a problem, the aphorism ends on a note of utter finality, due partly to the generality implicit in the formulaic pronouncement "Happy the person . . ." but also to the fact that the aphorism leads *nowhere* except to its own end. With this powerful but utterly inconclusive aphorism discharged, the narrative is free to go *anywhere*, and it does, back to a "new" episode of the Abraham story.

By virtue of its internal scenario of weaning, the above passage is in a privileged position to demonstrate why aphorism became the basic unit within Kierkegaard's overall strategy of disruption to conceptual and teleological continuity. As is the case with many of Kierkegaard's aphorisms, the above example *proclaims* its fragmentariness and *pronounces* its own finality. Kierkegaard's aphorisms are thus fragments of utterance that manage to end or close with a powerful sense of inevitability. As fragments, the aphorisms allow themselves to be assimilated only obliquely within wider schemes of argumentation. Because they tend to focus on only one or two facets of a problem, Kierkegaard's aphorisms gather *resonance* by means of a scattering or diffusion effect as opposed to assimilation within linear argumentative chains. Since Kierkegaard scrambles the sequences of aphoristic themes, interconnections between them occur randomly rather than by premeditated design.

If Kierkegaard's aphorisms arise and above all close in a studied sense of their own inevitability, this is to be sharply distinguished from any assertion of a more general truth. The inevitability that Kierkegaard's fragments generate is a limited as opposed to a general necessity, a necessity limited by the particularities of context. In their pronounced closure, Kierkegaard's aphorisms circumscribe a self-referential world apart. Because each aphorism generates its own context, limited necessity, and inevitability, each one declares its own self-sufficiency as a text.[9] Aggregates of aphorisms, such as the "Diapsalmata" with which *Either/Or* opens, thus do not reproduce preconceived lines of thought but rather form open-ended and textually determined echo chambers of association.

The main themes of the "Diapsalmata" to *Either/Or* may well be the isolation of the artist, the arbitrariness of sex identifications, the value of sound and music as models for the work of art, and the needs for passion, chance, and a renunciation of intention within esthetic and philosophical production, but we learn this only after the individual aphorisms discharge themselves and resonate openly and randomly with each other. There can be no more compelling proof of the power of aphorism as a metacritical notation or shorthand than the first of the "Diapsalmata":

> What is a poet? An unhappy man who in his heart harbors a deep anguish, but whose lips are so fashioned that the moans and cries which pass over them are transformed into ravishing music. His fate is like that of the unfortunate victims whom the tyrant Phalaris imprisoned in a brazen bull, and slowly tortured over a steady fire; their cries could not reach the tyrant's ears so as to strike terror into his heart; when they reached his ears they sounded like sweet music. And men crowd about the poet and say to him, "Sing for us soon again"—which is as much as to say, "May new sufferings torment your soul, but may your lips be fashioned as before; for the cries would only distress us, but the music, the music, is delightful." And the critics come forward and say, "That is perfectly done—just as it should be, according to the rules of aesthetics." Now it is understood that a critic resembles a poet to a hair; he only lacks the anguish in his heart and the music upon his lips. I tell you, I would rather be a swineherd, understood by the swine, than a poet misunderstood by men. (*E,* 19)

Although itself a self-contained and autonomous composition, this fragment combines a number of issues that will extend into Kierkegaard's work well beyond this section and even *Either/Or.* Not only does this aphorism appropriate the figure of the artist as a model and starting point for philosophical discourse; it criticizes the process of esthetic reception in cultural usage that dissimulates the origins of the work of art in suffering by attaching an aura of sublimity to esthetic appreciation. The brazen emperor Phalaris hears the end product of his political repression in the form of "sweet music." Like Phalaris's victims, the figure of the artist sketched by this passage is

unhappy, isolated, and misunderstood. The artist is destined to repeat his suffering, sacrificed by an audience that continues to con-
found beauty with platitudinous sublimation.[10]

Kierkegaard thus concentrates a number of his most vital philosophical and esthetic concerns in a brief fragment. The antagonism
between the artist and the state anticipates the fundamental Kierkegaardian deadlock between the countermetaphysics that will be
known as the esthetic and the ethical. That the victims' cries are transformed into the phonic art of music is suggestive of an ongoing
Kierkegaardian emphasis on music as a medium devoid of certain
deterministic, rational, and idealizing tendencies to which speculative
discourse is susceptible. The speaker's desire for a sympathetic relation between the artist or writer and the audience ("I would rather be
a swineherd, understood by the swine, than a poet misunderstood by
men") is indicative of the possibly ironic subjectivization of philosophical discourse that we have already observed. And the appearance in
the passage of the figure of the critic, who "resembles the poet to a
hair," underlines the close affinity in Kierkegaard's work connecting
an esthetically fashioned philosophical discourse to criticism in general and literary exegeses in particular. Closed with vehemence by the
proverb which is its refrain, this pregnant paragraph declares its discursive autonomy while retaining as potential energy an aggregate of
concerns that wait to interact with subsequent pronouncements.

Yet another quality proper to this fragment and to Kierkegaard's
aphorisms in general, then, is the manner in which they anticipate the
throw of dice at the heart of Mallarmé's poetics,[11] the multitude (if
not infinity) of avenues of pursuit that they leave in their wake. Each
theme and combination of themes touched upon by the aphorism
opens a channel for potential exploration. The multitude of open
directions is so great that they could not possibly be arranged in
logical sequence. Kierkegaard's aphoristic mode offers an enormous
diversity of themes because of the tangential nature of the links between the individual pronouncements. One instance of such a striking
associative leap occurs within pages of the beginning of the
"Diapsalmata."

> I am as shrunken as a Hebrew *shewa*, weak and silent as a *daghesh lene;* I
> feel like a letter printed backward in the line, and yet as ungovernable
> as a three-tailed Pasha, as jealous for myself and my thoughts as a bank
> for its notes, and as generally introverted as any *pronomen reflexivum.* If
> only it were true of misfortunes and sorrows as it is of conscious good
> works that they who do them have their reward taken away—if this held
> true of sorrow, then were I the happiest of men: for I take all my
> troubles in advance, and yet they all remain behind. (*E*, 22)

Filled with linguistic examples of marginality, hidden but discernible sources of affect, and deviations encompassed by the sphere of
writing, this fragment situates not only itself and the esthetic utterance but all of Kierkegaard's discourse in relation to prior philosophy.
The location of this discourse is precisely that of the Hebrew *shewa*
and *daghesh:* these are shifters decisive to the identity and pronunciation of letters and hence to the signification of entire words, yet assuming the form of a merely diacritical notation of dots. The *daghesh*
is a dot that when present *within* certain Hebrew consonants makes
their otherwise soft pronunciation hard. The *shewa* is the weakest
Hebrew vowel, appearing, like the other vowels, below the letters. At
the end of a syllable it merely indicates the close of the sound; at the
beginning it adds the soft intonation, *i*. The influence and power
exercised by Kierkegaard's aphoristic mode are those of a notation
which is nearly invisible and marginal but which nonetheless possesses
transformational capabilities. Although Kierkegaard's discourse occupies the marginal space relegated to the Hebrew *shewa* and vowels,
the power it hopes to exercise consists precisely in that dislocation.
From the neglected and possibly repressed hinterlands of both the
written character and speculation will issue the radical, if not purga-
tive, force of transformation. The brief passage indicates what the
nature of that metamorphosis will be: revolution ("ungovernable as a
three-tailed Pasha"), involution ("introverted as any *pronomen reflex-
ivum*"), and catastrophe ("misfortunes and sorrows").

The Hebrew marks in this aphorism comprise merely one instance
of an entire grammar of marginality, dislocation, and nearly imper-
ceptible sources of transformation running throughout Kierkegaard's
work. The Greek sensuality that "Esthete A" accuses Christianity of
having excluded in "The Immediate Stages of the Erotic" has sur-
vived nonetheless "as an enclitic"—an unstressed syllable or word
attaching its accent to an adjacent one—"assimilated by assonance" (*E*,
60). The figure of Socrates, who in many ways embodies what
Kierkegaard means by Greek sensuality—an unrestrained coupling
or associative displacement in language—"functions in world history
like a dash in punctuation" (*CI*, 222). The unsignifying yet crucial
dash, the silent enclitic, and the Hebrew vowels all define a discourse
that while issuing from the margin of isolation strives to release and
recall the motives and focuses that have been bypassed by the mainstream of inquiry.

Yet Kierkegaard advances the cause of this shadowy domain of
suppressed impulses not so much by exercising intellectual mastery as
by relinquishing this role and opening his discourse to less controlla-

ble factors. It is for this reason that the loss of control and chance become overt concerns of the "Diapsalmata":

> No one ever comes back from the dead, no one ever enters the world without weeping; no one is asked when he wishes to enter life, no one is asked when he wishes to leave. (*E*, 25)

> And so I am not the master of my life, I am only one thread among many, which must be woven into the fabric of life! Very well, if I cannot open, I can at least cut the thread. (*E*, 30–31)

Pervading these two aphorisms, which exemplify the terseness of statement of which Kierkegaard is capable, is a sense of utterly indifferent randomness surrounding the events and acts of existence. The first fragment, in the repetitive and mechanistic manner in which it presents the lack of volition surrounding four of the most basic experiences relating to life and death, dramatizes the very loss of intention that it describes. Each phrase centers around a subject that is so amorphous as to be almost negative: no one. And the most tangible quality possessed by this vaguest of agents is precisely never to act according to its own volition. The second aphorism suggests an alternative to the epistemological model in which thought and action are determined by the intent of the subject. If the speaker of this utterance is not master of his life, he does belong to a woven pattern that is akin to an artistic design or written text. This design takes the form of sequences or textual chains of association: "And thus I, too, am bound in a chain formed of dark imaginings, of unquiet dreams, of restless thoughts, of dread presentiments, of inexplicable anxieties. This chain is 'very supple, soft as silk, elastic under the highest tension, and cannot be broken in two'" (*E*, 33). Art and writing in general, but specifically the aphoristic mode, offer themselves here as alternatives to the model of premeditation in thought and action. Because "no one" wills even his most basic experiences, the textual alternative to volition comprised by aphorism accommodates the randomness and indifference of chance. The aphoristic mode thus incorporates within its program the need to bypass or undermine logic and systematic thought. "My view of life is utterly meaningless" (*E*, 24).

Within this program of marginality, loss of volition, and chance, music serves as an exemplary esthetic medium. For Kierkegaard music plays a number of parts. Its passionate sensuality renders it resistant to logical operations associated with vision and the eye. Don Juan's sexual effervescence, an outpouring of energy that will admit of no sequence or purpose and that is irreducible to the conjugal exclusiveness institutionalized by marriage, is what makes him an essentially *musical* figure. The imaginative projection that music, as a nonreferential language, demands of the auditor makes listening an esthetically active rather than passive function. Music transforms its auditor into an artist of sorts and thus, in a manner similar to Kierkegaard's, plays on narrative intimacy, confusing the distinction between activity and passivity, production and reception. This transformative capability of music is a fitting context in which to explain Kierkegaard's ongoing fascination with androgyny. Kierkegaard is less concerned with any inherent characteristics accruing to the genders than with the vacillation from passivity to activity, and vice versa, that narrative demands and music embodies. Hence it is with considerable deliberation that a page after the close of the "Diapsalmata," "Esthete A" declares, "I am still too much of a child, or rather I am like a young girl in love with Mozart, and I must have him in the first place, cost what it may" (*E*, 46). Mozart's music may inspire a profound admiration for Don Juan and even arouse some of his sexual appetites in the reader. But this does not preclude the ability of Mozart's music to awaken desire in another, possibly complementary form: the desire of a virgin to be marked and molded forever by an esthetic experience with the force of the first love.

Both attitudes, the aggressive and productive one as well as the more receptive one, are at play in Kierkegaard's characters and philosophical explorations. Unfolded, the complex narrative structures of both the *Either* and *Repetition* form sequences of exchanges between interlocutors assuming active and passive—"male" and "female"—roles in relation to each other. Kierkegaard's most interesting and enigmatic characters, such as Cordelia in the "Diary of the Seducer" and the narrator's male confidant in *Repetition,* are precisely those who assume both attitudes at the same time. This duplicity defines the seductiveness of such characters, and the dynamics of seduction itself. On the widest level, the androgyny so closely linked to Kierkegaardian music is indicative of the readerly and writerly functions that combine in the inscription and reception of the text.

Formally speaking, Kierkegaard's aphorisms are musical because they are errant motifs that may be haphazardly and repetitively recombined. In one of the "Diapsalmata," two "familiar strains of the violin," as they are played by a pair of blind beggars, are drowned out by the din of heavy wagons (*E*, 29–30). The anecdote combines the themes of esthetic misery and isolation, the deafness of the world of mundane concerns, and the almost unbearable receptivity awakened by music ("Does my ear, which from love of Mozart's music has ceased to hear, create these sounds . . . ?"). In their own musicality,

Kierkegaard's aphorisms become a musical notation in words. Not only *describing* music, randomness, and the dissolution of many kinds of epistemological roles effected by art, Kierkegaard's aphorisms *play* these themes, with all the variation of musical composition.

Irony and laughter are the performative effects of Kierkegaard's transformation of philosophical discourse into musical notation. The distance of the artist from the community and of the aphorism from the argument assumes the form of mockery. Thus, the aphoristic speaker compares himself to Parmeniscus, who "lost the power to laugh, but got it again" (*E*, 33). And this laughter, which intensifies as the esthetic isolation increases, makes the riddler in aphorisms a monster in relation to the community: "The disproportion in my build is that my forelegs are too short. Like the kangaroo, I have very short forelegs, and tremendously long hind legs. Ordinarily I sit quite still; but if I move, the tremendous leap that follows strikes terror in all to whom I am bound by the tender ties of kinship and friendship" (*E*, 37). The monstrous disproportion of the aphoristic speaker makes for the abrupt and discontinuous pace of fragmentary writing. There is no fuller measure of the capacity for jarring unevenness exercised by Kierkegaard's aphoristic mode than its very asymmetrical deployment of the two categories that might seem to lend his work some resolution and measure: the esthetic and the ethical. For although Kierkegaard may well have attempted to halt the ongoing progress of the Hegelian dialectic by means of a complex equilibrium between these categories, in his aphoristic mode the esthetic and ethical supplant each other with all the fitful irregularity of a kangaroo's leaps. Thus, the esthetic release of a phrase such as "My soul is so sick, so sound, so joy-intoxicated!" can be immediately succeeded by a smug moralism: "In itself, salmon is a great delicacy, but too much of it is harmful, since it taxes the digestion" (*E*, 41). Far more important than either the esthetic preciousness or the moral complacency is the license for discontinuity and inconsequential reversal that the aphoristic mode claims.

Kierkegaard's aphorisms, in their movement, operation, gestures, and choice of themes, constitute a program of disruption to Hegelian claims of resolution, continuity, and progress. Of prime importance here is that in the aphorisms, Kierkegaard synthesized a medium of articulation that implemented his ideological program through a variety of interrelated means. Like any set of strategies, Kierkegaard's general response to Hegel, his conscious or unconscious historical placement, is susceptible to involuntary deviations—in fact precisely of the sort that his aphorisms dramatize. Even though Kierkegaard devotes considerable energy to the fabrication of an equilibrium that is an end-all in itself, and that thus terminates the functioning of the Hegelian system, it is questionable whether his writings, either as a body or as separate works, ever supersede the fragmentariness enunciated by his aphorisms.

Displacement and Repetition

> Still, I had best proceed in order and explain how I came into possession of these papers. It is now about seven years since I first noticed at a merchant's shop here in town a secretary which from the very first moment I saw it attracted my attention. It was not of modern workmanship, had been used a good deal, and yet it fascinated me. . . . My daily path took me by this shop, and I never failed a single day to pause and feast my eyes upon it. I gradually made up a history about it; it became a daily necessity for me to see it, and so I did not hesitate to go out of my way for the sake of seeing it. . . . (*E*, 4)

Thus begins "Victor Eremita"'s fictive account of the production of the counter esthetic and ethical tests comprised in *Either/Or*. The cabinet, remarkable for the fascination it has for its owner even before he possesses it, will deliver its secret contents, the papers making up *Either/Or*, by chance and without warning one morning when "Eremita" is feverishly searching for something else. In this fictive allegory of writing, the text arises literally in the place of something other, by a movement of indirection.

If aphorism characterizes the tangible substance of the Kierkegaardian discourse, his texts proceed by displacement and repetition. Within the arenas opened up by Kierkegaard's individual works, the figures or structures that for him constitute the only basis of reality or thought shift from setting to setting. The narrator of *Repetition* may, like Kierkegaard himself in 1843, visit Berlin for a while and return to Copenhagen, but his concerns with seduction, marriage, and despair pursue him wherever he goes. This powerful and even uncanny combination of movement and persistence defines the interaction between displacement and repetition in Kierkegaard's work. *Kierkegaard's texts are organized by the displacement of relations or structures from scene to scene, where they are repeated but where, because of the prior movement, they are each time slightly different.* Kierkegaard's texts dramatize *displacement* because their relationship to any essential truth or reality is precisely one of substitution or distortion. But because of Kierkegaard's insistence on a figural as opposed to an ontological basis of reality, the relations or structures that his texts demonstrate are fated to *repetition*. In the absence of any final terminus or truth, the relations that proceed from a fictionalized philosophy can only move from situation to situation, where their repetition is both compulsive and imperfect.

In the above example, the account of the production of the countertexts of *Either/Or,* desire is surely a relation that is both decisive and repetitive. Yet no sooner is the desire for the secretary expressed than it is compounded by contrary wishes and compulsions that are displaced versions of itself. Already the above passage assigns the fascination aroused by the piece of furniture a distinctly sexual character and declares it powerful enough to induce the narrator to go out of his way for a peek at the object of his desire, literally to dislocate himself.

> But desire is a very sophisticated passion. I made an excuse for going into the shop, asked about other things, and as I was leaving, I casually made the shopkeeper a very low offer for the secretary. I thought possibly he might accept it; then chance would have played into my hands. . . . I continued to pass the place daily, and to look at the secretary with loving eyes. "You must make up your mind," I thought . . . . My heart beat violently; then I went into the shop. I bought it and paid for it. "This must be the last time," thought I, "that you are so extravagant." (*E,* 4–5)

Only with understatement and dissimulation does "Eremita" express his desire for the secretary to the shopkeeper, in the effort to obtain a low price and out of guilt for the intensity of his desire. "Eremita"'s desire for the secretary, already cast into sexual terms, quickly expands into a scenario of seduction. From his own point of view, "Eremita" is the seducer, attempting to lure the cabinet away from its owner at the least possible expense. But in terms of the outcome of the episode and anticipating the reciprocal nature of seduction throughout *Either/Or,* it is "Eremita" who is seduced, initially by the secretary and irreversibly by the shopkeeper, who holds out for his price. At the same time that this passage amplifies the dynamics of desire, however, it introduces complications that are displaced forms of the initial wish, which seemed at first so simple and attainable. Coexisting with the allure of the secretary, itself a displaced form of sexual lust, is a contrary yet closely interrelated desire: to obtain the object at the lowest price.[12] The sexual desire for the cabinet quickly transforms itself into "Eremita"'s anxiety about losing his money. The desire to *expend* is inextricably bound up with one to *retain.* The compulsion to resist the seduction and to save money, as well as the shame at the extravagance of the purchase, is a manifestation of the negative facet of "Eremita"'s desire. And conversely, the desire for gratification, for an ejaculation now economic as well as sexual, is bound to an impending sense of loss—loss of money and, as we shall see, time.

For "Eremita"'s conflicts are not resolved when the secretary is safely installed at home. To be sure, he initially delights in his acquisition's "rich economy, its many drawers and recesses" (*E*, 5). But his final agonizing confrontation with the secretary, the motivation behind his violent penetration of its female space, is a loss of time that aggravates "Eremita"'s sense of economic dissipation.

> In the summer of 1836 I arranged my affairs so that I could take a week's trip to the country. . . . I awakened at four, but the vision of the beautiful country I was to visit so enchanted me that I again fell asleep, or into a dream. . . . The postilion was already blowing his horn. . . . I was speedily dressed and already at the door, when it occurred to me, Have you enough money in your pocket? There was not much there. I opened the secretary to get at the money drawer to take what money there was. Of course the drawer would not move. Every attempt to open it failed. . . . The blood rushed to my head, I became angry. As Xerxes ordered the sea to be lashed, so I resolved to take a terrible revenge. A hatchet was fetched. With it I dealt the secretary a shattering blow, shocking to see. Whether in my anger I struck the wrong place, or the drawer was as stubborn as myself, the result of the blow was not as anticipated. . . . Whether the shock to the whole framework of the secretary was responsible, I do not know, but I do know that a secret door sprang open. . . . This opened a pigeonhole that I naturally had never discovered. Here to my great surprise I found a mass of papers.
> (*E*, 5–6)

It is only fitting that "the result of the blow was not as anticipated," that the secretary opens in an unexpected place and yields unforeseen contents, writing instead of money. For the untoward end products of the scene are merely the results of its prevailing economy of displacement. The boundless pangs of lust give way to monetary avarice, which is in turn transformed into a temporal compulsion and sense of immanent loss. The titillating allure of the secretary initially provokes a monetary inhibition but then instigates a violent act of entry exhibiting the sexual nature of the desire in its purest form. "Eremita"'s compulsions repeat themselves, albeit always in a slightly different form, even at the moment when he is supposedly leaving the scene, and perhaps its fascinations, behind.

For all its force, desire, which is a relation to something, is remarkably unspecific in its manifestations. This protean capability of desire is in keeping with its relational and structural, as opposed to substantial, nature. As lust becomes avarice, which becomes an overwhelming sense of tardiness, the force and structure of compulsion are able to maintain themselves even while the manifest stimuli and causes of "Eremita"'s actions change. This passage, then, which claims nothing less than to account for the sizeable portion of Kierkegaard's writings comprised in *Either/Or*, illustrates both the displacement and the repetition at the heart of Kierkegaard's poetics and philosophy.

The texts of *Either/Or* arise in the place of something else, whether love, money, or time. The only existence of the literary-philosophical work is that of a substitute. And what the work contains and stages are precisely the processes of displacement and distorted repetition by means of which it intervenes in the place of something else, whether life experience or a higher truth. There is no fuller evidence of the power exerted by this substantive and repetitive process than the fact that the richest source of motivation and images in the passage discussed above, the female body, has already been deleted when the passage begins. "Eremita" loves the secretary as a female body; he penetrates its internal space with the violence of a sexually deprived abductor. Yet the haggling with the shopkeeper and the frantic search for money are substitutes for a female figure that the narrative has already, and with great deliberation, replaced.

The story of "Eremita"'s seduction by and assault on the secretary is not merely a fictionalization or myth of the ensuing text's production. In the manner in which it stages the displacement and repetition of desire, the passage is very much *of* the text that it introduces. As the passage indicates, displacement, repetition, desire, and structures in general operate autonomously of volition, whether the characters' or the author's (especially since this text takes such pains to obscure who the "author" might be). "Eremita"'s compulsions seem to originate from nowhere, yet they are inextricably bound to the structures of desire and seduction that precede them. The displacement and repetition contained by the narrative of "Eremita"'s secretary thus characterize a writing that has become autonomous. Like the drawer that Eremita finds "as stubborn as myself," Kierkegaard's discourse declares its self-sufficiency and independence from intention or agency. It does not matter whether "Eremita" acknowledges the complex sequence of surrogates by which Kierkegaard distances himself from the book or whether he identifies himself with the writing of *Either/Or;* the textual structures that repeat and displace themselves do so by their own momentum. Because *Either/Or*, whether ascribed to "Eremita," "Esthete A," and "Judge William" or "Søren Kierkegaard," is a self-contained economy of relations and structures, it becomes a double of its "author," whoever that may be. And the doubling that gives not merely *Either/Or* but all of Kierkegaard's major works a "life" or "mechanism" of their own is the fullest extension of Kierkegaardian repetition.

It is in this context that "Eremita" both distances himself from the papers of *Either/Or* and occasionally slips into a close identification with them. His pronouncement that "I, who have simply nothing to do with this narrative, I who am twice removed from the author, I, too, have sometimes felt quite strange when, in the silence of the night, I have busied myself with these papers" (*E,* 9) underlines the involuted fictive narrative structure by which Kierkegaard has separated himself from *Either/Or.* But "Eremita"'s very next words retract this distance, identifying him with the seducer, who is a persistent character in the work. "It was as if the Seducer came like a shadow over the floor, as if he fixed his demoniac eye upon me, and said: 'Well, so you are going to publish my papers!'" (*E,* 9). Kierkegaard's posture toward his works varies from remoteness to intimacy. But as antithetical as these two positions may seem, they both emphasize the distorted way in which the text, by virtue of its structures' autonomy, describes and repeats its "author."

The resonances and conceptual ramifications of displacement and repetition echo throughout Kierkegaard's work. Music, irony, Don Giovanni, and Socrates—the predominant figures in Kierkegaard's work that challenge theology and idealism—all operate by displacement. Not merely one figure of speech in its own right, displacement describes the distortion in language whereby all words and other signs are dislocated from the things they would seem to indicate. For Kierkegaard, Greek eroticism was excluded by Christianity, was championed by Socrates, and found a modern descendant in Mozart's music. And yet when described, this sensuality appears far less as a carnal jubilation than as the type of displacement exercised by the metaphoric potential in all words.

> Eros was the god of love, but was not himself in love. In so far as the other gods or men felt the power of love in themselves, they ascribed it to Eros, referred it to him, but Eros was not himself in love. . . . If I imagined a god or goddess of longing, it would be a genuinely Greek conception, that while all who knew the sweet unrest of pain or of longing, referred it to this being, this being itself could know nothing of longing. I cannot characterize this remarkable relation better than to say it is the converse of a representative relation. . . . In the Incarnation, the special individual has the entire fullness of life within himself, and this fullness exists for other individuals only in so far as they behold it in the incarnated individual. The Greek consciousness gives us the converse relation. That which constitutes the power of the god is not in the god, but in all the other individuals, who refer it to him; he is himself, as it were, powerless and impotent. . . . (*E,* 61–62)[13]

In this passage it becomes evident that the displacement dramatized in the secretary episode is one manifestation of a general metaphoricity in language. Judeo-Christianity excludes Greek eroticism because the latter proclaims rather than dissimulates the disjunction between the embodiment or symbol of the thing (Eros) and the thing itself (love). The scandal for which Greek eroticism, Socrates, irony, and Don Giovanni are rejected by Western religion and all modes of thought that subordinate the word, sign, or symbol to some transcendental meaning or purpose is a scandal of displacement. Kierkegaard, in asserting that the very center of Greek eroticism is unerotic, implies that the Greeks accepted the disjunction separating their most intense emotions from the symbols of their emotions. Not only do the Greeks tolerate this disjunction, they conspire with it as well. Longing has a place in the Greek pantheon because it acknowledges and even cherishes the distance between the passions and the symbols, myths, and gods that men invent in order literally to come to terms with them.

As characterized in the above passage, the process by which the Greeks acknowledge the displacement of their most basic emotions is one of ascription. The Greeks revel in the absence of a transcendental entity to legitimate their erotic desire by ascribing or displacing the desire to a farcically impotent god. The farce, a subcategory of Kierkegaardian irony, is a celebration of the separation between the symbol and the thing. By displacing their most intense and perhaps primal emotion to Eros, the Greeks not only invent an ironic god but reserve a divine place for metaphor, the general rubric for displacement in language. Hopelessly bereft of the love that he symbolizes, Kierkegaard's Eros is far more a god of metaphor than one of passion. As a counterexample to the idealism implicit in Judeo-Christianity, bourgeois economics, and much of Romanticism, Kierkegaard holds up the Greeks of Socrates and Eros as a people whose deities, such as they were, were functions of language.

In the above passage, Kierkegaard opposes the deferral and "sweet unrest" of displacement to the grammar of representative relations and the theology of the Incarnation. Such a theology, implicit in Judaism as well as Christianity, restricts the displacement common to language and eroticism by ascribing it to a superior being. Only the Incarnation revels in the "fullness of life." The theology of the Incarnation shares the ascription belonging to Greek sensuality. But in the theological version the possibilities for movement and displacement are closed off rather than open-ended, and taken out of human hands. The grammar of representative relations serves this theological configuration, for in the aftermath of the ascription of all will, desire, and movement to a superior entity, language can only serve this external, absolute agency, although imperfectly. Thus, in the same process by which human passion, with its endless capacity for transformation, is transferred to a deity that closes it off, language finds that its own bottomless hovering between the thing and the symbol is terminated by the "representative relation"—the necessity of representing a reality higher than and external to it. The above passage provides a scenario for the fundamental antagonism between the general metaphoricity of language and the more restricted economics of theology and idealism.

Kierkegaardian displacement thus embraces the most general metaphoric process of transfer in language, as well as the transformation of desires and compulsions into variant forms. This displacement, in achieving its full affective capability, is often linked to a repetitive movement that demonstrates the persistence of relations or structures from scene to scene. Repetition, too, is inimically opposed to the theology of the Incarnation, for the obsessive recurrence of structures prevents them from ever attaining the finality of a superior being. No text could serve as a better example of Kierkegaardian repetition than the brief 1843 work bearing that name. The subtitle, *An Essay in Experimental Psychology,* suggests the close affinity between an *esthetics* of displacement and a *psychology* of obsession.

The crux of *Repetition,* the term as well as the book, is situated at the intersection between the same sort of involuted narrative structure that frames *Either/Or* and a farcical theater whose predominant activity is displacement. The book is—fittingly, given its subject matter—divided into two parts, which in certain senses repeat each other. The first part is narrated by the first-person narrator "Constantine Constantius," whose repetitive name protests only too much the constancy that this character never demonstrates. The two main characters in this part are "Constantius" and a protégé, whose lack of an identity belongs to the Kierkegaardian esthetics of concealment and secrecy. These two interlocutors collaborate in the matter of the presumably less experienced protégé's courtship of a young woman. The triangular configuration allows for the obvious possibilities implicit in the scenario of the younger man's confiding to a possibly ironic and not necessarily constant other. The text makes no effort to conceal either "Constantius"'s interest in the girl or his self-interest.

The second part of the text, entitled "Repetition," shifts from a first-person narrative to an epistolary mode. The part is introduced by a narrative statement by "Constantius," contains seven letters from the protégé to his mentor, and closes with a *letter* from "Constantius" to the reader. In the epistolary mode, the mediatory function of the narrator disappears and the fictional resources are concentrated upon an exchange of reading and writing between characters. There is observable, then, in the course of the text a transformation from *narrative,* in which the key themes of desire, trust, and deception take the form of *action,* to *epistolary correspondence,* in which these same terms operate within an allegory of reading and writing. "Constantius" shifts from the role of narrator to that of an epistolary editor, a role closely analogous to the one played by "Eremita" of *Either/Or.*

In the middle of this process, at the end of the first part, to get away from the complexities of the love triangle "Constantius" takes a trip to Berlin, where he stumbles upon a farcical theatrical presentation. But "Constantius"'s narration of this whimsical adventure of escape reinstates—or repeats—many of the circumstances involved earlier in the intense atmosphere of the love rivalry. Repetition thus enters the story at the moment when it opens itself to farce—when the passionate assertion of will in love gives way to an esthetics of accident, indirection, absurdity, and hilarity. Repetition is thus a way station or crux between narrative control and an open-ended, undetermined interaction between the readers and writers of letters. In the wake of the Berlin farce, plans, intentions, controls, whether on the part of the characters or of the "author," cannot be taken seriously, for a factor of indeterminacy has entered, in the form of repetition itself.

In light of the biographical circumstances surrounding Kierkegaard's life, it is highly ironic that the protégé and correspondent, rather than the I-narrator, plays the role of the suitor. For the protégé is closer to the wooing and abandonment performed by "Søren Kierkegaard" in his traumatic engagement to Regina Olson than is "Constantius," who at first glance would seem to be Kierkegaard's most direct "representative" in the text. What I am suggesting here is that the *structure* of interlocution is more important than the "identities" of the characters themselves. In the uncanny affinity of their tastes and desires "Constantius" and his protégé are in some senses doubles of each other, and in their experiences of deceit and remorse both are doubles of the historical "Søren Kierkegaard."

"Constantius" intersperses throughout his description of the initial collaboration between the young poet and himself two narrative strands that will be decisive both to the resolution of the story and in dramatizing the notion of repetition. The first of these is a tangential narrative, a seemingly random recollection of a brief flight of adventure that "Constantius" had made six years before (*R,* 51–52). This coach journey, during which "Constantius" had briefly encountered a girl, foreshadows the more elaborate and conceptually richer escape to Berlin and the farcical theater. The primary importance of this passage is to "seed" a set of seemingly inconsequential details, including coffee, cigars, and an effusive natural description, which in their recurrence will emerge as the very crux of the notion of repetition.

Closely related to this episode is "Constantius"'s discussion of the distinction between repetition and recollection. While opposed, these countermodalities are closely related. The recuperative act of recollection provides the material that will become unpredictably rearranged by the prospective and automatic act of repetition. "But here I sit and relate in full detail what really was addressed in order to show that the love of recollection does indeed make a man unhappy. My young friend did not understand repetition, he did not believe in it, and did not desire it with energy" (*R*, 48–49). The protégé's recollective stance is closely connected to the idealism of his love and the teleological aspirations that he holds for the affair. In order for the protégé to "desire" repetition "with energy," he would have to relinquish his nostalgia and embrace the purely inconsequential movement in language as well as love entertained by Greek eroticism. Underlying the pathos of the nostalgia in recollection is the desire to master and exploit the past. The prospective stance of repetition substitutes uncertainty for this control.

Although a temporal term, "repetition" is highly consequential to the possibility and nature of motion in general, and it is precisely at this point that repetition joins the Kierkegaardian program of disruption to the progress and resolution promised by speculative systems such as Hegel's. Were such a thing as a perfect repetition possible, it would question the possibility of any serial motion, including that claimed by philosophy. The perfect repetition of an event would question the actuality of any movement made subsequent to it. But since it is extremely difficult to deny the actuality of motion, just as Diogenes, in the first lines of this text, "*stepped* forth literally" in reaction to the Eleatic denial (*R*, 33), repetition may well imply not so much a total *halt* as a new kind of movement. "The dialectic of repetition is easy; for what is repeated has been, otherwise it could not be repeated, but precisely the fact that it has been gives repetition the character of novelty. . . . repetition is the *interest* of metaphysics, and at the same time the interest upon which metaphysics founders" (*R*, 52–53). The new movement qualified by repetition is situated in the interstice between simple progress and total paralysis, denying the domination of the past but just as equally questioning the possibility of predication. Repetition is, precisely, a movement that does not move, a movement inscribed as a necessity within desire and language but one irreducible to the simplicity of any actual movement. "Repetition is the *interest* of metaphysics" because as a form of movement it participates in the general teleological aspirations of all idealistic modes of thought. But by retracting the kind of progress that it seems to guarantee, repetition is also the submerged obstacle "upon which metaphysics founders."

"Constantius," having trapped his protégé within a web of self-defeating plans and having illustrated as well as broached the questions of recollection and repetition, has paved the way for his Berlin interlude. He has convinced the innocent to set up an arrangement with a seamstress in order to arouse the jealousy and desire of his true ladylove. Having personally engineered this scene of substitution from a bourgeois comedy, "Constantius" turns his back on it, undertaking a "voyage of discovery . . . in order to investigate the possibility and the significance of repetition" (*R*, 54). In Berlin, he gives himself over entirely to random recollections, uncanny repetitions, and a farcical stage that proclaims the figural constitution and domination of all reality.

The farcical play at which "Constantius" assists may be performed at the King's Theater, but as a medium the farce functions as a multifaceted foil to predetermined orders, whether social or esthetic, and to the idealism and teleological aspirations of the protégé's romantic love. If repetition is the undefinable motion that neither sanctions nor definitively halts progress, the farce is its medium, for it questions and ultimately dissolves both the social and esthetic contexts that would define its own place and meaning. The farce, in successfully attacking the frameworks that would make it intelligible, becomes a pure and self-contained play or image, a sign not *receiving* its meaning from but *imposing* its freedom and uncertainty upon its context.

If "Constantius" leaves behind in Copenhagen a bourgeois comedy of his own construction, in Berlin he finds a popular farce reaching Carné's *Les Enfants du paradis*,[14] a theater entertaining an "exceedingly diversified" audience (*R*, 63).

> The action generally takes place in the lower spheres of society, therefore the gallery and the second tier promptly recognize themselves, and their shouts and bravos do not express an aesthetic appreciation of the individual actors, but rather a purely lyrical explosion of their sense of contentment; they are not in the least conscious of being an audience, but want to take part in what is going on down in the street, or wherever the scene is laid. (*R*, 63)

Beloved by a constituency more general than the "real theatrical public," with its "narrow-minded seriousness" (*R*, 64), the farce challenges other conventions of classical theater as well. The "reaction" of its hybrid audience is "spontaneous" rather than refined or sublimated (*R*, 64). "The reciprocal regard of actors and audience, which commonly gives one such a sense of security, is here done away with" (*R*, 64). In this strikingly open intercourse between the viewer and the work of art, the spectator "asserts himself to an unusual degree" (*R*, 63). The farcical theater thus marks a disruption to the neat epistemological separation of the actors from the audience characteristic of more restrained art forms.

Just as the farce caters to an unorthodox audience that receives it in a manner inimical to classical decorum, it eludes the conventional generic categories of esthetics. "Every attempt at an aesthetic definition which might claim universal validity founders upon the farce" (*R*, 63). It is the bottom line in an esthetic degradation that proceeds downward from the time-honored genres, appealing to the individual who, "though neither tragedy nor comedy can please him . . . turns to the farce" (*R*, 61). The anomalousness of farce's audience and generic profile extends to its performance as well. The spontaneous relation between the audience and the actors is indicative, not of any spiritual immediacy or communion, but of the manner in which farce bypasses a self-reflexive mode of performance, in which roles and gestures are calculated for their effects. Like Kierkegaard's aphorisms, the performers of the farcical theater are free to interact unpredictably within an open-ended framework. Farcical performers are not so much agents performing their tasks within the encompassing design foreseen by the playwright or director as they are children placed upon the stage for the sake of their own unpredictable play.

> [The actors] must be the children of caprice, intoxicated with laughter, dancing for sheer humor and merriment. . . . they become transformed, and like the noble Arabian steed begin to puff and snort, their distended nostrils witnessing to the chafing spirit within them. . . . They have therefore hardly calculated what they will do, but let the instant and the natural force of laughter be responsible for everything. They have courage to do what the ordinary man dares to do only when he is alone by himself. . . . (*R*, 65)

In its whimsy, childishness, and capacity for sudden transformation, the farcical stage is an attempt to formulate a performative and imagistic purity and autonomy. The farcical stage destroys the technical and intellectual buttresses that would otherwise rationalize it. Grounded in the working classes and indifferent to inherited classical values, the farce reinstates a certain nature to art, "the farce" of spontaneous laughter, a farce as "natural" as any physical or climactic one.

Not only do "Constantius" 's visits to the theater confirm his esthetic detachment and the cynical posture that he has maintained toward his protégé, they open the work as a whole to a repetition, sometimes of minor details, that will eliminate any pretensions it might have maintained to completion, unity, or logical conclusiveness. At one of the performances he spies in the audience a young girl who, like the protégé (and his ladylove), is secretive and concealed (*R*, 71–72). The girl reminds him of yet another, whom he has furtively stalked in a "large shady garden with many trees and shrubs," "several leagues from Copenhagen" (*R*, 72). The haphazard discovery of the girl in the theater not only *repeats* the motifs of concealment, pursuit, and seduction elsewhere in the book; it elaborates the type of "natural" spontaneity that the farce reinstates into the theater. By implication, the several passages in the book in which there is a seemingly random free association of natural imagery all relate to the manner in which the Kierkegaardian esthetics dislocates the conventional positions of nature and artifice.

Having found an emblem in a farcical art form that defies all predetermined definitions and conventions of reception and participation, Kierkegaardian repetition proclaims its freedom to go about its business: to be the mode in which the relations and structures that shape perception and cognition replicate themselves. The repetition that this text dramatizes, on major and minor scales, is one that takes place independently of the empirical circumstances that might otherwise seem the "substance" or "significance" of experience.

Logical Deadlock

EITHER/OR

An ecstatic lecture

If you marry, you will regret it; if you do not marry, you will also regret it; if you marry or do not marry, you will regret both; whether you marry or do not marry, you will regret both. Laugh at the world's follies, you will regret it; weep over them, you will also regret that; laugh at the world's follies or weep over them, you will regret both; whether you laugh at the world's follies or weep over them, you will regret both. Believe a woman, you will regret it, believe her not, you will also regret that; believe a woman, or believe her not, you will regret both; whether you believe a woman or believe her not, you will regret both. Hang yourself, you will regret it; do not hang yourself, and you will also regret that; hang yourself or do not hang yourself, you will regret both; whether you hang yourself or do not hang yourself, you will regret both. This, gentlemen, is the sum and substance of all philosophy. (*E*, 37)

Perhaps more powerfully than any other single passage in Kierkegaard, this passage demonstrates the futility of dialectical logic and in so doing articulates the program by which Kierkegaard undermines Hegelian progress, by bringing it literally to a halt. The passage is rigorously patterned and repetitive. For a statement rife with imperatives, it is surprisingly negative. In each of four hypothetical situations—marriage, laughter, belief, and suicide—the four logical alternatives emerging all turn out to be futile. In each of the four cases, the logical alternatives follow the same sequence: assertion of the hypothesis, its negation, assertion of the hypothesis with its negation, and the negation of the hypothesis with its negation. Or in simpler terms, the sequences arising from the situations of marrying a woman, laughing at the world's follies, believing a woman, and killing oneself run: yes, no, both, neither. The invariable result of all four alternatives in all four situations is a regret that, as we have seen, is associated with the recollective or remorseful stance that is the double of the unrestrained esthetic expenditure of energy.

If all sixteen alternatives entertained by the passage abut on the same remorseful and futile conclusion, Kierkegaard is demonstrating an interruption of motion in a dramatic yet precise way. The sixteen varieties of choice are products of two, of the two possibilities comprising choice itself, Either/Or, yes or no. Sixteen is two to the fourth power: a basic choice situation squared (or repeated) and then squared again. The ease with which choices proliferate in mathematics is tantamount to the facility with which the exponent, the diacritical number whose status is akin to the Kierkegaardian *shewa* or enclitic, may be revised. Yet the bewilderingly numerous choices all find the same futile terminus. Once again the very possibility of motion has been subjected to denial.

Not only do the logical alternatives proceeding from the cases follow the same sequence but the sequence of the cases is interesting in itself. The first hypothetical possibility is marriage, the contractual exchange of material for conjugal possession and a pledge of exclusiveness in sexual relations. The two succeeding situations in the sequence are mirror images of each other. Within the sequence concern for the social institution of marriage is immediately succeeded by a concern for the interpretative problems that such a contract involves. Laughing at the world's follies and believing a woman are, respectively, ironic and naive modes of reading. Thus far in the sequence, then, all alternatives accruing from marriage as well as from an ironic or naive interpretative stance are grounds for regret. Suicide might seem the most viable way out of this impasse, occupying the antithetical pole to marriage. Suicide may well provide in decisiveness what it lacks in longevity—but even this final "out" falls prey to the ineluctable sequence: yes, no, both, neither.

Kierkegaard's sequence of situations is thus itself a pair of doubles: marriage/death and innocence/irony. And the principle by which each of these cases could multiply into four futile alternatives is the double Either/Or choice at the basis of multiplication itself. Yet this remarkably fecund and rapid doubling leads either nowhere or to the same dismal place. It is with the "ecstasy" of such *precisely* uneventful multiplication that Kierkegaard introduces some of the most overt formulations of the placement of his discourse.

> It is not only at certain moments that I view everything *aeterno modo*, as Spinoza says, but I live constantly *aeterno modo*. There are many who think that they live thus, because after having done the one or the other, they combine or mediate the opposites. But this is a misunderstanding; for the true eternity does not lie behind either/or, but before it. Hence, their eternity will be a painful succession of temporal moments, for they will be consumed by a two-fold regret. My philosophy is at least easy to understand, for I have only one principle, and I do not even proceed from that. . . . If it seems, therefore, to one or another of my respected hearers that there is anything in what I say, it only proves that he has no talent for philosophy; if my argument seems to have any forward movement, this also proves the same. But for those who can follow me, although I do not make any progress, I shall now unfold the eternal truth, by virtue of which this philosophy remains within itself, and admits to no higher philosophy. For if I proceeded from my principle, I should find it impossible to stop; for if I stopped, I should regret it, and if I did not stop, I should also regret that, and so forth. But since I never start, so can I never stop; my eternal departure is identical with my eternal cessation. Experience has shown that it is by no means difficult for philosophy to begin. Far from it. It begins with nothing, and consequently can always begin. But the difficulty, both for philosophy and for philosophers, is to stop. (*E*, 37–38)

If Kierkegaard's aphoristic voice speaks from eternity, this is an eternity radically different from the one toward which theological experience tends. Kierkegaard's use of the term "eternity" here is indicative of a predicament throughout his work. In his attempt to articulate a discourse founded on structures rather than concepts, Kierkegaard cannot avoid recourse to certain of the terms of the system that he attempts to dislocate. The disfigured eternity of the above passage thus joins the aphoristic finality that was distinct from philosophical necessity, and the spontaneity of the farcical theater that was similarly different from spiritual immediacy.

The perspective of the eternal mode of Kierkegaard's discourse is that of a paralysis or inertia that precedes, conditions, and ironizes all subsequent progress. The eternal mode is the temporal condition defining the marginality of Kierkegaard's aphoristic utterance. The "true" eternity of a marginal discourse that is indifferent to transcendental purpose, historical progress, and conceptual unity is a form of unmitigated, unjustified stillness. Whereas theological and teleological modes of eternity reproduce the "painful succession of temporal moments" that they ostensibly succeed, Kierkegaard attempts to formulate an inertia that resists all relapses into a progressive mode.

In the above passage, the eternal mode, because it is fundamentally antagonistic to the opposition that is the basis of all logical progress, remains self-contained and confined to a single principle. This principle is itself consistent throughout its duration. "True" eternity anticipates rather than succeeds the logic of Either/Or: rather than being a theological moment of moratorium or sublimity reserved for the end of experience, this stillness originates and preconditions all activity.

Within this framework, dialectical logic becomes not so much a source of motion as an instrument of stasis. At the end of the above passage, dialectical logic is reduced to an object of parody. "Stopping" joins marriage, irony, naiveté, and suicide in the futility of its logical sequence: yes, no, both, neither. Kierkegaard's primary attack against Hegelian progress may be described as a subjection and subordination of dialectical logic to the eternal mode. Whether on the microscopic level of the aphorism or in the structural framework encompassing entire works, Kierkegaard halts logical progression by confining it to a single dialectical cell governed by the logic of Either/Or. Opposition is viable for Kierkegaard to the extent that it manages to *confine* motion to a single, uniform stage of development.[15]

The Kierkegaardian program of *halting* dialectical progress by *containing* it to a single stage, one qualified by the complications resulting from a situation of *choice*, influences virtually every aspect of his work. On the thematic level, the notions of fear and trembling, dread, and despair all describe the emotional states accompanying situations of unresolvable duality. The variety of these agonizing situations in Kierkegaard's work—whether Abraham's decision to sacrifice Isaac in *Fear and Trembling* or the recurrent choice between seduction and marriage in *Repetition* and *Either/Or*—suggests that the structure of choice itself is far more fundamental and significant than the specific alternatives weighed. In Kierkegaard's narrative works, the reciprocal interplay between paired characters, who vacillate between aggressiveness and passivity in relation to each another, is the *dramatic* correlative to the paralyzing indecision of certain choices. The possibility that Cordelia may be as seductive as Johannes the seducer in the "Diary," or that by the end of *Repetition* the protégé has become as cynical as his mentor, creates a tension between fictive personae every bit as immobilizing as dread or anxiety. Yet there is no fuller measure of the paralysis created by logical deadlock in Kierkegaard's work than the framework of *Either/Or* itself. In composing this massive work, Kierkegaard literally enclosed the reader within the structure of choice. The esthetic papers of *Either*, while extolling the pleasures of excess, often verge on a Faustian nostalgia for a limit or end to shifting movement. In a complementary fashion, "Judge William" of the *Or* can describe the prosaic beauty that occasionally surfaces in the moral life only in terms of esthetic excess. *Either/Or* imprisons its readers within the structure of indecision just as its movement is confined to what would be in Hegel a single dialectical stage not by virtue of the simple opposition between the esthetic and the ethical but because each of these models tends toward the other. It is because of this more complex opposition, one invading both the esthetic and ethical alternatives, that *Either/Or* as a whole serves as the ultimately passive agent of the eternal mode.

While for the moment whether *halting* dialectical progress is sufficient to undermine the logical principles of such movement remains an open question, the conclusion that Kierkegaard devoted considerable resources to the achievement of such a logical equilibrium is difficult to avoid. And to the extent that logical deadlock impedes progress, it joins Kierkegaard's plays on narrative objectivity, his aphoristic mode, and his notion of repetition within a multifaceted attack on the Hegelian system. One element of this challenge is so general and pervasive that thus far it has been overlooked in pursuing specific points of opposition: Kierkegaard's stylistic parody or pastiche. But in the exaggerated deliberateness with which Kierkegaard is capable of assuming an ostensibly objective rhetoric of opposition and inference, he levels at the Hegelian system the wide but no less pointed cannons of mockery.[16]

With the instruments of aphorism, repetition, and an excruciating logical suspense, Kierkegaard executed his program of disruption to the Hegelian system. It is hoped that the following readings of *The Concept of Irony* and *Either/Or* will clarify the extent to which he did and did not succeed.

[II]

THE IMPASSE OF IRONY

If Kierkegaard, through his explorations into the fragment and his sabotage of the machinery of dialectics, anticipated much of the agenda of modern esthetics, he labored no less under the burden of his

Romantic patrimony. Although Kierkegaard tested the limits of logic and narrative reliability in the ways suggested in the preceding section, he had recourse largely to concepts operative within the systems that he debunked. Kierkegaard's work on irony exemplifies this impasse. His 1841 thesis for the degree of Masters of Arts in Theology at the University of Copenhagen, entitled *The Concept of Irony: With Constant Reference to Socrates,* is a battleground between the radical potentials that he unearthed within fiction and philosophy and the long-standing speculative conventions that were his primary means of conducting his experiments. If this particular battle remains indecisive, if irony's dependence on near-archaic notions of subjectivity, freedom, individuation, and negation is not definitively overcome by ironic undecidability, this in no way obliterates the innovations made both by the term and the treatise.

Surely, among the work's most persistent contributions is that irony, rather than a specific trait or figure of speech, comprises a *complex* of qualities and activities. Anticipating Freud, Kierkegaard assembled a set or complex of traits that as an ensemble could account for a wide range of literary moments and psychological states. The components of irony recur together with a gravitational force that is uncannily their own. As an ensemble, irony is as much an energy field as it is a composite of substantive elements. The combinatorial force with which such qualities and activities as hovering, freedom, and negativity recur is as vital an ironic element as any more tangible quality.

Virtually all of the traits and activities that Kierkegaard ascribes to irony have linguistic correlatives, that is, they characterize processes occurring within the domains of the literary and discursive text. The seductiveness that Kierkegaard ascribes to Socrates, the exemplary *eiron* at the core of the Western tradition, for example, falls under the ironic categories of freedom and negativity. Yet Socrates' playful attitude toward his students, the yearnings and curiosities that he awakens with his detachment, is matched by a verbal copulation, a linguistic capacity for random and promiscuous associations, that irony also puts into play. Because of the dual substantive and linguistic status of the elements comprised in the complex of irony, the treatise constitutes a major contribution to Kierkegaard's grounding of being and reality in figural relations.

Not only does irony resist reduction to a single trait or identity but certain of its elements remain truer to the patrimonies of subjectivity, reflection, and representation than others. Not only is irony a differentiated figure or metatrope but it is compounded by the varying degrees to which its constituents violate the imperatives of logic and representation. This complexity is what places Kierkegaardian irony at a true impasse: it falls both inside and outside the systematic thought that it would disfigure and supplant. It violates to varying degrees of intensity, preempting and disqualifying virtually any generalizations that could be made with regard to its placement.

These difficulties in assimilating irony did not escape Kierkegaard; rather, he appropriated and inscribed them within irony's composite profile. The double enterprise of couching a radical countertradition to dialectical formalism in terms derived from that very system inscribes a rift that carries through the treatise on irony. Instead of hiding this fissure, Kierkegaard makes the theme of bifurcated or doubled irony a recurrent one in the work. The split between conventional usage and radical redefinition that characterizes several of the major elements of irony is analogous to the doubling of characters in *Repetition*. This inherent rift prepares irony for what may well be its final, even ultimate, emanation: irony's feigned capitulation to and disappearance within the very speculative tradition from which it separated itself and which it undermined. There is a victorious weariness in this gesture: irony finally submits to philosophical procedures that it knows, by virtue of a more comprehensive knowledge, it has defeated. Kierkegaard compares this feigned capitulation to Socrates' acceptance of a death sentence by the Athenian state that he knows rests on insubstantial grounds and to a monarch's happy abdication of power. Of all the elements of irony, this feigned submission to closed operations that have already been debunked may be of the greatest consequence for Kierkegaard's work as a whole, for it is this gesture that questions the ingenuousness of the retreat to the ethical at the end of this dissertation, or the *Or,* and in Kierkegaard's later writings. The ironic nature of this submissive act suggests the superficiality of the logical and moral equilibrium attained by Either/Or logic. The complex of irony supplants existential indecision as the telos of Kierkegaard's work.

Although in *The Concept of Irony* Kierkegaard experimented with several ways of organizing his material, it is primarily a lexicographical and rhetorical work. In subsequent texts this encyclopaedic treatment is replaced by a dramatic one, literally acting out irony and its many potentials for indeterminacy, hovering, and subversion. The 1843 *Either/Or* and most of Kierkegaard's major subsequent works, I am suggesting, even when they appeal to theology, are dramatic explorations into the linguistic qualities that were initially assembled under the rubric of irony.

The treatise on irony is divided into two parts, "The Standpoint of Socrates Conceived as Irony" and "The Concept of Irony." The latter is by far the shorter, little more than a third the length of the former, and it contains the astonishing development that after outlining a model for an ironic tradition in Western thought continuous since Socrates, Kierkegaard repudiates the Romantic irony "after Fichte." This rejection of such masterful practitioners of irony as Friedrich Schlegel, Tieck, and Solger is particularly shocking because it reveals a certain conservatism, an attempt to protect Socrates from his heirs and reinstate him to preeminence that has silently coincided with Kierkegaard's synthesis of irony as a complex of subversive operations. Kierkegaard's sudden reversal at the end of the treatise, his backing away from the most immediate historical context for his ironic awareness, may indicate some moral or theological reservations regarding the esthetic undermining that so captivated him. But a more fruitful if less familiar avenue of pursuit to follow in examining this incongruous gesture may well be to consider Kierkegaard's seeming retreat as the final and consummate irony of the work, a reversal leaving the entire work in an agonizing state of hovering. Of necessity, the present discussion will return to the anomalous ending of the treatise, but at this stage we can already discern in the suspended animation of the final moment the dualistic structuring that will so fully inform such works as *Either/Or, Fear and Trembling,* and *The Concept of Dread.*

The ostensible organization of the far longer first section of the work is a pursuit of irony along the sequence of stages from "possibility" through "actuality" and "necessity." But the movement along this succession does not so much transform irony as serve as a pretext enabling Kierkegaard to reorganize his material differently at each stage. After paying brief attention to Xenophonic and Platonic accounts of Socrates' bearing, the first major subsection, "The Conception Made Possible," examines a number of Platonic texts in generating a wide range of observations concerning irony. Crucial to this subsection is the fact that it consists of a sequence of *readings.* The texts examined include the *Symposium,* the *Protagoras,* the *Phaedo,* the *Apology,* the first book of the *Republic,* and Aristophanes' *Clouds.* Because this extended passage is constructed around exegeses rather than arguments, Kierkegaard makes little attempt to organize or place in consecutive sequence the observations that emerge. Kierkegaard's strategy is not to force the diverse texts into a substantive agreement or uniformity but rather to exploit their heterogeneity in providing different perspectives on irony.

The basic assertions of the second subsection of the work, "The Concept Made Actual," are in substantial agreement with the observations that emerge in the course of Kierkegaard's readings, but they are cast quite differently. What becomes actual in this subsection is not so much irony or any theoretical category as the person of Socrates: the concentration of discursive materials around Socrates as both a dialectical thinker and a mythological character enables Kierkegaard for the first time to formulate positively the complex of irony, which could not coalesce amid the diffusion of the earlier readings. Although Kierkegaard makes constant reference to the historical events in the life of Socrates that have been passed down above all by Plato, Socrates is for him far more than a historical personage. Kierkegaard considers Socrates' mythological daimon, which as an internalized oracle is exceptionally well-suited to his own ideology of a subjective philosophical discourse. He then follows Socrates through his accusation by the Athenian state, the ironic and seductive stance that he maintains toward his students, his trial, and ultimately, his execution. What emerges from this discussion is the image of a Socrates who is an embodiment or incarnation of irony. Socrates combines and performs the ironic functions of negativity (in relation to the official ideology of the state), seduction, dissimulation, hovering, and an infinite, that is, indeterminate and open-ended, reflection. Socrates thus becomes the personification of the multiple and uncoordinated activities of irony, a figure appended to another and even more complex trope. If irony goes a long way in accounting for the Socratic arguments and deeds, Socrates is no less essential in making irony possible, by serving as a manifold linking its varied activities.

The disproportionately large first half of the work concludes with an attempt to assess, rather than crystallize, the places of Socrates and irony in the development of Western thought. "The Conception Made Necessary" views Socrates' posture and influence as a *fait accompli*. If the readings of Plato and Aristophanes that open the work, as well as the ironic complex that configures itself around Socrates, emerge in a present tense of crystallization, Kierkegaard views irony's necessity from the retrospective stance of historical hindsight. Irony's necessity is not so much a new logical condition as an assertion of the continuity of irony's operation throughout the history of Western philosophy and literature. Irony attains *necessity* at the moment when it is granted historical facticity, when it is afforded the insulation and protection of posterity. In an appended section to the first half of the work, "Hegel's Conception of Socrates," Kierkegaard identifies Hegel as a forerunner who observed the ironic vacillation in Socrates' arguments and postures, but he repudiates the Hegelian morality that assigns a negative value to such indeterminacy (*CI*, 248, 253). Even where Kierkegaard departs from Hegel's assessment of Socrates, he appeals to Hegel as a historical arbitrator whose even partial appreciation of irony bestows it with retrospective necessity.

As they have just been outlined, the organization and economy of the first section of *The Concept of Irony* are not merely extrinsic framing devices but are located at the crux of irony's theoretical ramifications. The "positive" identification and combination of the elements in the complex of irony becomes possible only after a sequence of readings that loosely indicate irony's *negative* attributes. Irony's *linguistic* facet, as a complex trope demonstrating language's negative relation to logic and order, is inextricably linked to the *historical* scenario in which the person of Socrates embodies the activities excluded by the mainstream of Western thought. The negativity that Kierkegaard identifies as an element of irony asserts itself in the constant participation of the ironic complex in an attack on a metaphysical system every bit as formed as itself. Irony is thus both a rhetorical complex and a historical tradition, or rather an ongoing countertradition to the intellectual history of the West, with its assertions of progress toward ideal conditions, orderly procedure, consistency, and consummation. In its division of irony into linguistic and historical manifestations, *The Concept of Irony* anticipates the organization of "The Immediate Stages of the Erotic" at the beginning of *Either/Or*.

Like its own inherent vacillation, the notion of irony hovers between positive and negative articulations of its potential. For all this congenital instability, however, traits emerge that if for no reason other than their persistence comprise the complex of irony. Among these qualities the following may be numbered: (1) a fissure within the epistemological field; (2) subjectivity; (3) freedom; (4) hovering or vacillation; (5) infinitude; (6) negativity and its ultimate extension, nothingness; (7) seduction and its affects, which are based on absence rather than presence; (8) secrecy or concealment; (9) the image as a model for a nonrepresentational language; and (10) a feigned capitulation to the ideational, representational, and deterministic operations already undermined by the other elements of irony. Together, these elements comprise a grammar of the complex trope irony.[17]

If there is an oracle from which the other elements in this catalog proceed, it is the initial entry, the epistemological split within the field of knowledge that makes Kierkegaard's works, and ultimately all narratives, unreliable. As was suggested in the earlier discussion of the feigned intimacy of the Kierkegaardian narrator, the different levels of knowledge delineated by Kierkegaard's involuted narrative frameworks are themselves residues of an even more fundamental divergence: between symbols and things, signifiers and their significations.

Emanating from the fundamental epistemological divide marked by irony are both a set of positive or positivistic qualities well grounded in the history of philosophy and a *via negativa* of subversive activities, some of which are every bit as venerable. The positively articulated qualities of subjectivity, freedom, and hovering set the stage on which nothingness, concealment, secrecy, and seduction act out their negative potentials. Although irony is the manifold joining these positive and negative trajectories, the scheme is complicated by the fact that the various elements either regress to or trespass the limits of systematic thought to different degrees. The infinite subjectivity attributed to Socrates represents irony's closest point of contact to a transcendental metaphysics in which the choice exercised by the individual subject is a private manifestation of divine will. The Socrates in whom "we see . . . the infinitely exuberant freedom of subjectivity, that is, irony" (*CI*, 233) is the classical speculative subject, reveling in a freedom whose ultimate source is the Judeo-Christian God.[18] In this formulation, irony is in apposition to, or equivalent to, subjectivity. The close connection between ironic subjectivity and freedom and infinite volition not only forms an ironic configuration within the compass of this treatise: it becomes a psychological profile of the esthetic personality throughout Kierkegaard's writings.

> Irony is free, to be sure, free from all the cares of actuality,but free from its joys as well, free from its blessings. For if it has nothing higher than itself, it may receive no blessing. . . . This is the freedom for which irony longs. It therefore keeps watch over itself, and fears nothing so much as that one or another impression may overwhelm it. For when the individual is free in this way, only then does he live poetically. (*CI*, 296–97)

Yet the scenario of irony as the quintessence of personal whim exists at an extreme within the treatise. Virtually all of the categories and activities attributed to irony other than subjectivity and freedom are a good deal more complicated, encompassing both conventional and marginal intonations. A reading of the complex trope irony demands an apprehension of the full range of the nuances accommodated by the ironic elements. The general impasse of irony, in other words, extends to the specific ironic traits, themselves divided between their systematic and radical potentials.

Negativity

Negativity and its adjective, *negative*, constitute the single most persistently applied attribute of irony, appearing in the treatise almost as often as *irony* itself. Yet this recurrence impedes rather than enforces the consistency or unity of the signification of the term. The usages of ironic negativity extend from simple *negation* in the sense of logical refutation to varieties of absence and displacement that we have already observed in relation to "Eremita"'s secretary and *Repetition*. Like the rhetoric surrounding the image, ironic negativity remains partly within the compass of dialectical procedures and partly outside it. This in-between location, on the border of systematic thought but pointing toward an indefinite beyond, may well constitute the enduring contribution of Kierkegaardian irony as a general category.

On the most specific level, ironic negativity derives from the heartland of dialectical refutation; while characterizing the types of order and consistency that irony refuses to sustain, the negative nonetheless owes its activities to logical negation.

In his interpretations of the Platonic dialogues, Kierkegaard observes the philosophical implications of the displacement effected by irony. In his attempt to postulate the formal discursive implications of negativity, Kierkegaard considers such issues as the inconsistency of Socratic arguments, their failure to be resolved, the reversal of arguments and interlocutors' positions in dialectical disputations, the failure of the disputants to achieve their intentions, and the fundamental amorality of such playful exchange. Even though dialectical thought will serve as a foil to the indifference and autonomy of myth and the image, it contains its own varieties of subversiveness: in the form of its reciprocal organization and capacity for infinite reversal of positions.

It is in the context of the formal implications of ironic negativity that Kierkegaard emphasizes the ending of Plato's *Protagoras* "without a result" (*CI*, 92). Kierkegaard characterizes the dialogue as a perpetual motion machine of reciprocal exchange and reversal of positions.

> After the two antagonists . . . have tried their hand at every kind of wrestler's hold, in as much as Socrates first asks then Protagoras answers, then Protagoras asks and Socrates answers, and finally Socrates asks and Protagoras answers, so that . . . they have tested each other's salt repeatedly, there occurs the strangest phenomenon, namely, Socrates defends what he had intended to refute, and Protagoras attacks what he had intended to defend. (*CI*, 93)

Not only does this scenario describe an infinite reversibility of positions within dialectical disputation that precludes any progressive culmination but it suggests a loss of the interlocutors' control over their positions and even their argumentative wills once they have entered the reciprocal exchange of discourse. The reciprocity of the argumentation supersedes and subsumes any particular position or volition.

The infinity that Kierkegaard here observes as it percolates from the center of logical refutation is very close to the infinite cycles that Hegel inserts within his discourse at certain key moments of logical deadlock. The Hegelian cycles of necessity, life, and infinity itself in the early *Phenomenology*[19] take place when the opposed dialectical pairs, in the inability of establishing any clear relationship of dominance and submission, begin to repeat on themselves endlessly. What this implies for Kierkegaardian irony is that the ubiquitous category of negativity, despite its mystical overtones, has its origin in logic, in an infinity that arises in the despair of achieving choice or resolution. It is questionable whether the ironic infinity that characterizes the ironic subject as well as the Platonic dialogues ever fully severs its ties to dialectical logic.

In addition to this specifically logical context, ironic negativity exists on a far more general level, as a comprehensive negative relation to everything or as nothingness. It is important to note that as a general category, ironic negativity shares the infinite extension of a transcendental entity. Yet from this mystical and mystified dimension of nothingness emerges a type of ironic indifference that is quite congenial to the radical displacement that we have observed in *Repetition* and *Either/Or*.

As the embodiment of ironic potential, Socrates is the professor of a comprehensive negative knowledge, and it is for this reason that Kierkegaard stresses his negative relation to virtually everything, the state, the Sophists, his students, and ultimately even the concept of being ("*bestehenden*") itself. "Not a point on the periphery of the state gravitating toward its centre, but instead a tangent constantly touching only the peripheral manifold of the state" (*CI*, 208), Socrates acquired and disseminated a kind of knowledge appropriate to this type of incidental relation (*CI*, 199).

The fullest extension of the multifaceted negativity that Socrates installed within Western philosophy even during its classical moment is the notion of nothingness itself. Kierkegaardian nothingness is an affirmation of the license on the part of philosophical reasoning and intellectual history to be purely nonproductive, to produce precisely nothing—save a random movement in which structures and configurations crystallize only to disintegrate and reform within a flow of images.

> With irony, on the other hand, when everything else becomes vain, subjectivity becomes free. And the more vain everything becomes, so much the lighter, more vacuous, more evanescent becomes subjectivity. . . . For irony everything becomes nothingness, but nothingness may be taken in several ways. The speculative nothingness is that which at every moment is vanishing for concretion, since it is itself the demand

for the concrete, its *nisus formativus.* The mystical nothingness is a nothingness for representation, a nothingness which yet is as full of content
as the silence of the night is eloquent for one who has ears to hear.
Finally, the ironic nothingness is that deathly stillness in which irony
returns to 'haunt and jest' [*spøger*] (this last word taken wholly ambigu-
ously). (*CI,* 275)

This passage is merely one of many instances in the treatise where a
major segment of the elements in the ironic complex reconvene, a
coincidence of factors that will become increasingly evident in the
material extracted from the treatise. The varieties of nothingness that
Kierkegaard articulates in this passage are based on a distinction that
we will be pursuing shortly, between the dialectical, which he here
terms "speculative," and the mythical. These different formulations
do not oppose so much as supplement each other. "Speculative" nothingness, which is an ongoing dissolution of the concrete, releases
philosophical discourse from any preconceived imperatives to productivity and finality. The nothingness arising out of the mythical
strand of Socrates' thought is more linguistic in nature, akin to a
language that has rejected its representational function and thrown
off its subservience to an external reality. The sound of the silence in
the night is like the upheaval that takes place in language when its
representational function is replaced by nothingness.

And yet there is a third and distinct level on which ironic negativity
operates, one having little to do with either logical disputation or an
encompassing metaphysics of nothingness. It is on this level that the
rhetoric of ironic negativity intimates the absence in which the text
arises, where it initiates an economy of substitution and displacement.
This emanation of ironic negativity as absence displays the negative at
its highest level of literary potential. It is in the context of the negative
relation that instigates the sequence of substitutions epitomizing literary activity that Kierkegaard offers the suggestion that Socrates'
power as teacher and eroticist derived from his ability to arouse a
sense of absence, rather than presence, in knowledge and love. This
image of Socrates emerges in the discussion of the *Symposium,* where
"Irony is the negative in love, the incitement of love" (*CI,* 88), making
tolerable and even intellectually edifying the fact that "love is the
absence of something" (*CI,* 82). As an illustration of the ironic negativity that takes the form of loss and longing, Kierkegaard gives images of hollowing and emptying a prominent place in his interpretation of this dialogue. "Socrates gets at the nut not by peeling off the
shell but by hollowing out the kernel" (*CI,* 82). "The ironist is a vam-
pire who has sucked the blood out of her lover and fanned him with
coolness, lulled him to sleep and tormented him with turbulent

dreams" (*CI*, 86). In such passages, the absence and substitution at the heart of desire and the process of learning are cast in terms of the negative relations of hollow to full space, dreams to consciousness, femininity to masculine assertiveness, and parasitic dependence as opposed to productivity.

Ironic negativity thus runs a full gamut of significations from logic and existential mystification to the absence at the basis of literary production.

The Image

The ironic image arises in the space opened by the indifference that Kierkegaard repeatedly ascribes to mythical thought (*CI*, 110–14). Yet for all the reverence in which it is sheathed, the image is caught in the same crossfire that sundered ironic negativity. One flank of the ironic image is held fast within the closed systems of dialectical reasoning, idealism, and iconic religiosity. Yet the image also serves as the basis for the radically nonrepresentational language whose paradigm Kierkegaard locates in Aristophanes' *Clouds*. In his rhetoric of imaging in the treatise, Kierkegaard certainly continues a Romantic tradition in which the image is invested with virginal and sacred properties, a tradition encompassing works as diverse as Wordsworth's *Prelude* and Nathaniel Hawthorne's *Marble Faun*.[20] Yet it is precisely the *frame* around the image, the possibly theological separation allowing the image to relate purely to itself, that is the foundation for its operation within a drastically different order. The remoteness of the image is the origin of the self-referential and completely autonomous network of language that it forms.

There is perhaps no more striking illustration of irony's impasse than the double-duty to which Kierkegaard relegates the image. On the one hand, the image is in collaboration with dialectical logic and the metaphysics of reflection and representation. This becomes particularly evident in a passage in which the Hegelian rhetoric of sublation (*Aufhebung*) is deployed in characterizing the manner in which the image appropriates the mythical.

> If, after consciousness awakens, the imagination again desires to return to these dreams, the mythical exhibits itself in a new form, that is, as image. A change has now occurred, for the mythical is here taken up into consciousness, that is, the mythical is not the Idea but the reflection of the Idea. This is the case, I believe, with the mythical representations in the constructive dialogues. The mythical is there for the first time assimilated into the dialectical, is no longer in conflict with it, no longer concludes like a partisan; instead, it alternates with the dialectical, and in this way both are lifted up into a higher order of things. (*CI*, 134)

In this scenario, the mythical repudiates its prior indifference to dialectical compulsion in the interest of a higher purpose. The collaboration, rather than opposition, between mythical apprehension and dialectical mechanics places the image, myth's successor, in the ideal position of being both *within* systematic thought and *free* of it. In this passage, Kierkegaard defines the image as alien to neither dialectical thought nor what falls outside it. The image is a go-between. Its mediatory function is stressed by the characteristic Hegelian gestures: the mythical is "taken up into consciousness"; "both are lifted up into a higher order of things." Closely allied to the image's dialectical facet is its participation within the economics of reflection and representation. The image captures that moment of the myth when it is "the reflection of the Idea." On one of its double faces, then, the image subordinates itself to a metaphysics in which symbols themselves serve higher realities. It *resolves* the qualifications of logic with the broader apprehensions that nullified them. It *affirms* the idealism at the basis of the metaphysics of reflection and representation.

Yet at the same time the image is the building block within a language that definitively effects the break with dialectics. The image is the rubric for the potentials and activities that enable this break. And Aristophanes' *Clouds* is the incubator for the radical potentials of the ironic image. Like the images of the opera and farcical stage that recur in Kierkegaard's work, this play is an artwork within whose compass the negativities of mockery and dispersion are endowed with a positive dramatic elaboration. The clouds are not merely a telling image from the play; they constitute an image for the image itself, for a self-referential, nonrepresentational language.

> But if we omit all this, it becomes even more important to dwell on the symbol in which the poet has enveloped the chorus, viz., the clouds. . . . Manifestly, it illustrates all the empty and vacuous activity that goes on in the Thoughtery, and it is therefore with deep irony that Aristophanes, in the scene in which Strepsiades is to be initiated into this wisdom, allows Socrates to call upon the clouds, the airy reflex of his own hollow interior. Clouds describe perfectly the completely directionless movement of thought, which, with incessant fluctuation, without foothold and without immanent laws of motion, configures itself in every which way with the same irregular variation as do the clouds, which now resemble mortal women, now a centaur, a leopard, a wolf, a bull, etc. (*CI*, 163)

The image of Aristophanes' clouds, nebulous as they may be, provides Kierkegaard with an occasion for articulating the dispersion, hovering, decentering, and fluid transformation that he has previously characterized as loss. Clouds ground a metaphysics of association rather than one of growth or development toward revelation. The Socrates of the play is not the cornerstone and symbol of the quest for truth in Western thought but a buffoon, the target of his own irony. The nebulousness for which the image of clouds and Aristophanes' play both provide a positive expression is the model for a combinatorial language whose deep structure is resonance rather than fidelity to the ideal. Just as "clouds describe perfectly the completely directionless movement" of this thought, Kierkegaard would hope that irony would describe perfectly the activities of a nonrepresentational language and countermetaphysics.

Aristophanes' *Clouds* furnishes Kierkegaard with an image for the nonrepresentational vacuity preceding, underlying, and qualifying all human activities, whether communal or personal. To their limitation and chagrin, the political state and its individual members are founded on a shifting emptiness. This is felt more acutely by no one than by the thinking subject at the center of philosophical speculation.

> Indeed, this correspondence between the clouds and the world to which they belong, a fact which it seems to me interpreters have so far overlooked, is expressed even more definitely when it is said: 'These become just what they please. . . .' Here the Aristophanic irony undoubtedly lies in the reciprocal impotence: that of the subject who, in seeking the objective, obtains no more than his own likeness; and that of the clouds, which grasp merely the subject's likeness and produce this only so long as they continue to see the object. (*CI*, 164–65)

Even the sense of selfhood at the root of personal experience as well as philosophical conjecture is based on a misapprehension. The "objective," which is the stable ground for subjectivity, is itself vacuity and whim. The fundamental epistemological confrontation that grounds the self turns out in this passage to be a component of irony. Irony is closely linked to the dramatic scenario of a confrontation between characters with incomplete knowledge. Abstract as their names may be, these characters, "subject" and "object," fabulate a certainty to which they are not entitled because of their reciprocal vacuity. In a scenario whose characters are the fundamental categories of epistemology, Kierkegaard associates irony with the epistemological difference in knowledge disqualifying what the "subject" thinks it knows.

The Feigned Capitulation to the Already Debunked Categories of Western Thought

The impasse of Kierkegaardian irony is closely analogous to the philosopher's ambiguous attitude toward Hegel. Just as Kierkegaard challenged but in other ways acceded to his predecessor, to some extent irony retreats back to terms deriving from the philosophical system it has attacked.

In order to distinguish and protect his reformulations of such terms as *negativity, myth,* and the *image,* Kierkegaard devised the strategy of bifurcating the speculative system into which the illogical tendencies of irony might otherwise disappear. Kierkegaard's act of division, of course, originates in the same dialectical procedures with which irony is at odds. But such a movement is instrumental in the delineation of the ironic potentials that Kierkegaard's text would release.

> That irony and dialectic are the two great forces in Plato will surely be admitted by all; but it is no less obvious that there is a double species of irony and a double species of dialectic. There is another irony that is both the agent and terminus towards which it strives. There is a dialectic which, in constant movement, is always watching to see that the problem does not become ensnared in an accidental conception; a dialectic which, never fatigued, is always ready to set the problem afloat should it ever go aground; in short, a dialectic which always knows how to keep the problem hovering, and precisely in and through this seeks to solve it. There is another dialectic which, since it begins with the most abstract Ideas, seeks to allow these to unfold themselves in more concrete determinations; a dialectic which seeks to construct actuality by means of the Idea. (*CI,* 151)

In this passage, Kierkegaard differentiates between two versions of irony and dialectic, privileging in each case his first formulation. He prefers a Mephistophelean irony of goading and constant attentiveness to an irony with teleological aims, directed at a "terminus." He similarly rejects an Idea and therefore solution-oriented model of dialectical process in favor of one that effects a sustained resonance and interpretative multiplicity in approaching a philosophical problem. Kierkegaard associates the radical emanations of irony and dialectical thought with the breadth and indifference of the mythical mode. The preemptive gesture of distinguishing the radical nuances of ironic terms from their conventional usages within speculative thought becomes a compulsive necessity within Kierkegaard's treatise: the bifurcation of the system and the concomitant doubling of irony recur at several points in the work (*CI,* 98, 260, 331).

Despite Kierkegaard's own compulsive distinction-making, however, there is a moment at which the radical potentials of irony do vanish into the speculative system from which they took off. Seemingly a defeat, this gesture is the movement by which irony claims a permanent place for itself in philosophy and holds its indeterminacy in ongoing reserve. "Hence irony lapses into the very thing it most opposes, for the ironist acquires a certain similarity to a thoroughly prosaic person, except that he retains the negative freedom whereby he stands poetically above himself" (*CI*, 298). With this statement, the secrecy and conniving of the Kierkegaardian seducer gain a new meaning. The concealment of irony consists not so much in the specific seductions that it effects as in the permanent place that it establishes for subversion within philosophical discourse.

In this feigned renunciation of its negative attributes and reconciliation with metaphysics, irony pushes toward the limits of its own dramatic potentials. The close affinity between irony and dramatic acting has been intimated in the treatise since Kierkegaard's reading of the *Apology*, in which there is an emphasis on Socrates' joy in performance and exaggeration for their own sake (*CI*, 120–24). In this interpretation, Kierkegaard reads Socrates' acceptance of the death sentence imposed upon him by the Athenian state as an ironic rather than idealistic act: "One cannot help but approve of that apparently guileless and good-natured yet freezing irony with which he ignores the terrible argument and amicably converses with the Athenians" (*CI*, 123). Irony's highest expression is its capacity to relinquish its own combativeness, to give the assertion of power and reason over to the dialectically organized systems that it opposes, whether logical necessity or the Athenian state that executes Socrates. In another passage Kierkegaard will compare irony's displacement of power and reason away from itself, and by implication away from language and rhetoric, to "a king without a country who delights in the sheer possibility of renouncing everything at the moment of apparent possession, though both the possession and renunciation are illusory" (*CI*, 165). The Socrates who welcomes his absurd punishment is thus a king who happily abdicates his throne and, as the same passage continues, a runaway child. All three of these images suggest that even if it were possible for irony to take itself back, to retract its critical questionings, waverings, and undecidabilities, the act of renunciation, as well as dialectical assertion, would be "illusory."

If it is merely apparent, what does the swan song that irony sings as the curtain falls on its performance accomplish? For one, irony's vanishing act, the assertion that its doubt is a "vanishing moment in the system" (*CI*, 192), assures a place for irony in the yet empty horizon of philosophy. In making Socrates a personification of irony, Kierkegaard insinuates ironic negativity into the classical foundations of Western thought. When irony disappears into the lineaments of that philosophical system, its historical course runs full cycle. It becomes the key to the repetition within a perpetual-motion machine, a permanently installed potential energy for subversion. In its seeming retreat, irony invades the future of philosophy as ineluctably as it penetrated the origins in the figure of Socrates. By means of its henceforth invisible workings within philosophy, irony attains the mythical dimension of an eternally recurring cycle.

Yet irony's feigned renunciation of its capabilities is as instructive a key to *The Concept of Irony* and Kierkegaard's work in general as it is to the history of philosophy. For just as Socrates might appear to sanction his death, and irony might appear to submit to logic and reason, Kierkegaard's model of esthetic excess might appear to subside into the moral pronouncements of the prosaic life. But "the mischievous face of irony is occasionally allowed to peep out" of Ast's stolid reading of Socrates in the same way that the black border that intrudes between the Madonna and the angels below her in a religious engraving is ineffectual (*CI*, 124–25). In a similar vein, one may say that the priority of esthetic decentering shines through the dual structure that Kierkegaard imposes on his works. If at the end of such works as *Either/Or* moral judgment and restraint seem to reclaim a control temporarily usurped by the esthetic mode, this is as much to secure the position of irony's "minute, invisible personage" (*CI*, 111) as it is to prolong any logical equilibrium. Like irony's pronounced acts of renunciation, then, the dualistic structure of Kierkegaard's works and the logic of Either/Or are ploys imperfectly dissimulating the predominance of the esthetic mode in his writings.

The theatrical rejection, on the part of irony, of the effervescent, hovering, self-contained, and nonsequential potentials that it has labored with such effort to formulate and combine not only explains the ending of this work: it *is* the ending, entitled "Irony after Fichte." At the same time that Kierkegaard exploits the ending of his work as an occasion to *consolidate* certain key aspects of irony—above all, its attack on actuality (*CI*, 296, 341) and its continuity as a countertradition to Western metaphysics (*CI*, 294–95)—he also *repudiates* those theorists of irony who were his immediate forebears. In sundering his treatise from the works of Friedrich Schlegel, Tieck, and Solger that would constitute its most immediate context, Kierkegaard's motive is that of purification: to protect first Plato and then Hegel from the degradations of irony of which he accuses the three Romantic authors. An inevitable moralism creeps into the oedipal act of defending the two philosophical patriarchs against the sins of the literary fathers. The moralism to which Kierkegaard reverts is precisely what irony, with its freedom, hovering, and undecidability, was designed to undermine. Kierkegaard's regression to the idealism of morals would seem to close the treatise in the dualistic suspension that structures so much of his writing. Yet as we have observed, this equilibrium is itself merely a screen concealing the finality or ultimatum of the esthetic mode.

Although the predicates of freedom and hovering that Kierkegaard assigns to the ironic subject are close to Friedrich Schlegel's parabasis, he accuses Schlegel of an egotistical nihilism and stupor that is beyond the compass of irony (*CI*, 304, 312, 316). So lyrical and decadent is Tieck's poetry that it evaporates before it can achieve any substantive effect (*CI*, 318, 320, 322). Solger's irony, on the other hand, is so concrete and vigorous that it attacks even its own esthetic qualities, leaving nothing in its wake (*CI*, 328, 330, 335). This turning upon Kierkegaard's most immediate predecessors as theorists of irony is curious on at least two different levels. On the one hand, the repudiation of these authors because they arrive, in different ways, at a moral anomie is strongly reminiscent of Hegel's critique of the states of "free self-consciousness"—Stoicism and Skepticism—as he sets the stage for the emergence of the minister who bonds the sensible to the supersensible world by sacrificing the pleasures of the former. Stoicism and Skepticism are culpable because they are the primitive stages of a consciousness that has for the first time become internal *self*-consciousness. Having just penetrated the threshold of interiority, they are *too free*, Stoicism because of its own brand of nihilism and Skepticism because of its mystification. Not only do Kierkegaard's criticisms of F. Schlegel, Tieck, and Solger repeat Hegel's objections to these stages of consciousness: Kierkegaard holds Hegel up as representing the happy medium between negativity and actuality that the other authors somehow missed.

Kierkegaard's repudiation of F. Schlegel, Tieck, and Solger forces him into a filial relation with Hegel, whose assurances of continuity and resolution in philosophical discourse were the foundation that his esthetic mode set out to destroy. An even deeper irony of these alliances is that Kierkegaard, while he identifies with Hegel as an opponent of nihilism, describes F. Schlegel, Tieck, and Solger precisely in the terms that he has employed to characterize irony and Socrates throughout his treatise. Schlegel's *Lucinde* "cancel[s] all actuality" (*CI*, 306), Tieck's work is musical and opposes the "ossification" of the prosaic life (*CI*, 318, 322), and Solger reaches toward an ultimately nonproductive nothingness (*CI*, 328–29, 331). Kierkegaard is thus inseparable from the predecessors from whom he emphatically recoils in horror. By means of a contrived alliance with Hegel, Kierkegaard seemingly retreats from a position of ironic negativity to one of ethical judgment. But the synthesis between irony and ethics completes the architectural framework from whose gaps the "mischievous face of irony," its "minute, invisible personage," will mockingly peep.

Even if Kierkegaardian irony is itself ambiguous in its relation to the speculative and reflexive tradition that it would supplant, both drawing upon and disfiguring that system, it is remarkable for the wide range of literary and linguistic qualities that it embraces. Kierkegaard's treatise makes the outstanding contribution of distinguishing between ideational and deterministic philosophical procedures and a large set of linguistically based potentials that evade their grasp. Not only does Kierkegaard extrapolate and collect these potentials all the while that he reinterprets Socrates as an ironic figure: he calculates in historical terms the stakes of the battle between idea-based speculation and language-based poetics. From his variegated use of his material, *we* may extrapolate a scenario in which the idea-based mainstream of Western thought suppresses irony and its poetics but cannot exclude them entirely. Irony is too well entrenched at the beginnings; too permanently installed at the end, when it has disappeared seamlessly into the systematic limits.

Although with varying degrees of comprehensiveness, *The Concept of Irony* embraces virtually all of the characteristics that Kierkegaard will discern in language, as well as the main lines of battle between ideation and poetics. In its wake, Kierkegaard's works act out or dramatize various of the potentials explored in it. *Either/Or* is precisely such a work, more a *theater* of irony's activities than a compendium.

[III]

EITHER/OR: THE THEATER OF IRONY

Although possessed of a formidable volume, *Either/Or* is a magnum opus less by virtue of its size than by virtue of the prodigious variety of roles and disguises that philosophical discourse assumes within its compass. From its paean to Don Juan's ebullience to "Judge William" 's prosaic moral pronouncements, to its exegeses of the *Antigone* and Scribe's *The First Love, Either/Or* is a showcase for the bewildering multiplicity of rhetorical, argumentative, hermeneutic, and fictive functions that philosophical discourse can perform. Even with its thrusts in the direction of morality, the work is a celebration of writing and the possibilities that writing liberates, a fact borne out by the irony and equivocation that penetrate as far as "Judge William" 's prose. On a substantive level, there is very little in *Either/Or* that is not taken into account by previous and contemporary works of Kierkegaard: *The Concept of Irony, Fear and Trembling, Sickness unto Death,* and *Repetition.* This vast work owes its distinction, then, to the relentlessness and creativity of its exploration into the potentials of discourse, fiction, poetics, and performance.

Our discussion of other Kierkegaardian works has necessarily touched upon many of the arguments and thematic areas appearing in *Either/Or.* Rather than recapitulate these concerns, we will, like the fictive editor "Victor Eremita" first surveying the secretary from which the texts of *Either/Or* emanate, delight in its "rich economy," the appropriation of the materials rather than the materials themselves.

Either/Or, or more precisely, the economy of its resources, *performs* what *The Concept of Irony* assembled. If irony is a complex trope encompassing a wide variety of practices that indicate the linguistic constitution of reality, the appropriation of materials in *Either/Or* dramatizes many of those same figurative usages. As we will observe in greater detail, the dualistic structure that seems to send the *Either* and the *Or* off in diametrically opposed directions is highly questionable: there is much to suggest that the esthetic and ethical modalities, rather than negating one another, are in substantial agreement.[21] Any difference between the modalities is perspectival, not logical or substantial. The counterperspectives supplement rather than detract from each other. In its widest dimensions, then, *Either/Or* performs the disruption to dialectical logic announced by the myth and consummated by the image in *The Concept of Irony.*

We have already observed the involuted narrative structure that Kierkegaard fashioned for *Either/Or.* The work bears the name of "Victor Eremita," who turns out to be merely the discoverer and editor of its two countertexts. In the virtual absence of "Eremita" from the text, it is "Esthete A" and "Judge William" that the reader confronts as authorial surrogates. Complicated by the work's narrative structure, *Either/Or* thus pursues a rather indirect trajectory from its author to its readers:

$$\text{Søren Kierkegaard} \to \text{"Victor Eremita"} \begin{array}{c} \nearrow \text{"A"} \longrightarrow \textit{Either} \searrow \\ \longrightarrow \\ \searrow \text{"Judge} \qquad \qquad \nearrow \\ \text{William"} \to \textit{Or} \end{array} \text{reader}$$

Each stage of this sequence offers new discrepancies and complications within the epistemological field. In comparison with "Kierkegaard," the surrogate "Eremita" is a bit limited in his perceptions and even simple-minded. Yet it is precisely his naive absorption in his editorial role that enables him to deliver his marvelously suggestive, both psychologically and literarily, confession of how the texts ostensibly came into his hands. By knowing less, "Eremita" is able to reveal more, certainly more than "Søren Kierkegaard" could have divulged under his own name. Similarly, read individually, the esthetic and ethical modalities set forth, respectively, in the *Either* and the *Or,* are surrounded by apparent limits—temperamental and conceptual. Since the ethical mode repeatedly defines itself as a voluntary choice of existential limit, above all through the institution of marriage, it in particular begs to be apprehended as a perspective of repression and constraint. But in relation to each other, the *Either* and the *Or* resonate far differently than they do alone. In the way they play themselves off against each other, in the way their interaction encompasses a full range of relations, from opposition to collusion, together the *Either* and the *Or* define a knowledge vastly more expansive and ironic than that evident in either of their particular invectives. As the last link in the communicative sequence or allegory conjured by the work, it falls upon the reader to consummate or totalize this fragmented field of knowledge. Yet the only act left to the reader is closer to capitulation than omniscience: the admission that all levels of knowledge delineated by the work are by nature limited and irreconcilable.

Either/Or thus joins the notion of irony in challenging dialectical logic and in establishing a divided and inherently ambiguous field. So too do the qualities of the aphoristic utterance which are celebrated by irony and with which the *Either* begins carry over into the work as a whole. Just as Kierkegaard's individual aphorisms are fragmentary in their scope, arbitrary in their finality, and oblique in their interrelation, the subtexts comprising the *Either* and the *Or* may touch common themes, but their emphases, organizations, and polemical thrusts are markedly heterogeneous.[22] In accordance with the tenets of the esthetic mode, the subtexts of the *Either* are particularly so. These essays vary in the historicity of their approach, in the degree of their hermeneutical commitment, and in their emphasis on their own fictive qualities.

We have already observed how "Victor Eremita"'s Preface establishes a shifting economy of displacement and metaphoric transformation for the work as a whole, applying to the ethical as well as the esthetic papers. And in the first of the esthetic writings, the "Diapsalmata," aphorism emerges as the basic medium for esthetic undecidability. And yet, if any characteristic from our earlier discussion accounts for the heterogeneous economy of *Either/Or,* it is Kierkegaardian repetition, the unique persistence of linguistic structures as they advance from scene to scene. When in a late section of the *Either* entitled "The Rotation Method" "Esthete A" takes up the problem of repetition, he offers us at the same time a key into the organizational principles of the entire work.

The rotation method is a model for a methodological and situational shift of field. Kierkegaard is well aware of the agricultural roots of the metaphor.

> My own dissent from the ordinary view is sufficiently expressed in the use I make of the word, "rotation." This word might seem to conceal an ambiguity, and if I wished to use it so as to find room in it for the ordinary method, I should have to define it as a change of field. But the farmer does not use the word in this sense. I shall, however, adopt this meaning for a moment, in order to speak of the rotation which depends on change in its boundless infinity, its extensive dimension, so to speak. (*E*, 287)

Kierkegaard's hesitations, as he grapples for the agricultural conception of rotation but momentarily settles for the "ordinary method" involving a simple change of location, are indicative of his own semantic fluctuations. Rotation is a fundamentally circular movement. The change of field that is its provisional definition adds the potential for reversal to this circularity. Yet a simple movement from field to field does not provide the extension of a "boundless infinity" that "Esthete A" wishes to incorporate into the method.

> My method does not consist in change of field, but resembles the true rotation method in changing the crop and the mode of cultivation. Here we have at once the principle of limitation, the only saving principle in the world. The more you limit yourself, the more fertile you become in invention. (*E*, 288)

It is in this passage that "Esthete A" suggests the analogy between Kierkegaard's discursive methods and rotation. The "true" rotation practiced by the farmer is substantive *and* methodological. Not only do the crops change but so does the "mode of cultivation." In *Either/ Or*, many of the different papers derive from common thematic roots: desire, deception, seduction, and interpretation. But as these thematic strands "rotate" from section to section, Kierkegaard subjects them to radically different modes of treatment. The rotation method is a metaphorical rubric for the relentless movement of structures and themes from scene to scene that took place in *Repetition.* From the writerly point of view, this marked transformation constitutes the only form of extension or infinity that can be transported from the agricultural to the textual field. But this imperative to variation imposes a burden as well. The law of rotation constitutes a statute of limitations in the sense that variation places a severe esthetic demand—in terms of style, genre, and composition—on the writer. If this statute of limitation is responsible for an increase in creative fertility, it is because of the additional esthetic ingenuity that rotation demands.

"Esthete A" goes on to compare the methodological as well as the substantive change involved in "true" rotation with the creative form of forgetting vital to poetry. Like Proust's "mémoire involontaire,"[23] this form of forgetting is not so much a loss of consciousness as a productive interruption placed within a compositional sequence, a lapse in the interest of unpredictable tangents and associations. "The more poetically one remembers, the more easily one forgets; for remembering poetically is really only another expression for forgetting" (*E*, 289). Writing borders on farming precisely at the point where lapses and interruptions are vital to the fertility of each. This separation point is also where forgetting and remembering vanish into each other, where the seemingly vacant space of forgetting is endowed with creative activity. "Forgetting is the shears with which you cut away what you cannot use, doing it under the supreme direction of memory. Forgetting and remembering are thus identical arts, and the artistic achievement of this identity is the Archimedean point from which one lifts the whole world" (*E*, 291). Forgetting thus joins the statute of limitations as a negative moment essential to esthetic indirection and variation. Just as forgetting becomes indistinguishable from its opposite, the statute straddles both sides of the divide between the esthetic and the ethical. For the esthetic mode, the *limits* on such constructs as memory, consciousness, and totality constitute an impetus for creative elaboration. Yet the notion of limit as the stability attained through the *elimination* of choices is equally crucial and positive to the prosaic existence of the ethical domain.

Whether defined as a creative statute of limitations or an ultimately constructive forgetting, the rotation method defines the interrelation of the various papers and sections comprising *Either/Or*. The first major expository section of the esthetic papers, situated after "Eremita"'s preface and the "Diapsalmata," is entitled "The Immediate Stages of the Erotic: Or the Musical Erotic." This is a crucial piece of writing for two reasons: on the one hand, it furnishes a close reading of the Mozart-Da Ponte opera *Don Giovanni*, becoming a model for textual exegesis in Kierkegaard's work; at the same time, it lays both the conceptual and the historical groundwork for the scenario in which music expresses the repressed potentials in Western thought. The metaphorical and nonrepresentational quality ascribed to music in this section constitutes the concept of irony in

Kierkegaard's treatise. If Socrates was irony's primary personification and promulgator, the operatic character Don Juan performs these functions in relation to music. If Don Juan is "effervescent as champagne" (*E*, 134), this bubbling and decentering describe not merely his almost infinite sexual exploits but his functioning as the copula of coupling itself, a figure for unlimited metaphoric association or copulation in language.

In terms of the structure of *Either/Or* as a whole, Don Juan's position is central. He is the effervescent link between the theoretical and historical contexts for music and repression early in the work and the scenarios of seduction, deception, and marriage that inform all subsequent sections. "The Immediate Stages of the Erotic" plays a fundamental role in articulating the *theoretical* distinction between music as a nonrepresentational, nonreflexive language and the type of conceptual language that assists in the processes of determination and ideation. It also establishes the *historical* context in which the traits of irony, here attributed to music, have been systematically excluded from and repressed within Western thought, at least since the dominance of Christianity.

Yet the figure of Don Juan does not merely step forth onto this theoretical and historical platform. In his amorality, charisma, and complete lack of introspection, he initiates processes of seduction and deception that will never be quelled, despite "Judge William"'s efforts, in the course of the work. Seduction becomes the field in which the metaphoric copulation of music plays itself out. Just as Don Juan is not only an empirical sensualist but a figure for the general metaphoric copulation in language itself, the solicitations, refusals, and dissimulations involved in seduction are not merely the preambles to physical pleasures but moments structurally inherent to all communicative acts. The figure of Don Juan resides halfway between a theoretical and historical placement of language in relation to Western thought and an allegory of reading and writing whose multiple versions revolve around the dynamics of seduction.

"The Immediate Stages of the Erotic" is a title with Hegelian resonances. For Kierkegaard to commence his vast work with the erotic suggests that within the system that ostensibly follows, sensuality is as fundamental a starting point as the more formal "Sense-Certainty" was to the development of "consciousness" in the *Phenomenology of Spirit*. Yet the "stages" of this supposed sensuality-based evolution can hardly be described as rigorous. The stages themselves are vastly overshadowed by their "Insignificant Introduction" (*E*, 45–73), and when they are finally elaborated, we find that they correspond to operatic characters—the page in *Figaro* and *The Magic Flute*'s Pa-

pageno—rather than to defined cognitive levels. "Esthete A"'s invo-
cation of Hegel at the beginning of his papers enables him both to
declare the quintessentiality of eroticism and music to his discourse
and to parody the earlier philosopher. The "Immediate Stages" thus
provides the same contrapuntal accompaniment to Hegel that opera
and Don Juan offer to the representational and deterministic cur-
rents of Western thought.

Both as an eroticist and as a figure for the unlimited metaphoricity
of language, Don Juan embodies the antithesis of marriage. "So Don
Juan is an image which constantly appears, but does not gain form
and substance, an individual who is constantly being formed, but is
never finished, of whose life history one can form no more definite
impression than one can by listening to the tumult of the waves" (*E*,
91). Marriage is the institution of sexual exclusiveness and the social
sanctioning of sensuous experience that applies the moral statute of
limitations to the various forms of ironic indeterminacy embodied by
Don Juan. It is not accidental, then, that both in the remainder of the
esthete's papers and throughout the moral treatises of the *Or* marriage should be the point of tension at which ironic negativity should
collide into moral and social speculation. In the wake of "The Immediate Stages of the Erotic," all of the esthetic papers are concerned
with marriage, its promise, and its violation. As an institution, marriage demands that a literal reading, a single and permanent interpretation, be imposed upon the variegated erotic and linguistic
possibilities released by music. Marriage constitutes an interruption, a
decisive break, in an otherwise continuous sequence of erotic expenditure. The endless prolongation of random experience is precisely
what Mephistopheles offers Faust in Goethe's tragedy.[24] Faust will
violate his pact only at the moment when he desires to halt this erotic
flux, that is, when he imposes the conditions of Kierkegaardian marriage upon himself. It is in this sense that "Esthete A" takes the marvelously unpredictable step of appropriating *Faust* as a theologically
oriented counterexample to *Don Giovanni* (*E*, 89–90).

In their markedly heterogeneous execution, the remaining esthetic
papers in the *Either* focus on different aspects of the conflict that takes
place at the intersection between ironic indeterminacy and marriage,
with its ideology of identity, exclusiveness, and permanence. The esthete's treatment of this opposition varies from the expository distinction between ancient and modern tragedy in "The Ancient Tragical
Motif as Reflected in the Modern," to the textual exegeses of Goethe's
Clavigo and *Faust* and Mozart's *Don Giovanni* in "Shadowgraphs," to
the fictive invention of the "Diary of the Seducer." This latter text is
in effect a semiautobiographical, semiepistolary novella.

As has already been suggested, there are close similarities between the argumentative schemes of *The Concept of Irony* and "The Immediate Stages of the Erotic." In both cases a ruling ideology, whether described as the Athenian state or Christianity, strives to exclude or eliminate certain erotic tendencies, which, on closer inspection, imply a language-based constitution of reality or existence as opposed to a foundation in transcendental ideals or logical procedures. Also, in both cases a central figure—Socrates or Don Juan—embodies and personifies the qualities of the suppressed linguistic undercurrent in culture. Rather than these major similarities, what will concern us here are the specific points at which "The Immediate Stages of the Erotic," as the argumentative foundation of *Either/Or*, diverges from the ironic thesis.

The strategic requirements of "The Immediate Stages of the Erotic" vary from those of *The Concept of Irony* in two major areas. Whereas in the earlier work the ideological mainstream undermined by irony was limited to the Athenian state and the abstract philosophical procedures of ideation and determination, in *Either/Or* the predominant cultural current assumes the far more concrete form of marriage, and an entire complex of assumptions and expectations accompanying it. In *Either/Or*, music must relate more tangibly to the themes of seduction and marriage than did irony in *The Concept of Irony*. A second new emphasis emerges from the dialectical structure of *Either/Or*. Since the consummate irony of this work will be that both the esthetic and ethical modes are ultimately reflected, that is, articulated and qualified, by language, the speculative notion of reflection becomes more crucial to the economy of "The Immediate Stages of the Erotic" than it was in the earlier text.

These two points of divergence become particularly important in relation to the historical and theoretical frameworks that buttress the argumentation of "The Immediate Stages of the Erotic." Not only does "Esthete A" regard the erotic as a cultural undercurrent excluded by Christianity; he observes how in its own way Greek thought was inimical to musical genius as well. *The Concept of Irony* prepares us for the paradoxical assertion that in driving "sensuousness out" Christianity "has brought sensuousness into the world" (*E*, 54). But if Christianity determined sensuality as a power to be bluntly repressed, the Greeks took love away from their exemplary lovers, and out of their own hands as well. Eros's love is not based "upon the sensuous but the psychical" (*E*, 61). In psychologizing love, the Greeks exiled it to the domain of the individuated, speculative subject inhabited by abstract thought. Even though Don Juan will himself, as the decentered source of erotic energy in Mozart's opera, be close to the Greek model of displaced love, the esthete's performative act of accusation stands: in terms of *Either/Or* the exclusionary policy of Western thought with regard to eroticism and language extends to the Greeks.

"The Immediate Stages of the Erotic" diverges even more significantly from the patterns established in the work on irony with respect to the theoretical redefinition of the function of language. The role played by irony in the earlier text as a complex rubric for language's release from its representational and referential functions is here assigned to music. The decisive formulation of the "Insignificant Introduction" to the "Immediate Stages," and one that may be taken as an epigraph for the section as a whole, is the following paradoxical statement: "The most abstract idea conceivable is sensuous genius. But in what medium is this idea expressible? Solely in music. It cannot be expressed in sculpture . . . nor in painting . . . it is a storm, impatience, passion" (*E*, 55). Although other languages privilege external ideals and truths, which they purport to represent, music is a counterlanguage in which sensuality is granted the highest importance. Music gives credence to sensual experience, and in fact assigns it an authority that in other forms of language is reserved for abstraction. It is in its sense of receptivity to nonsequential physical experience that music joins the abstract to the sensuous and that sensuous genius becomes the "most abstract idea conceivable."

"Esthete A" devotes a lengthy exposition to distinguishing music from other forms of language. Although at first he seems to posit the rather naive categorical distinction making music the only language entirely free of reflection or mediation, music's distinction evolves into its unique hovering between sensual immediacy and self-consciousness. The esthete's first position in separating music from other forms of discourse is to assert a unique musical receptivity to pure immediacy. As opposed to painting, for example, music refuses to yield to the program of representation, "for it cannot be apprehended in precise outlines" (*E*, 55). Yet no sooner does the esthete attempt to characterize music in words than he is forced to fill in its *terra incognita* with images and metaphors imported from other discourses.

> If I imagined two kingdoms adjoining one another, with one of which I was fairly well acquainted, and altogether unfamiliar with the other, and I was not allowed to enter the unknown realm, however much I desired to do so, I should still be able to form some conception of its nature. I could go to the limits of the kingdom with which I was acquainted and follow its boundaries, and as I did so, I should in this way describe the boundaries of this unknown country, and thus without ever having set foot in it, obtain a general conception of it. . . .

> The kingdom known to me, to whose utmost boundaries I intend to go in order to discover music, is language. If one wished to arrange the different media according to their appointed developmental process, one would have to place music and language next to one another, for which reason it has often been said that music is a language, which is something more than a genial remark. (*E*, 64–65)

This passage discloses the contradictions in the esthete's attempt to separate music from language. On the one hand, he would like to keep the border between the adjacent realms guarded. If music is the only medium in which sensuous genius is expressible, in "language the sensuous is as medium depressed to the level of a mere instrumentality and constantly negated. . . . The sensuous is reduced to a mere instrument and is thus annulled" (*E*, 65–66). The "language" to which the esthete opposes music in his effort to keep the separation between the territories clear is a limited notion of language as instrumentality. As the esthetic medium that eschews the vague "inwardness" of sculpture and the "precise outlines" of painting, music resists any instrumental function of language, that is, any notion that language represents, that it implements, that it reduces the manifold of possibility into irreversible action. Music is no more a spiritual medium than it is an instrument. "Esthete A" posits that music conveys a certain immediacy, but this is a sensuous immediacy, not one emanating from any transcendental or theological essence. The belief that music conveys a theologically sanctioned spirituality is yet another instrumental notion of language. "But the immediacy which is thus excluded by the spirit is sensuous immediacy. This belongs to Christianity. In music it has its absolute medium. . . . Music is, then, the medium for that species of the immediate which, spiritually determined, is determined as lying outside of the spirit" (*E*, 69). By means of this formulation, the esthete asserts a musical intensity having the force of a hypothetical immediate expression, but detached from any metaphysical or theological entities or values.

One element of the esthete's characterization of music is thus a rigorous separation of it from the limited notions of language as an instrument and as a spiritual medium. But as a medium, music also participates in a general linguistic economy. Music is a language itself. While distinct from the restrained usages of language described above, music has close affinities to the general economy of language. Music, for example, "is the only" medium other than language "that takes place in time" (*E*, 67). The esthete describes the relation between music and the general economy of language as that between two adjacent lands. The relation between music and the wider sense of language is thus metonymic. The nonreferential sequences of music may be translated into words only through the metonymy that describes music in terms of linguistic operations.

Upon close examination, then, the seemingly impermeable barrier that the esthete constructs between "language" and music breaks down. Music is inimical to instrumental and spiritual uses of language, but then it is describable only in terms of the full system of linguistic operations. "Language" thus expands from a limited code to a set or manifold of usages. There are, for example, degrees of musicality in language, genres that are "more" and "less" musical.

> Now if I take language for my point of departure, in order by moving through it, as it were, to spy out the land of music, the result appears about as follows. If I assume that prose is the language-form that is farthest removed from music, then I notice even in the oratorical discourse, in the sonorous structure of its periods, a hint of the musical which manifests itself more and more strongly at different levels in the poetic form, in the structure of the verse, in the rhyme, until at last the musical has been developed so strongly that language ceases and everything becomes music. (*E*, 67)

Here oratory and even more so poetry are linguistic media more musical than the prose that will become the most basic style that "Judge William" attributes to the ethical life.

But language is not merely more or less musical; music is a language itself. As such, while expressive of "sensuous genius," it is itself articulate, mediated, reflected. As was suggested above, one of the distinct innovations of the "Immediate Stages" is the connection between the ironic language of music and the problematic of reflection, a decisive step in the construction of a dialectical work whose opposed countermodalities finally agree, at least in the sense that they are both articulate. As is befitting a medium that is neither so immediate that it precludes articulation nor so abstract that it instruments logic or spirituality, "Esthete A" places music halfway between a zero point and a totality of reflection.

> The more the drama is self-reflective, the more the mood is explained in the action. The less action, the more the lyrical element dominates. This is quite proper in opera. Opera does not so much have character delineation and action as its immanent goal; it is not reflective enough for that. On the other hand, passion, unreflective and substantial, finds its expression in opera. The musical situation depends on maintaining the unity of mood in the diverse plurality of voices. This is exactly the characteristic of music that it can preserve the diversity in the unity of mood. When in ordinary conversation one uses the word *majority*, one commonly means by that a unity which is the final result; this is not the case in music. (*E*, 117)

Opera, or musical theater, is situated between passion, which as a purely physical experience is untranslatable into any language, and the presentation of characters, which are artificial surrogates endowed with the properties of identity. The musicality of opera questions both the identity that defines characters and the implicit representational model by which characters are simulated on the stage. Yet as an art form too deliberate and contrived to be simple eroticism, opera is necessarily reflected and thus joins the other languages of art as a semiological subsystem with its own conventions.

As the expository introduction to *Either/Or,* "The Immediate Stages of the Erotic" establishes two theoretical fundaments upon which all subsequent sections are based: the *historical* scenario, in which music and the figure of Don Juan embody the analogous erotic and linguistic potentials excluded by the mainstream of Western thought; and the philosophical implications of a music described as a linguistic basis and constitution of reality. The precise definition of music suggests that no experience is too personal, no immediacy too immanent, to bypass linguistic articulation. Although in subsequent sections the work considers the thematics of desire, deception, and marriage, it is never far from the recognition that these interactions are allegories for linguistic activity.

Within the historical and theoretical contexts formulated by "The Immediate Stages of the Erotic," the figure of Don Juan emerges as the constructive alternative to the Greco-Christian exclusion of sensuality and restricted economies of language. Like the Socrates who precedes him in Kierkegaard's work, Don Juan positively enacts the negativity of irony. In keeping with his particular variety of indeterminacy, Don Juan defies specific historical placement. He emanates from the murky kingdom of the early Middle Ages, where language—as an instrument—"has no place, nor sober-minded thought, nor the toilsome business of reflection. There sound only the voice of elemental passion, the play of appetites, the wild shouts of intoxication" (*E,* 88). As opposed to the "psychical" love of the Greeks, Don Juan radiates sensuous love, whose medium is seduction. Sensuous love, as opposed to psychological love, renounces the principles of individuation and identity at the basis of the individual personality (*E,* 91–92). Don Juan does not love in a premeditated, reflexive way, nor does he love individuals. Don Juan seduces, but not with the method or intention suggestive of an individuated or formed psyche: "To be a seducer requires a certain amount of reflection and consciousness . . . cunning intrigues and crafty plans. This consciousness is lacking in Don Juan. Therefore he does not seduce. He desires, and this desire acts seductively" (*E,* 97). Just as such a persona can hardly be called a subject in the Cartesian or Hegelian sense, the object of desire is not so much a specific beloved as a general sexual manifold. "Psychical love does not exactly move in the rich manifold of the individual life, where the nuances are really significant. Sensuous love, on the other hand, can lump everything together" (*E*, 94). Anticipating the Marcel of Proust's *Recherche,* who selects Albertine from the wide frieze of girls at the seaside, Don Juan moves in a sexual field of generality, but not abstraction, without, however, succumbing to the torments of individual love.[25]

Not only does a sensuous love, as opposed to psychological love, challenge the integrity of the subject and the object and therefore undermine the foundations of individual psychology and epistemology. The open sexual field of seduction requires a time scheme radically different from that of the closed field of marriage, a temporality of repetition as opposed to one of consummation. "Sensuous love, in terms of its very concept, is essentially faithless. But this, its faithlessness, appears also in another way; it becomes in fact only a constant repetition" (*E*, 93). In terms of eroticism, the temporality of repetition is indicative of the unlimited desire for more of a good thing. The operations of seduction, which open a potentially endless sequence of different experiences, require a temporality in which new beginnings emerge even during the moments of the most intense gratification. "Only in this manner can Don Juan become epic, in that he constantly finishes, and constantly begins again from the beginning, for his life is the sum of repellent moments which have no coherence, his life as moment is the sum of the moments, as the sum of the moments is the moment" (*E*, 95). Within the mathematics implied by this repetitive motion, there is no sum of moments distinct from the moments. No total summarizes and exceeds the erotic moments. There is nothing but the discrete moments themselves. As the esthete's personification of an erotic repeater, Don Juan neither refers his activities to an origin nor defers them in the name of marriage's ultimate contractual bond. Predicated on the temporality of repetition, his activity describes a prospective, linear, nonevolutionary, nonteleological annexation of experience.

If "The Immediate Stages of the Erotic" devotes few resources to elaborating the theological and metaphysical systems against which the sensuous genius of music arises, it is because this task is left to "Judge William" and the ethical essays of the *Or.* Yet already in Don Juan's movement, the expenditure of his energy, and his relation to time is intimated the dialectical superstructure encompassing the work as a whole. If *The Concept of Irony* situated itself in the between-space separating the procedures of ideation and logic from mythical and ironic negativity, *Either/Or* hovers between the countermetaphysics of eroticism and marriage. In keeping with the hovering motion that Kierkegaard painstakingly elaborated in the earlier treatise, neither seduction nor marriage ever definitively gains the upper hand, although "Judge William" 's rosy pronouncements on marriage may well be ironic. The relation between the two models is *rhythmic* rather than logical, a factor adding to the importance of the musical motif in this and other works.

The figure of Don Juan embodies the type of language operative within the esthetic domain. This is a musical language, inimical to the types of constraint implemented by marriage. The language in which eroticism is issued forth is metaphoric rather than literal: it operates by displacement, deferral, and ventriloquism. This music disavows consistency and uniformity, whether of person, place, or context. It is in the sense of such a metaphoric language that the figure of Don Juan, like the Greek Eros, deflects rather than concentrates love, functioning as the decentered source of energy in Mozart's opera.

> In *Don Juan* the keynote is nothing other than the primitive power in the opera itself; this is Don Juan, but again—just because he is not character but essentially life—he is absolutely musical. Nor are the other persons in the opera characters, but essentially passions, who are posited with Don Juan, and thereby become musical. That is, as Don Juan encircles them all, so do they in turn encircle Don Juan; they are the external consequences his life constantly posits. It is this musical life of Don Juan, absolutely centralized in the opera, which enables it to create a power of illusion such as no other is able to do, so that its life transports one into the life of the play. Because the musical is omnipresent in this music, one may enjoy any snatch of it, and immediately be transported by it. One may enter in the middle of the play and instantly be in the center of it, because this center, which is Don Juan's life, is everywhere. (*E*, 118–19)

The Don Juan of this passage not only personifies the erotic language of music that works by indirection and ventriloquism. As an encompassing and ever-shifting power who animates all around him only to be moved by them, Don Juan is himself a metaphor, the first great figure of speech in a work whose motif of seduction invariably involves metaphoric displacement.

By the end of the *Either*, Kierkegaard's expository distinctions, such as between music and "language" or between ancient and modern tragedy in the "ancient Tragical Motif," give way to the full-fledged fictive composition of the "Diary of the Seducer." Kierkegaard's logical distinctions, however parodic they may be, become part of a wider exploration into the dynamics of reading and the dimensions of the literary text. The deceived women who abound in the *Either* after the "The Immediate Stages of the Erotic" function as exemplary readers. The game of seduction becomes a model for the strategies and battle plans available to the fictive writer. The erotic and marriage are not antithetical philosophical positions so much as complementary narrative modes: both are deployed by the fictive text in arousing the sympathies of the reader, who in position, but not gender, is feminine in Kierkegaard's work, as our earlier discussion indicated. The erotic is the battery of ironic and poetic devices that convince the reader to suspend her disbelief, just as the figure of the deceived woman is cajoled into relinquishing her virginity. The institution of marriage, on the other hand, is the house organ of the reality principle, the voice of logic, restraint, commitment, and finality. Yet even in its banality, marriage joins the fictive allegory of *Either/Or*. The order of marriage corresponds to the community of accepted usages, the Saussurian *langue*, which is the basis of the intelligibility of any text. Marriage may comprise the exposed and delightfully vulnerable foil against which the esthetic mode may commit its excesses; but within the fictive economy of *Either/Or,* marriage is also the foundation on which individual esthetic improvisations, corresponding to the Saussurian *parole*,[26] become intelligible and join the general system of signs.

If the exemplary readers within the internal allegory of reading of *Either/Or* are feminine, they are not women in the proper sense of the word. They are, rather, female literary characters including the venerable Antigone and her modern descendents, Marie Beaumarchais from Goethe's *Clavigo*, Margaret from *Faust*, Donna Elvira from *Don Giovanni*, and Emmeline from Scribe's *First Love*. In this sequence of feminine characters the most significant organizational principles of the *Either* are to be discerned. In the esthete's discussion of the *Antigone* in the "Ancient Tragical Motif" the categorical exposition that appeared in "The Immediate Stages of the Erotic" is for the first time combined with critical exegesis. In the wake of the partially parodic logical distinction between ancient and modern tragedy in that section, the emphasis on logic declines and the essays' absorption in fictive texts and characters deepens. The climax of this line of development occurs in the "Diary of the Seducer," where roles and actions formerly attributed to the *literary* works of Sophocles, Goethe, and others appear as characters within a fictive work in its own right. The *exegeses* that take up the middle of the *Either* may be said to comprise rehearsals for the break from critical reading to fictive invention.

Another form assumed by the development in the *Either* from philosophical exposition to fiction may be described as the choice of increasingly comic or ironic models for the allegories of seduction and reading. The esthete's initial model of feminine disappointment is an Antigone who is a somber and withdrawn character indeed. "Although she is living, she is in another sense dead; quiet is her life and secretive, the world hears not even a sigh, for her sigh is hidden in the depths of her soul" (*E*, 155). Yet by the discussion of Scribe's *The First Love,* in the last substantial section preceding the "Diary of the Seducer," the female character is in the comical situation of selecting between two seducers, one more and one less ironic, who have complicated the matter by exchanging identities. Not only do the superimposed scenarios of seduction and interpretation in this progression gradually acquire the exuberance of the music in *Don Giovanni* but the feminine figure passes from being the passive object, or victim, of seduction to a willful participant in the scenario of deceit. The fact that Scribe's Emmeline is in the position of choice between her two crossed and more and less ironic lovers prepares the way for the possibility that the seducer's Cordelia is as manipulative and dissimulating as he is. The esthete's final version of the basic scene of seduction and interpretation, the "Diary," terminates in a stand-off between the designing seducer and the seemingly innocent object of desire, anticipating the far wider equilibrium between the esthetic and ethical modes.

Within the maturation of the esthetic mode, then, the transformation of philosophical exposition into fiction is tantamount to a farcical dimension that opens within the scenario of seduction and interpretation. The flight into fiction is made possible by an ironic disinterest that interrupts the stage machinery of tragedy, governed by extrinsic laws of necessity. The trajectory from "The Immediate Stages of the Erotic" to the "Diary of the Seducer" is ultimately a rotation, for the flight of philosophical discourse into the fiction of the "Diary" repeats the passionate exuberance that the esthete attributed to Mozart's music and the figure of Don Juan. "Reflection" is a term decisive to the movement from exuberance to exuberance. As opposed to what Kierkegaard regards as the entirely closed system of Greek tragedy, in which volition is subordinated to fate or chance, self-reflection is a necessary precondition for self-consciousness, choice, and the subjectivity predicated by choice. But the escape into fiction from philosophical reasoning and the music of *Don Giovanni* share the abandon that signals the limits of self-reflection. The full trajectory of the *Either* is thus self-contradictory, defending self-reflection in relation to the external necessity attributed to ancient art but renouncing it at the moment when fictive and musical release become possible.

Kierkegaard's notion of reflection is thus self-contradictory in the same way that his use of the term "language" vacillates between blunt instrumentality and the wider economy of symbolic exchange. When the esthete describes feminine characters such as Antigone and Margaret as "reflective" he is drawing on a rather conventional sexual model in Western thought in which the woman is too sublime to act. In such statements "reflection" is analogous to thought as opposed to action. The esthete's purely reflective women exist on too high a spiritual plane to exercise their volition. Yet the notion of reflection also exists in Kierkegaard's work on the more general level of articulation. In this broader sense, all linguistic and erotic activity is reflected, even the most strenuous efforts at moral restraint. By implication, if the figure of the woman is the generic locus of reflection in Kierkegaard's writing, both esthetic excess and moral choice fall under the aegis of the feminine.

It is on the continuum linking the esthete's initial paean to reflection with his repudiation of it at the portals of musical abandon that we may situate his interpretations of four exemplary female characters: Antigone, Marie Beaumarchais from Goethe's *Clavigo*, Donna Elvira from *Don Giovanni*, and the Margaret from *Faust*. On the basis of female characters rather than logical categories, the esthete organizes a sequence of feminine relations to men that turn out to be different versions of the fictive relationship between the reader and writer.

In a sense, all of these dramatic situations in which women are disappointed by men fall under the rubric of the distinction between ancient and modern tragedy posited by the esthete during his reading of the *Antigone*. In his interpretation, the esthete, placing the character Antigone against a backdrop of ancient esthetics in which anxiety, doubt, and individual volition played no role, nonetheless designates Antigone as the first character to undergo the fear and trembling of modern experience. Antigone becomes the epitome of ancient esthetics who still points in the direction of modern undecidability, and specifically toward the interpretative problems raised by the scenario of seduction. In a lengthy exposition, the esthete distinguishes ancient art by its objective quality. Ancient tragedy is grounded in the historical record provided by the epic (*E*, 141), and it is therefore in the service of the categories of "family, state, and race" (*E*, 147). Within this historical and social context, the ancient tragic hero or heroine suffers external torments. Her suffering is sorrow at the inevitability of tragic circumstances rather than pain because of any personal guilt (*E*, 145). The tragic sorrow of the ancient heroine is in proportion to her innocence, not her guilt (p. 147). Because the denouement of the ancient tragedy is taken so much out of the heroine's hands, "the

wrath of the gods had no ethical character, but only esthetic ambiguity" (*E,* 148). This is the same ambiguity that the writer of the esthetic
papers has celebrated in his praise of *Don Giovanni* and that he will
himself fashion as the author of the "Diary of the Seducer." But
before completing the rotation, he will pass through a stage in which
the feminine embodies the processes and pains of reflection. The
modern tragedy, anticipated by the figure of Antigone, is situated
within the internal conflicts of the heroine rather than in the external
conditions of history. The suffering undergone by the heroine is
ethical in character, deriving from her sense of personal guilt. In a
telling formulation, the esthete compares modern tragic torment to
the helplessness experienced by an adult in watching a child suffer,
and the sorrow of ancient tragedy to the necessity of a child's witnessing the demise of adults (*E,* 146).

Born in antiquity, Antigone becomes the first in a sequence of
female characters subjected to the interpretative uncertainties of seduction. Although in the course of this sequence the seductive situations become less tragic, and the women less passive, Antigone joins
Abraham as a Kierkegaardian paragon of anxiety. "At an early age,
before she was fully developed, dim suspicions of this horrible secret
had at times gripped her soul, until certainty with a single blow cast
her into the arms of anxiety. . . . For anxiety is a reflection, and in this
respect is essentially different from sorrow" (*E,* 152). Antigone is an
instance of anxiety because she is party to the subliminal semi-aware-
ness of the horrible secrets surrounding the house of Oedipus. In the
esthete's interpretation of Oedipus and Antigone, Kierkegaard concurs almost exactly with Hegel's reading and use of the Sophoclean
characters. In the Hegelian commentary, Antigone embodies the
feminine irony assuming the form of the possibilities excluded by
Creon's autocratic decision to deny Polyneices a proper burial and
defend his brother Eteocles. According to Hegel, the selective process
that intervenes between thought and action is invariably reductive.
Antigone represents the compassionate possibilities excluded by the
hierarchical actions of Creon, which come to haunt him in the down-
fall of Thebes in a way remarkably similar to the irrepressible intervention of the unconscious in the Freudian psychology. As yet another bearer of the anxiety-arousing knowledge that plays on the
border between awareness and repression, Kierkegaard's Antigone
also carries a knowledge that circumvents the efforts to contain it: the
knowledge of her incestuous lineage. Antigone's subliminal knowledge, which places her in the position of Don Juan and Socrates, runs
through the history of her family like a delayed reaction and an
uncontrollable repetition. The crux of the tragedy is, "so to say, the

after effects, the tragic destiny of Oedipus, ramifying in every branch of his family" (*E*, 154).

With enormous subtlety, the esthete transforms Antigone, the ancient tragic heroine, into a modern lover. The secret knowledge that is the basis of her anxiety becomes the divided knowledge of the ironist. Already the ancient character possesses the capacity for dissimulation that the Cordelia of the "Diary" will demonstrate. Her dowry of sorrow (*E*, 153, 163) will, amid the modern trappings of the "Diary," be transformed into the economic basis for the marital contract prescribed by engagement. The esthete's most masterful stroke in this adaptation is to metamorphose Haemon, Antigone's betrothed and Creon's son, from a victim of the tragedy into a seducer.

> He knows he is loved, and boldly presses his suit. Her reserve puzzles him. . . . What is all important to him is to convince her of how much he loves her. . . . With every assurance of his love, he increases her pain, with every sigh he sinks the dart of sorrow deeper and deeper into her heart. He leaves no means untried to influence her. (*E*, 161)

With the addition of the element of Haemon's seductiveness to the esthete's scenario, Antigone's profile as the prototype of all subsequent deceived women in the *Either* is complete. In her double characterization both as a victim to Creon and Haemon and as a secretive, self-contained ironic figure, Antigone encompasses the full range of feminine potential in the volume, from the pathos of Marie Beaumarchais and Margaret to Cordelia's possible dissimulation in the "Diary." The esthete's "Shadowgraphs" are precisely what their names imply: silhouettes, profiles, feminine characters represented by outline drawings that owe their flattening to the fact that only certain selected characteristics are examined (*E*, 171). In the esthete's argument, which proceeds from feminine character to character rather than from point to point, the qualities being profiled are the degree of tragedy in the seductive scenario and the extent to which the exemplary women/readers are active and ironic as opposed to passive and naive.

Within this sequence, the Goethean characters reside at an extreme of reflection and feminine passivity. Both Marie Beaumarchais and Margaret define themselves and their situations purely in terms of the men who abandon them. Their fictive existences do not long outlive their relations to the men who effectively define them. As readers, Marie Beaumarchais and Margaret are naive. They transparently reproduce the emotions affected by their lovers; they contribute little affect of their own; they are purely receptive and uncreating readers. Kierkegaard supplements Marie Beaumarchais with Margaret only to reinforce his observation that the Don Juan figure and his exploits comprise the secular and ironic version of the tragic romance played out in *Faust I*. By implication, the character Faust is a paradigm of the seducer, but one confined to the constraints of Western theology and ethics and to a dialectical stage machinery that must destroy him.

As is clear in the interpretation of the opera in the "Immediate Stages," Donna Elvira affords the esthete with an instance of some divergence from passivity, some capacity for dissimulation and irony. In her desire for revenge and her transformation into an even more beautiful woman, this single object of Don Juan's desire within an endless sequence becomes an ironic actor in her own right. "It is a young woman he has seduced, but her life is not ruined . . . she has been transformed, and is more beautiful than ever. . . . This woman is armed . . . she carries an invisible weapon, for her hate is not to be satisfied with speeches and declamations, but it is unseen, and this weapon is her hate" (*E*, 195). Donna Elvira is the shadowgraph for a reader who has become ironic in the course of her reading, a reader who has to some extent become a text. This textual potential is fully realized in the "Diary of the Seducer," which contains a woman who is not only as enigmatic as her lover but a fictive text in her own right.

As the final segment of the *Either* and the gateway into the moral scriptures of the *Or*, the "Diary of the Seducer" recapitulates the major components of the esthetic mode while arranging them so that they are a direct provocation to "Judge William"'s pronouncements. But if certain of the esthetic positions—almost dogmas—reappear within the "Diary," they are cast in a new light by its overtly fictive bearing and form. Its characters owe their recognition not to their roles in widely read masterworks but to their actions within the "Diary" and the motifs that their actions touch. To be sure, *Johannes* is the Germanic form of *Giovanni*, and as the seducer, this character is the final esthetic version of Don Juan, who lives in the contemporary milieu of nineteenth-century Copenhagen. Similarly, Cordelia, the desired woman of the "Diary," derives her name from *King Lear*, but while this name may be appropriate to one of her roles as an initially faithful and receptive reader, it does not begin to exhaust her complexity. Both characters define themselves far more significantly in terms of their activities within the "Diary" than by virtue of any literary associations that they may carry. In this regard Cordelia is quite distinct from earlier feminine characters in the *Either* such as Antigone and Margaret, who achieve, for illustrative purposes, the flatness of annotations.

Formally regarded, the "Diary" is a journal or diary occasionally diverging into an epistolary novel or novella. As a bizarre hybrid of literary genres, it is similar to *Repetition*. Yet the forms to which the "Diary" pretends are less important in their own right than as occasions for the display of the characteristic Kierkegaardian discursive modes. The main part of the text is indeed a diary. It consists of entries by one Johannes regarding his desire for, approaches to, and broken engagement with Cordelia. The events to be read between the lines of Johannes's entries are hardly complex. Johannes spies Cordelia in his ramblings through the city and pursues her with the deliberation of a hunter until he learns her name and other basic facts about her residence and family. He follows Cordelia to her meetings with a young merchant named Edward Baxter and insinuates himself into the relationship as Baxter's confidant, thus occupying the pivotal position in a triangular relationship, similar to "Constantius"'s role in *Repetition*. At the same time, Johannes enters the domestic milieu of Cordelia's family. By using the mundane merchant as a foil to his own esthetic qualities, which fall under the category of the "interesting," he engineers the termination of Cordelia's engagement to Baxter. Shortly thereafter, he enters his own engagement to Cordelia, which is as tormenting in its visions of stultifying domesticity as his machinations were gratifying. The engagement ends in an uncertainty that fictively dramatizes the hovering to which major segments of the treatise on irony were devoted: a complete lack of certainty as to who terminates the engagement and on what grounds. The final images of Cordelia describe her engaged to a certain "John," and in this name alone must reside the ambiguity as to whether she has fallen prey to yet another seducer or whether she has liberated herself from the designs and plots of active masculine seduction.

The diaristic element of this narrative is written in the style of the narrated monologue, or in German, the *erlebte Rede*. This is a first-person narration of events taking place in an extended present tense, and the narration is presumably simultaneous with the events being described. This style has been widely recognized as a hallmark of twentieth-century fiction and is closely associated with such writers as James Joyce and Franz Kafka.[27]

This subjective narration is interspersed, at both ends of the "Diary," with letters—from Cordelia to Johannes at the beginning and in the reverse direction near the conclusion. Yet far more crucial than the epistolary nature of these communications is the fact that they belong to Kierkegaard's aphoristic mode. "Johannes! There was a rich man, he had great herds, and many cattle, small and great; there was a poor little maiden, she had only a single lamb . . . ," writes Cordelia as an allegory of the difference between the sexual multiplicity available to Johannes and the limited possibilities for love afforded by her passive feminine position (*E, 308*). The "Diary" is thus a discourse under the control and direction of a single male figure, a monologue occasionally punctuated with a far more compressed, energetic, and poetic discourse which may emanate either from the male or female character. The fact that the aphoristic meta-utterance may issue from masculine or feminine sources indicates that within the "Diary" the male-dominated and neatly epistemological model of seduction—in which the male is the actor, and the feminine a purely reflexive form of passivity—is undermined by a reciprocal interplay between the parties.

The journal and letters comprising the "text" are introduced by "Esthete A," who in introducing the "Diary" assumes the same editorial role adapted by "Victor Eremita" in presenting and accounting for the production of the texts comprising *Either/Or*. The esthete's introduction of the "Diary" is the most sustained narrative intervention into the action of the *Either* since "Eremita"'s preface. The elaborate narrative machinery surrounding the "Diary" draws attention to the close analogy between narrative involution and triangular love. The esthete's ambiguous position, both outside the "Diary" as its editor and within the text as a model for Johannes, closely parallels Johannes's own position: not only does Johannes engage in a direct effort to provoke and attract Cordelia; in a design to manipulate her obliquely, he intervenes within her relationship with a third party, Edward Baxter, who is his prosaic double or counterpart. Johannes hopes to "author" Cordelia's fate and her relations with other men just as the esthete, acting as editor, "composes" the "Diary" and as Kierkegaard "writes" *Either/Or*. But something interrupts this sequence of authorities and authorships. Cordelia breaks away from the tradition of two-dimensional feminine "shadows" established prior to her in the *Either* and in the culture of the West. To the extent that she is reflected, or articulated, by language, she becomes as ambiguous and ironic as any written text. To the extent that as a fictive character she has actions assigned to her, she becomes as designing as any "male" character. In a similar fashion, *Either/Or* breaks the gravitational field determined by the intentions that may be attributed to "Søren Kierkegaard" and constitutes its own sustained dissonance in the mutual reading and interpretation that transpire between the esthetic and ethical modes.

The "Diary of the Seducer" is the center stage for the drama of doubling and duplicity that dominates and structures Kierkegaard's work. The "Diary" juxtaposes two models of seduction, two allegories of reading, and two notions of authority. In each case, manipulative

and intentional designs to achieve affect, whether in love, communication, or art, are undermined by reciprocal models of mutual interpretation. The seductive model with which the "Diary" begins, in
which Johannes is the master-seducer and Cordelia is a naive and
vulnerable receptor to his designs, gives way to a countermodel in
which Cordelia is as much of a writer and actor as Johannes. The
more reciprocal model of seduction *coexists* with the more classically
intentional and manipulative one. In this coincidence of active and
passive models of seduction and reading, the voice of the male-dominated and manipulative model may at first drown out its quieter
counterpart, but the softer voice of interchange and dissonance will
be heard in the end. It is in this sense that an attempt to "identify"
Kierkegaard with either his esthetic or his ethical mode is futile. In
terms of the movements set into play by the "Diary" and the overall
framework of *Either/Or*, the structure of the suspense and dissonance
between sustained double voices is far more vital to Kierkegaard's
work than is the crystallization of any single, coherent position.[28]

The elements of a paternalistic, authoritarian model of seduction,
in communication as well as in love, readily present themselves in the
"Diary"'s fiction. Within this configuration, Johannes is an active,
planning (and therefore speculative) subject, while Cordelia is a passive, reflexive image incapable of any volition. It is within the male-
oriented and paternalistic model of seduction in the "Diary" that
Johannes hunts Cordelia and, in terms of his own rhetoric, wages a
military campaign to win her. Bearing the military banner of esthetic
interest, he speculates that "the strategic principle, the law governing
every move in this campaign, is always to work her into an interesting
position. The interesting is the field on which the battle must be
waged" (*E*, 341). In this ambivalent picture of a love assuming the
form of battle rather than tenderness, Johannes is the soldier, while
Cordelia becomes a piece of the booty. The soldier of love exercises
the power to conjure up and dismiss the image of his beloved at will.
"The image I now have of her shifts between being her actual and her
ideal form. This picture I now summon before me" (*E*, 330).

Cordelia's image quality is what links her to the linguistic economies of irony and signification and will therefore be the basis of her
ultimate liberation. But in terms of Johannes's military model of seduction, Cordelia is never more fragile, passive, and manipulable
than as an image. The "infinite depth [of her gaze], impossible to
fathom" (*E*, 328), suggests the quiet and withdrawn reflexivity of
Antigone. Such a docile entity naturally submits to the jurisdiction of
a variety of legal codes: the laws of nature, sex, and even the imagination. "Woman is the weaker sex, and yet she needs far more essen-

tially to be alone in her youth than a man does; she must be self-contained, but that in which and through which she is self-contained is an illusion; this illusion is the dowry Nature has bestowed upon her, like that of a king's daughter. But this resting in illusion is just what isolates her" (*E*, 335). As the image at the soldier's command ("she *must* be self-contained"), Cordelia, and with her the notion of femininity, becomes literally a prisoner of war. The feminine image is imprisoned—in solitary confinement within herself. The illusion that is the imaginary key to her future release is subjected, in this passage, to the laws of some absolute and ubiquitous nature. Cordelia, the esthete has indicated by his references to Goethe, although daughter to a king, is sister to the great woman figures of Romantic literature. Like Wordsworth's Lucy Grey and the sister of "Tintern Abbey," Cordelia harbors an unknown and possibly savage strength which is recognized but then held under control by the applicable laws. Although Cordelia's reflexive quality makes her sublime, it also restricts her by taking her out of the fields of action and volition. She becomes the slave to the reflexive economy that is presumably at her service. "A mirror hangs on the opposite wall; she does not reflect on it, but the mirror reflects her. How faithfully it has caught her picture, like a humble slave who shows his devotion by his faithfulness" (*E*, 311). Cordelia is as much the prisoner of the frame around the mirror of reflection as the mirror is her slave.

To the authority conferred upon Johannes by the rhetorics of warfare and slavery that invade the narrative must be added the authority of authorship, his functioning as a writer. Within an intentional model of writing that is analogous to a sadistic model of seduction, Johannes writes the script of the events that control his and Cordelia's lives. In the wake of revealing that in order to arouse Cordelia's jealousy he has circulated around town the rumor of his attachment to someone else, he explains both his strategy and his authorial method.

> Today I introduced the subject [of the rumor]. I believe I can tell a story so that the point is not lost, *item*, so that it is not revealed too soon. To keep those who listen in suspense, by means of small incidents of an episodic character, to ascertain what they wish the outcome to be, to trick them in the course of the narration—that is my delight; to make use of ambiguities so that the listeners understand one thing in the saying, and then suddenly notice that the words could also be interpreted otherwise—that is my art. (*E*, 365–66)

This passage, describing Johannes's ploys in narrative terms, is parallel to the "Madamina, il catologo è questo" aria in *Don Giovanni*, in which Leporello proudly enumerates his master's exploits to an indignant Donna Elvira. So effective is his skill in translating intentions into actions, Johannes boasts, that he evokes exactly the reactions that he desires, whether suspense or deception, in his readers. The degree of control over writing implicit in Johannes's assertion of his mastery obviously belongs to the economy of seduction by domination. Yet the passage effects a far more important translation in its own terms, for it designates writing and narrative as the media of seduction. Seduction is tantamount to the designs of textuality. With this recognition, a second, hidden economy of seduction insinuates itself into the narrative, one in which the seducer loses his control to the language in which he speaks and to the characters to whom he makes his protestations. Within this undecidably reciprocal model of seduction, Cordelia is the author of the circumstances and the master of deceptions to the same extent as Johannes.

There are subtle intimations of this second seductive mode, which eschews the principles of intentionality and manipulation, from the outset of the narrative. Even in the passage in which Johannes notes the self-contained profundity of Cordelia's gaze, he cannot resist noting the "mischief" of her smile (*E*, 328). This mischief describes the relation between the masterful model of seduction and the reciprocal one. Already in his entry of the "fifth day," presumably the fifth day since chance has pointed out the existence of Cordelia to him, he associates her with texts by picturing her as a reader of novels (*E*, 313). If Johannes envisions himself in his machinations as an author, Cordelia is no less the image he reads and the text he desires to compose. Cordelia's existance as an image and reader is no less linguistically structured than Johannes's role as an author. It is the characters' collaboration within the exchange of reading and writing that finally gives them parity, despite Johannes's protestations of his control.

In the course of their collaboration in the "Diary"'s allegory of reading and writing, Cordelia and Johannes assume a variety of readerly and writerly roles in relation to each other. As an image, Cordelia confronts Johannes with the enigma of a riddle. "How significant, how pregnant our Danish language is: *to solve*, what an ambiguity it implies. . . . As the wealth of the soul is a riddle . . . so, too, a young girl is a riddle" (*E*, 326). Yet in accordance with the undecidable parity afforded in the readerly-writerly intercourse, Johannes characterizes himself as a riddle to Cordelia. "I am a riddle to her, a riddle that she has no temptation to solve, but which provokes her, and almost makes her indignant" (*E*, 346). Once the motif of provocation enters the narrative, however, it becomes virtually impossible to ascertain who agitates whom. "I scarcely recognize myself. My mind is like a turbulent sea, swept by the storms of passion" (*E*, 320). If the mirror frame of reflexivity is the locus of the depths, the turbulence of the immediately preceding formulation has somehow shifted from the feminine image to the sea in Johannes. A similar displacement takes place with regard to the possibility of self-division implicit in reflection. Within the naively epistemological model of seduction, the feminine subordination to reflection opens a potentially endless sequence of internal divisions. Yet when Edward Baxter confides to Johannes the anxiety that Cordelia arouses in him (*E*, 343), he in effect takes on Johannes's turbulent emotional reaction and becomes his double. Despite Johannes's coy disclaimer, "I have never observed this condition in myself, this fear and trembling" (*E*, 343), he and Edward *reflect* each other's emotional states in a manner befitting the fragmentation of female reflexivity.

Not only are Johannes and Cordelia enigmatic to each other and do they share certain qualities of reflection and bifurcation but they mutually interpret each other to the same degree. In this mutual exegesis, they relate to each other in both roles involved in correspondence, as readers and writers. Although Johannes claims the sanction of the interesting (*E*, 348) and describes Cordelia's reactions to him as the "still unpublished but announced commentary to my book" (*E*, 370), Cordelia also emerges as a writer, a poetess, whose "execution" and appearance are "dithyrambic" (*E*, 339, 428). In light of the nearly systematic reversal of roles that the characters undergo in their reciprocal performances and assessments, the indications of Cordelia's seductiveness that emerge in the end hardly come as a shock. These occur during the decline of their passion for each other. During a game of Ring, Cordelia ignores Johannes's wish to act out a mock exchange of the game rings as would occur in the marriage ceremony and throws the rings, with "a glance full of boundless audacity," beyond everyone's reach (*E*, 428). In this gesture, she rejects the confining rings, or bands, of marriage in favor of the exuberant rotation and sexual multiplicity characteristic of Don Juan and the esthetic mode. A few pages later, Johannes's apprehension of the seductiveness of a female penitent's posture in an engraving indicates that he has recognized a similar provocativeness in Cordelia's behavior throughout the romance (*E*, 432). With these signs, Cordelia joins Johannes as a seducer, just as she joined him as a writer and as he repeated her splitting and articulation.

The "Diary of the Seducer" occupies a pivotal position within the work as a whole, both in relation to the motifs introduced fragmentarily in the earlier sections and in anticipation of the moral discourse of the *Or*. In the manner in which the "Diary" recombines, and thus imperfectly repeats, strands of argumentation and imagery that have appeared prior to it, it is a veritable laboratory of the rotation method. The "Diary"'s return to and marshaling of the fragmentary quality of the earlier sections comprises a final vindication of Kierkegaard's aphoristic mode. The constructive forgetting of "The Rotation Method," the expository lapse that makes way for the unanticipated resonances of fiction, reappears within the "Diary" when Johannes's yearning for his beloved is intensified by his forgetting her (*E*, 319–20, 334). The exhortation in "The Rotation Method" "never to stick fast," for "everything will doubtless return, though in a different form" (*E*, 292), resurfaces in Johannes's formulation of a mainstay of the tradition of aggressive seduction: "No love affair should last more than six months at most . . . every erotic relationship should cease as soon as one has had the ultimate enjoyment" (*E*, 364).

Yet the recombinatory activity of the "Diary of the Seducer" is not limited to its technological application of rotation. Within the compass of the "Diary," the rudimentary opposition in "The Immediate Stages of the Erotic" between erotic displacement and the mainstream of Western thought is transformed into the confrontation between the countermetaphysics of seduction and marriage, linked by the ambiguous institution of engagement. Johannes is a not-so-distant descendant of Don Juan; if erotic metaphoricity manifested itself to the operatic seducer in an almost endless succession of couplings, for Johannes the dynamics of seduction has crystallized around the readerly-writerly correspondence characterizing his interaction with Cordelia. In a similar fashion, the esthete's lengthy explorations into the nature of femininity and the reflexivity that he identifies as a feminine trait ultimately reappear within the "Diary." Cordelia may be regarded as the final "shadowgraph" in the work, but one breaking both the two-dimensionality and the obscurity ascribed to the feminine spiritual domain. In keeping with his own mission of instability, "Esthete A" presents in Cordelia a model of femininity that radically subverts his earlier stereotypical formulations.

In taking up and combining the motifs disseminated throughout the *Either*, the "Diary of the Seducer" becomes a metatext: a text woven of prior textual strands. Yet the "Diary" is no less suggestive in its relation to the lengthy coda that follows, as an introduction to the *Or*. In its finality and utter ambiguity, the parity between Johannes and Cordelia eludes dialectical logic. Their relationship is an ultimatum. No higher level of development will proceed from it. The reciprocal deadlock between Johannes and Cordelia defines the relationship between the *Either* and the *Or*. To be sure, a certain equilibrium does exist between the two volumes. But it is highly questionable whether this stand-off may be converted into the symmetry and progressive movement of rigorous logic.

If the group of variations, or variant texts, comprising the *Either* have considered such philosophical themes as desire, repetition, and consummation from the perspective of linguistic and erotic displacement, the wisdom pronounced in the *Or* considers the same question—but from an idealistically and theologically structured perspective of judgment. It is fitting that the "William" who is the author of the ponderous sermons addressed to "Esthete A" should be an assessing judge (*O*, 328), for as much as any crucial theme, his discourse delineates the preconditions of the act of judgment itself. Kierkegaard's placing the final verdict in the mouth of the judge might seem to give the entire ethical mode the upper hand, to decide the esthetic-ethical opposition in favor of the latter. Yet our earlier discussion of Kierkegaard's curious repudiation, at the end of *The Concept of Irony*, of his immediate predecessors as theorists of irony would suggest that this judgmental gesture is as much an *extension* of esthetic irony as a suppression of it.

The consummate irony of the judge's pronouncements and the work as a whole is that the esthetic and ethical modes, while on divergent sides of a metaphysical divide, are in substantial agreement. In tone, orientation, and perspective the esthete's and the judge's remarks could not be more antithetical, yet this opposition is undermined by substantive agreement extending to virtually all thematic areas common to both volumes of the work. Despite the oppositional structure of the work, there is little that the judge pronounces with which "Esthete A" would disagree. In many regards, both fictive surrogates are saying the same thing, but from opposite sides of a perspectival watershed. In constructing a work whose dialectical opposition is sustained perspectivally but disappears on the level of the particular observations, Kierkegaard anticipates modern experiments into the impact of perspective on narrative made by authors as diverse as James Joyce, Virginia Woolf, and William Faulkner.[29] The implantation of mutual agreement within a superstructure of logical opposition is yet another tack within Kierkegaard's systematic strategy of disruption to Hegelian progress.

"Judge William" addresses his moral sermons to the esthetic writer and editor of the *Either*. A striking example of the agreement that undermines the ostensible opposition between the esthetic and ethical modes is to be found in the assessment that the judge makes directly to his interlocutor.

> The reason why the man who lives esthetically can in a higher sense explain nothing, is that he constantly lives in the moment, yet all the time conscious only in terms of a certain relativity and within certain

bounds. . . . You are witty, ironical, a close observer, a dialectician, experienced in pleasure, you know how to calculate the instant, you are sentimental or heartless according to circumstances; but beneath all this you are constantly only in the moment, and therefore your life dissolves, and it is impossible for you to explain it. (*O*, 183)

While he can hardly accede to the judge's conclusions, the esthete could not agree more wholeheartedly with the moralist's observations: from all the evidence presented in the *Either*, it would seem that the esthete is indeed relativistic, ironic, opportunistic, and calculating. Where the interlocutors part company in relation to this passage is at the point when the judge's observations slip into evaluations that imply his systematic ideology. While the esthete may live for the moment, and although this absorption in the present may define his attitude toward time, this does not imply that he is devoid of means of accounting for his own activity. This passage is emblematic of the difference that separates the esthete's discourse from the judge's. Again and again a substantial agreement on the level of observation is transformed into ideological conflict. The opposition between the positions emerges primarily on the level of invective.

Because of the interpretative twisting of common data that is the basis for the ideological warfare of *Either/Or*, it is essential to the design of the work that there be certain pivotal conceptions common to both the esthetic and ethical modes in terms of which the opposition between the positions may be gauged. The most prominent and possibly most significant of these pivotal points linking the two volumes is "first love," which is both the title of a play by Eugène Scribe for which the esthete provides a gloss in the *Either* and a conception vital to "Judge William" 's "The Aesthetic Validity of Marriage" in the *Or*. "Esthete A" 's commentary on both the play and the term begins with the narrative involution that is a hallmark of Kierkegaard's recognition of the fictive dimension of all discourse. In this case, the narrative frame around the esthete's interpretation of the play consists in an autobiographical introduction explaining the play's place within his experience. This introduction is itself double, for it claims two vital significations of the play to the author: as the national anthem of his passion for his own first love, whom he happens to meet during his engagement to another woman; and as the occasion for a seduction in literary terms. An editor employing techniques of coercion that would be worthy of the most brazen seducer prevails upon the esthete to publish his critique of Scribe's play (*E*, 244–45). Scribe's *The First Love* thus serves as the impetus for a double seduction in the esthete's life, by his long-lost first passion, whom he sees again at a performance of the play, and by an editor, who is described as a sexual *provocateur* of writing.

The esthete's entire interpretation of the play hinges on the meaning of one line, provided by Emmeline, the woman sought by the two opposed yet conspiring lovers, Charles and Rinville: "The first love is the true love, and one loves only once" (*E*, 252). The significations of "first love" and "once" not only determine "Esthete A"'s reading of the play but also demarcate the border between the esthetic and the ethical, between the two countermetaphysics. A first love is an original love, and the moral sphere dedicates itself to the location and preservation of a primal condition of transcendent innocence. For "Judge William," "first love" is a serious term indeed. It is the definitive term that determines marriage's "esthetic validity," the element of the beautiful that uniquely pertains to marriage.

> The sensuous factor as such comes to evidence only through reflection, but first love lacks reflection and is therefore not simply sensuous. This gives the character of necessity to first love. Like everything eternal it has the double propensity of presupposing itself back into all eternity and forward into all eternity. This is the element of truth in what the poets have often sung so beautifully, to the effect that the lovers even at first sight feel as if they already had loved one another for a long while. (*O*, 43)

In terms of this passage, ethical first love is the experiential manifestation of an eternity that is both an absolute origin and an ultimate end. In the ideology elaborated by "Judge William," the institution of marriage and the entire ethical sphere are at the service of the transcendental origin, purpose, and destiny revealed by the first love. Ethical first love is the expression of an entire system that goes back to a beginning. This is a far cry from esthetic first love, which is the indifferent first point of a potentially endless succession, a sequence that must begin somewhere. If the first love retains a certain allure on the esthetic side, this is the aura of an ongoing supplement to the pairing of marriage.

There is no more fundamental indication of the complex cooperative and divisive relation between the esthetic and the ethical than the choice that is the implicit imperative in the logic of *Either/Or*. Within the compass of the work it is possible to discern at least three varieties of choice. There is the indifferent Either/Or of the seducer, whether masculine or feminine. The seducer can pick this one or that one. Kierkegaard coyly intimates the existence of a structure of choice, however indifferent, on the side of the esthetic when he names the possibly duplicitous inspiration of love in the "Diary" Cordelia *Wahl*, or Cordelia Choice, the pick of the seducer in more ways than one. Even "Judge William" appreciates the randomness of esthetic choice: "For the aesthetical is not the evil but neutrality" (*O*, 173).

But also functional in the work is the Either/Or shouted by "Judge

William," an ultimate choice, an ultimatum to choose—the exclusionary, selective act by which the speculative and ethical subject is born. In this moment of moral choice, experienced by the individuated subject, the act of choice takes precedence over the outcome. "My friend, what I have so often said to you I now say once again, or rather I shout it: Either/or, *aut/aut*. For a single *aut* adjoined as a rectification does not make the situation clear" (*O*, 161), the judge impresses upon his interlocutor. A decision situation in which two alternatives are more important than one, the Either/Or of the judge leaves the subject no out. "For although there is only one situation in which either/or has absolute significance, namely when truth, righteousness, and holiness are lined up on one side, and lust and base propensities and obscure passions and perdition on the other; yet it is always important to choose rightly, even as between things which one may innocently choose; it is important to test oneself" (*O*, 161). While there is a premium on the subject's undergoing the act of selection, the "right" choice is preordained. Truth and the other ideals are known quantities. The Either/Or of the judge is the bottom extreme of a metaphysical system whose ideals, purposes, imperatives, and outcomes are preordained. Personal decisions, like the words, signs, and gestures comprising language, are at their service.

Finally, there is the Either/Or posed by the work as a whole, the perspectival choice between the modes articulated, respectively, by the esthete and the judge. And this choice is, by virtue of the complex mixture of collusion and mutual criticism that joins the modes at different levels, all but impossible. The moral, speculative, and theological ideology implicit in the judge's remarks on marriage and personal choice is the positive expression of the system that irony, music, eroticism, and the figures of Socrates and Don Juan have undermined. In the words of the judge, Kierkegaard has placed the dominant line in the ongoing counterpoint between the ideological and teleological orientations of Western thought and those processes, primarily linguistic in nature, that evade such predetermination. The judge's sermons thus comprise Kierkegaard's summary and recapitulation of the mainstream of Western thought. That marriage is the occasion for this reaffirmation, the central image around which the argumentative resources are allocated, is in accordance with Kierkegaard's general subjectivization of philosophical discourse. Within Kierkegaard's summation of the mainstream of Western thought as enunciated by the judge, marriage is the basis of a personal transcendental system. Marriage is the selective act by which the individual, and by implication the family and the community, is aligned with a predetermined historical and teleological necessity. It is highly significant that this scenario—in which the structure of marriage duplicates the movements of philosophical and historical necessity—takes place *in the wake* of the ravages to systematic thought effected by Socrates and Don Juan. There is a retrospective, almost futile quality to the judge's system, whose neatness parallels that of the tidy household maintained by his wife,[30] a futility ultimately falling under the aegis of irony.

The *Or* is divided into three papers, two lengthy discourses and a final "Ultimatum," or summation. Of the two substantial sections, the first, "The Aesthetic Validity of Marriage," effects the crossover from esthetic to ethical thinking. The "Aesthetic Validity" furnishes the complementary ethical vision of the same data and themes treated in the *Either:* love and marriage, permanence and change. As its title indicates, this discourse attempts to locate that element of esthetic intensity and jubilation which not only survives within the prose of marriage but shapes and informs it. Within this section marriage serves as the point of transfer between erotic energy and stability—in terms of both individual self-definition and societal endurance. In a fashion strikingly similar to the place within the psychic economy occupied by the Freudian ego, marriage sublimates the eroticism awakened by the "first love" into the foundations of social order and speculative progress.

The notion of marriage in the "Aesthetic Validity" is an exceptionally well-developed metaphor in several ways. Marriage not only serves as a locus around which the philosophical issues raised in the esthetic papers may be arranged. It functions literally as a *vehicle* between the particular complexities of the choice situation and the wider philosophical issues that accrue to subjectivity. In the second major segment of the *Or,* "Equilibrium," the judge elaborates the wider philosophical implications of the sublimation and resolution achieved through marriage. It is in the "Equilibrium" that the judge formulates the implicit attitudes within the ethical mode toward such issues as history, temporality, and the oppositions between free will and predetermination and interiority and exteriority. The resolution achieved within the state of "Equilibrium" enables the judge to annex an entire metaphysical system of destiny to the resigned sublimation of marriage.

And yet through all the judge's celebrations of a domestic tidiness whose widest implications extend to a metaphysics of personal and historical destiny, there are suggestions of an ironic wavering that not only collaborates with the ethical but subverts it as well. Just as in "The Diary of the Seducer" there is an unostentatious economy of seduction that coexists with the more male-dominated and intentional model, questioning and supplanting it, there is a variety of self-contradiction within the ethical that does not ultimately serve ethical ends. Within the ethical, there is an ironic moment that verges toward the esthetic, just as the esthetic could not avoid appealing to classical tragedies and models of reflection in formulating the esthetic and linguistic operations that bypassed them. The ultimate model for the relation between the esthetic and the ethical entertained by the *Or* is that of complementary antagonists on opposite sides of a modal watershed verging toward each other. If any equilibrium is achieved by this configuration, it is not the sensuous and moral resolution instrumented by marriage but the equilibrium providing for the continuity of a perpetual-motion machine whose movements have been adjusted to include ongoing dissonance.

Our last gaze at *Either/Or* will be in the direction of those nonconstructive remains of irony that invade and subvert the ethical mode. But before we consider that final irony, ethical prudence suggests that we pursue the wider lineaments of the speculative and teleological system set out in the *Or*. Although the three papers comprising this volume organize their material somewhat differently, there is a set of ethical propositions running through them, and these account for a wide variety of the observations and assertions made in the course of the *Or*. The basic units of the ethical mode are pronouncements, judgments, judicial sentences—rather than aphorisms or marginal utterances. It is with this in mind that our own formulation of the key architectural elements in the argumentation of the *Or* assumes the form of proposition-sentences.

The Individuated Subject Is Born in an Act of Choice

The heavy emphasis on the act of choice at the beginning of the "Equilibrium" is the cornerstone of the entire ethical metaphysics because it removes subjectivity from the sphere of *possibility* to that of *actuality*. Although in *The Concept of Irony* the artist's subjectivity was a function of the manifold of possibilities in which he danced; according to the judge, subjectivity and action, which always result from a reduction of possibilities, are synonymous. Within the metaphysics of the ethical mode, the subject *acts* by eliminating possibilities and is the *product* of an analogous process of exclusion.[31]

"The choice itself is decisive for the content of the personality, through the choice the personality immerses itself in the thing chosen, and when it does not choose it withers away in consumption" (*O*, 167). Here the personality is pictured literally as an insubstantial spirit that dies unless rooted to a specific choice. According to this description, subjectivity is a bond linking the transcendental spirit to the concreteness of a choice. In the judge's excursus on marriage, the wedding ceremony occupies an exactly analogous position, as that which bonds the spiritual substance of love to the order of conjugal existence.

By an Orwellian logic, the necessity of choice provides the only *freedom* thinkable within the ethical sphere. While this freedom does not decide the nature of the good, the right, or the beautiful, it is the only form of decision available to the subject. As a manifestation or illusion of choice within a scheme of necessity, freedom thus shifts from its role as the principle of uncertainty within the esthetic to that of an instrument of predetermination.

By virtue of its origin in the choice act on the side of the ethical, subjectivity acquires a substantiality lacking in the esthetic. The judge has recognized this when he declares to the esthete, "In fact you are nothing; you are merely a relation to others, and what you are you are by virtue of this relation" (*O*, 163). Once again making a pronouncement with which the esthete could only agree, the judge here distinguishes between the rooting of the ideal in the concrete which characterizes the ethical and the purely *relational* or relative nature of esthetic associations. Esthetic associations, whether erotic or assuming the linguistic form of metaphor, demand neither a transcendental sanction nor a concrete ground. It is in this sense that the judge can brand his interlocutor impetuous, haphazard, and insecure (*O*, 7–10).

History Is Collective Choice:
The Structures of Subjectivity and History Are Analogous

Within the ethical mode, the predetermined issue of the choice situation is that it forges a bond between the individual subject and collective destiny, as it has been formulated in Christian theology. The judge's term for this destiny, which has moral, theological, and philosophical facets, is "history." The individual's trajectory from an open sexual field through choice, engagement, and marriage closely parallels the collective course that begins with an absolute origin and proceeds through history toward a revealed and predetermined telos. The bond between the personal choice of the subject and the historical destiny of the community is the pivot upon which the ethical mode stands or falls.

One strategy that the judge attempts in order to secure this bond is to define history in so multifaceted a manner that it encompasses both subjective and collective dimensions.

> I do not create myself, I choose myself. . . .
>
> The man we are speaking of discovers now that the self he chooses contains an endless multiplicity, in as much as it has a history, a history in which he acknowledges identity with himself. This history is of various sorts; for in this history he stands in relation to other individuals of the race and to the race as a whole, and this history contains something painful, and yet he is the man he is only in consequence of this history. Therefore, it requires courage for a man to choose himself. (*O*, 220)

As opposed to the esthetic sensibility that evades choice, the subjectivity forged by the reductive transition from sensibility to actuality is historical in nature. And of the "various sorts" of history to which the judge alludes, two vital, if not exhaustive, varieties are the personal history that is synonymous with one's choices and the collective history here attributed to race. The notion of history is thus the connector that binds the drama of subjectivity so prominent in the literature and theory of Romanticism to a Judeo-Christian teleology of far more ancient ancestry.

Within such a historical scheme, two decisive points are the origin and the end. If the errant wandering of Kierkegaard's ironists and seducers preempts any progress, the judge's historical subjectivity is unambiguous in its linearity.

In extrapolating formal temporal qualities implicit in metaphysical attitudes, Kierkegaard's work is uncannily ahead of its time, anticipating the temporal explorations of modern phenomenology.[32] The temporality of the ethical mode includes an absolute origin and an ultimate end. Because the temporal continuum between these terminal points refers back to an origin, ethical time is governed by specific causal relations. The judge is obsessed with the notion of "first love" as an ethical category, as the sensuous awakening sublimated, spiritualized, and preserved by marriage, because his program of personal and collective history requires an origin. Ethical "first love" is the sensuous origin of marriage and the cornerstone of the social order organized by marriage, occupying a position within the ethical sphere analogous to that of "Sense-Certainty" within the development of the Hegelian *Geist*.

> Hence, when one has talked with a certain sad seriousness of the first love as of something that could never be repeated, this is no disparagement of love but a lofty eulogy of it as the eternal power. . . . God only once became flesh, and it would be vain to expect this to be repeated. . . . The first green, the first swallow, we hail with a certain solemnity. (*O*, 41)

As regarded by this passage, "firstness," whether of love or creation, is an origin that is absolute by virtue of its unrepeatability. "First love" is thus the origin of the entire speculative and theological system that proceeds from the birth of subjectivity out of personal choice.

Yet the causal and linear history that governs the ethical domain would be incomplete without a specific end toward which human activity aspires. The judge does not omit to supply this telos. On the level of personal activity, the goal toward which the subject strives is a happy marriage, the issue of prudent choice. "Have not knights and adventurers undergone incredible pains and trouble in order to come to harbor in the quiet peace of a happy marriage?" (*O*, 17). And at the wider reaches of moral speculation, the structure of ending or resolution is an end in its own right. Although the judge acknowledges that mystics have submitted to choice, he denounces the absence of development in their contemplations (*O*, 246–47). Not only does the progressive movement of history move in its linear course toward a predetermined telos but such movement is the goal of personal and collective history itself. "If there is to be any question of teleology there must be a movement, for as soon as I think of a goal I think of a movement; even when I think of one who is at the goal I always think of a movement, for I reflect that he has reached it by a movement" (*O*, 278). The history that reinstates the individuated Romantic subject within the Judeo-Christian destiny thus runs a full and uninterrupted course from an origin to a consummation.

Marriage Effects the Bond between the Subjectivity Determined by Choice and Historical Destiny

If the central moral treatise of the *Or*, the "Equilibrium," synthesizes the philosophical postulations that constitute the ethical mode, it is preceded by a lengthy paper whose primary subject is marriage. "The Aesthetic Validity of Marriage" strives for an encyclopaedic range. With a seemingly unflagging steadiness, the judge explores in this essay the nature, justifications (*O*, 65–89), ceremony (*O*, 90–110), economics (*O*, 133–36), historicity (*O*, 136–46), and even difficulties (*O*, 121–33) of marriage. Since marriage may be construed as merely one element or complex comprising the ethical world, the judge's obsessive concern with its every aspect is disproportionate.

Yet the judge's obsession is understandable not only in light of the momentary circumstances surrounding the engagement of one "Søren Kierkegaard" but also in terms of the teleological system that he himself formulates. Marriage is the public reenactment of the birth of the subject in choice that endows him with an historical dimension. Through the marriage ceremony, the sensuous residue that survives in the "first love" is sublimated and converted into social order and utility.

The widest challenge that the judge assumes in "The Aesthetic Validity of Marriage" is to demonstrate the persistence of some esthetic quality within marriage despite the metaphysical and transcendental values that the institution carries. This program explains the judge's self-appointed "task of showing that marriage is the transfiguration of first love, not its annihilation, that it is its friend, not its enemy" (*O*, 32). Yet for all the judge's insistence on marriage's esthetic quality, history and personal morality assert their values within its domain with a vengeance. Having asserted the congeniality between esthetics and marriage, "I will show that it is essential for first love to be historical, and that the condition for this is precisely marriage; and with this I will show that romantic first love is unhistorical" (*O*, 47).

Even more than the institution of marriage itself, which is too attenuated in time to be characterized by concrete actions, the wedding ceremony serves the judge as a metaphoric vehicle that demonstrates the superimposition of a teleological superstructure upon individual actions. "What, then, does the wedding ceremony accomplish? It provides a survey of the genesis of the human race, and therewith it grafts the new marriage upon the great body of the race. Thereby it presents the universal, the essentially human, and evokes it in consciousness" (*O*, 91). In this passage the coordination between personal action and collective destiny effected by the wedding ceremony is presented literally as a graft or a superimposed weaving. The individual marriage is a representation in miniature, a synecdoche, of the genesis of the human race, whose theological account begins with Adam and Eve. Crucial to this account are its philosophical resonances. The human-transcendental bond secured by marriage is tantamount to the revelation of the philosophical universal on the way to absolute knowledge. The passage thus equates philosophical with divine revelation within the system crystallizing around marriage.

In order to emphasize the revelatory quality of marriage, the judge compares the act of personal choice consummated in the wedding ceremony to the leap of faith at the bottom of religious conviction. In some regards, the wedding ritual actually impedes marriage, such as by imposing the publishing of the banns. Yet the purpose of such barriers is actually to enhance that element of marriage which is a leap of faith (*O*, 98). In accordance with the wedding ceremony's communal and historical nature, such procedures as the publishing of the banns endow marriage with a dimension of publicity and openness sharply contrasting with the secrecy of seduction. From the judge's point of view, the esthete's residence is a death chamber of secrecy with "big, cool, high-vaulted halls" and "mysterious half-obscure chambers. . . . Your principle evidently was mysterious, refined coquetry. Not only the walls of your chambers . . . but even your world of consciousness must be diversified by similar refractions of light" (*O*, 108). As opposed to such esthetic concealment and secrecy, which the judge calls "petty effeminacy," marriage is a place of "open-hearted-ness" (*O*, 114), where in spite of the female frailty that marriage was designed to protect (*O*, 93), the wife possesses unlimited strength as a confidant: "Only confide to her everything!" (*O*, 115). The bond between personal choice and history supplied by marriage thus implies an entire speculative and theological system with its own model of revelation and its own poetics, whose principles include openness and a plain style.

Underlying the Metaphysics of Marriage Is a Representational Concept of Language

The above discussion should make clear that marriage and the metaphysical system that it implies are grounded in a sequence of couplings or bonds: between subjectivity and collectivity, between self-determination in choice and history. Yet underlying these transcendental bonds is one so fundamental that it is almost invisible, one that exists on the symbolic plane and fuses the word and the thing. Implicit in the judge's paeans to matrimony is a scenario that has marriage as a symbol linking its parties to the transcendental ideal of love.

The judge is himself aware of the symbolic implications of the set of couplings that marriage effects. "Every marriage, like every human life, is at the same time this particular thing and yet the whole, at once an individual and a symbol" (*O*, 92). Within the symbolic order that marriage abbreviates, love is the ideal essence or meaning that marriage symbolizes; and the partners of the marriage and their household and offspring may be taken as a proof or a sign of such love. The offspring of the marriage serve as a useful index to this reproductive scheme: they are living and genetic proof of the reproduction by which the family configuration duplicates the ideal of love. "Children belong to the inmost and most hidden life of the family" (*O*, 74). Within the symbolic order of marriage, love comprises the ideal signified, and the wedding ceremony and conjugal relations emanating from it constitute the sign or signifier.

In terms of the ethical mode, marriage functions as a symbol within a transparently representational model of language, effecting a perfect link between the signified and the signifier. It is in his detailed explanation of the relation between love (the signified) and marriage (the signifier) early in "The Aesthetic Validity of Marriage" that the judge acknowledges the dependence of the ethical order on a representational model of language, one in which people as well as discursive units are subservient to a higher meaning (*O*, 34–38). Although in the course of this discussion he briefly allows himself to question the causal sequence of love and marriage by asking, "Is love the first, or is marriage, of which love then is the sequel?" (*O*, 35), he resolves this chicken-and-egg uncertainty with a formulation at the heart of any representational symbolic order. "So then love," as the essence served and implemented by marriage, "comes first" (*O*, 34). Any threat to the representational sequence in which love precedes and marriage signifies, any discrepancy between love and marriage that the partners experience, the Judge dismisses as "a poor outlook," confined to "the empty heads of foolish humans" (*O*, 34).

Behind the more conventional and explicit themes of personal choice, marriage, and community comprising the ethical mode, then, there resides a linguistic order of representation. If this model is not often formulated in terms of its symbolic operations, it is nonetheless the point at which the misusages comprising the complex of irony and the esthetics of seduction take off. Representation is thus the generally veiled center of the transcendental order that the esthetic mode violates, all the while compiling a lexicon of linguistic excesses. The spawning ground and native home of these violations is the space between love and marriage, the discrepancy between the signified and the signifier, which for the judge and all metaphysical thinkers must not be allowed to exist.

The Metaphysics of Marriage Expands into a General Moral Imperative

In its widest dimensions, the metaphysical system initiated by the wedding ceremony reaches a point at which the prescriptions of marriage no longer relate to any of the issues or themes specifically associated with conjugal domesticity. The logic of marriage extends to a sphere of neutral and general moral responsibility that the judge terms "duty." Duty is simply a domain in which the *imperatives* of marriage prevail but where they are no longer applied to the domestic economy's conjugal compatibility and the rearing of children. The judge articulates his duty as a creed of faith. "I recognize that it is a man's duty to seek a definite profession in life, I regard it as his duty to be faithful to his calling, and, on the other hand, when he violates his duty he suffers well-deserved punishment. Here is duty. I undertake something definite, I can state precisely what it is, I promise to perform it dutifully" (*O*, 153). In its lucidity and precision, duty represents the teleological, moral, and theological system emanating from marriage at its fullest logical extension and clarity of vision.

As a general moral imperative, duty dictates not merely actions but tastes. Duty demands its own *style,* and to the extent that it touches on esthetic concerns, the esthetic mode may be said to harbor its own poetics. This poetic code, or concern with style, that penetrates the esthetic mode is the basis for the judge's insistence on an *"aesthetic validity of marriage."* Yet the judge's esthetics limits itself to questions of taste, to questions of usage not substantially different from those of manners or etiquette, while the esthetics of seduction and writing substitutes language-based notions of reality, movement, and time for the transcendental couplings we have observed at the basis of the ethical order.

While at a certain point the ethical mode verges on esthetic concerns, it is not to be confused with the Kierkegaardian esthetics, which is a complete restructuring of speculative and teleological presuppositions. As the dialectical structure of *Either/Or* would enable us to anticipate, the rules encompassed by the ethical style sheet are in direct response to the esthetic principles of irony. Where Kierkegaard's esthetes and ironists advance as stylistic values ambiguity, inconclusiveness, and variation in love as in art, the judge prizes solidity, coherence, constancy, and rationality. For the esthete's "multiplicity" of pleasure (*O,* 188), the judge would substitute the constancy of friendship (*O,* 324). Where the esthete suffers from incoherence and insatiety (*O,* 206–7) and allows his existence to be shaped by accident (*O,* 264), the judge would assert "the rational order of things" (*O,* 297). As opposed to the poetic excess systematically dramatized by the esthete (*O,* 277), the judge chooses the quiet prose of the domestic life (*O,* 281, 302).

The ethical voice in Kierkegaard is Hegelian in the sense that it calls for the emergence of all values and goals from *within.* "The individual has his teleology in himself, has inner teleology, is himself this teleology" (*O,* 279). And yet for all the subjectivity of the choices, aspirations, and imperatives advanced by the judge, they are structured by a hierarchical system in which transcendental values precede and determine all experience. In spite of the judge's precaution to qualify his values by their interiority, they emanate from above whether they are stylistic or moral in nature.

Men and Women Occupy Predetermined and Nontransferable Functions and Roles

The absolute fixity of sexual roles, a presupposition running throughout the judge's papers, is a corollary to the transcendental model of signification at the heart of the ethical mode. A marriage is a complex signifier composed of a man and a woman who are themselves signs in the sense that they express a discrete sexual essence. It is indicative of the judge's intellectual operations, not to mention his bias, that although himself a man, he finds it far easier to articulate the sexual essence of the woman. "In general woman has an innate talent, a primitive gift and an absolute virtuosity for explaining finiteness" (*O*, 315). "A woman comprehends finiteness . . . from the bottom up" (*O*, 316).

The judge's model of sexual definition, in which masculine and feminine roles are in accordance with a predetermined scheme, is close to the scenario articulated by Hegel in a section of the *Phenomenology* entitled "The Ethical Order." As in the Hegelian scheme, the judge situates the woman at the level of particularity and places her at the service of others. For Hegel, the sister defends the divine law within the sphere of particularity encompassed by the household, while the brother progresses from the family's allegiances to the service of the state and the universal consciousness that such duty conveys. But while in Hegel such sexual roles are ambiguous enough to eventually afford the figure of the sister an irony penetrating the entire system of allegiances, Kierkegaard's ethical judge will entertain no irony or sexual uncertainty. It is for this reason that he continually denounces the esthete's activities, whether specifically sexual or in the realm of art, as "effeminate" (*O*, 114, 124). More than the feminine nature of effeminacy, the judge rejects the sexual indeterminacy that homosexuality would suggest. Such a mixture, or crossing, of sexual roles is a threat to an entire system determined by a perfect compatability between identities and essences. The judge's rigidity with regard to sexual roles is a response to the type of sexual reciprocity and interplay dramatized in the "Diary of the Seducer."

In the above postulations of the judge, Kierkegaard has formulated the lineaments of the metaphysical system that irony and the esthetic mode disfigure, dismantle, and radically restructure. Yet it would be reductive to suggest that the esthetic simply destroys what the ethical erects. The judge himself dismisses as naive the proposition that "the ethical . . . is something totally different from the aesthetical, and when it prevails it destroys the other entirely" (*O*, 276), an attitude that he ascribes to the esthete. The reciprocal exchange of reading and interpretation involving the ethical and esthetic modes is too complex to be accommodated by a model of simple negation. The moral teleology of the judge is so riddled with inconsistencies and contradictions as to suggest that it is an ironic reprise appended to the esthetics of the *Either* at a moment when any vision of hierarchical and causal order is hopelessly belated. The intense and possibly facetious innocence of the *Or* is the last act in the play of irony, the moment when through its feigned gestures of self-horror irony invisibly rejoins the philosophical system that it has already interrupted. In this gesture, the double work known as *Either/Or* completes the cycle of ironic acts codified and rehearsed in *The Concept of Irony*.

In spite of the architectural substantiality of its system, the *Or* is filled with a string of intimations suggesting that the judge is himself an *eiron:* that he conceives of himself as a seducer, fancies himself an artist, and manipulates the nuances of his language. Of that element of the *Or* which retracts the idealism and purity of its metaphysical system, two areas are particularly prominent: the *self-contradiction* that pervades the moral treatise, both in the use of specific terms and in the reversal of argumentative positions; and the stage machinery of the text, the *dramatic* roles that the judge *plays* as an actor and *orchestrates* as a director internalized within the text.

For all the tranquillity that the judge attributes to his domestic life, there remains a touch of the artist in him. "I, too, sometimes saunter about the sheets, abandoning myself to my own thoughts and the impressions momentarily made upon me by the surroundings" (*O*, 75). In his emanation as a *flâneur* the judge is also pleased to visit the esthete in the latter's decadent but funereal den of seduction (*O*, 108). Employing a metaphor that is telling in terms of both his own self-conception and the *Or*'s irony, the judge pictures himself as "a solitary artist upon the stage of life" (*O*, 291). Yet the judge's functioning within the esthetic mode is not limited to the superficial plane of his assertions. Above all, in his use of terms, philosophical as well as moral, he luxuriates in a poetic license, a freedom in the manipulation of meanings, as extreme as any that the esthete professes.

Particularly striking in the judge's paradoxical use of terms is the manner in which he approaches the Orwellian *doublethink*, the application of a meaning to a word that is diametrically opposed to its conventional usage.[33] Even where the judge's doublethink is in the service of transcendental values, the liberty that he takes with words bespeaks an ironic posture. With reference to the birth of subjectivity, for example, the judge's repeated assertion that the predetermined necessity of choice constitutes the only available freedom (*O*, 178–82) shifts a measure of esthetic willfulness over to the ethical domain. Yet this advertisement for the ethical life and the metaphysical superstructure that it carries with it is predicated on a violent shift in signification.

This doublethink, the forceful wrenching of meanings in accordance with a predetermined scheme, is one of the judge's characteristic rhetorical gestures. By the same token that determination is freedom, there is a happiness in despair (*O*, 217), beauty is a kind of plainness (*O*, 277, 279), and the extraordinary is in reality the ordinary (*O*, 333). There is a blunt force in these redefinitions, yet to whatever extent they implement a teleological necessity, their license derives from the multivalence of meaning in irony.

The self-contradictory nature of the judge's use of language is not limited to his reversing the conventional usages of words. The judge also tampers with the conceptual cornerstones of the metaphysical system that he himself propounds. For all its austerity, the system that he represents is filled with contradictions in the very terms that serve as its underpinnings. Having devoted considerable discursive resources, for example, to formulating a subjectivity that derives its teleological thrust from history, at one point the judge places historical awareness on the side of the freethinker, who opens "the door to historical infinity" (*O*, 270). There is a similar breakdown in the judge's simplistic but fundamental system of sexual identities and roles. The judge, having repeatedly accused the esthete of an effeminacy that constitutes a clear sexual deviance, complains that he is not womanly enough. According to the judge's wife, whose opinion he shares or would not repeat, the esthete lacks "a certain degree of womanliness. You are too proud to be able to devote yourself to anyone" (*O*, 331). This conspicuous violation of the judge's sexual metaphysics is complemented by one in his esthetics. For all the judge's invective against incoherence, inconstancy, and disorder in art as in life, he acknowledges the role that chance and contingency play within the accomplishments of the ethical life. "So what I accomplish follows upon my job as a piece of good luck in which I may well take delight but which I dare not impute absolutely to myself" (*O*, 300). Having railed against the accidental quality pervading the esthete's activities, the judge now incorporates luck within the ethical life-style.

In a work so dialectically patterned as *Either/Or*, and in an ethical treatise ascribed to a fictive surrogate so cognizant of modal borders, such conceptual lapses or inconsistencies do not occur haphazardly. The judge's inconsistent attitudes toward history, sexual determination, and chance are not outside, but fall within the compass of the *Or*'s design. No less than the esthetic papers, the *Or* is a site of self-contradiction and paradox. When the judge describes marriage, the emblem of the ethical mode, as a "unity of contradictions" (*O*, 62), he is giving testimony to the ironic gesture of self-denial that invades even the sanctuary of moral restraint. Briefly assuming a stance of autobiographical recollection, the judge recounts how this ironic self-contradiction patterned the primal scene of his ethical life. As a boy, the judge, confronting the basic childhood task of lesson learning, perceived that "it was as if heaven and earth might collapse if I did not learn my lesson, and on the other hand as if, even if heaven and earth were to collapse, this would not exempt me from doing what was assigned to me, from learning my lesson" (*O*, 271). For all the direction supplied by the moral imperative, the boy experiences his duty as a paradox, a double bind, a wavering between achievement and apocalypse.

Of all the contradictions woven into the design of the *Or*, none has wider theoretical implications than the judge's attempt to define and locate the notion of reflexivity. In securing a strategic advantage for the ethical ideology, the judge ascribes the delusory hope for immediate experience to romantic love and places reflection on the side of moral restraint. This position is diametrically opposed to the one maintained by the esthete, who identifies spiritual immanence with ideals similar to those propounded by the judge and who analogically links the erotic chain of seductions to metaphoric displacement in language. Within the judge's metaphysics, the first love "lacks reflection" (*O*, 43); "no reflection molests it" (*O*, 48); it is destroyed "the moment it reflects" (*O*, 56). First love shares the chastity of the idealized innocent bride. Reflection, which for the judge is tantamount to restraint and prudence, is supplied by marriage and the entire metaphysical system that it predicates.

> First love is strong, stronger than the whole world, but the instant doubt occurs to it, it is annihilated, it is like a sleep-walker who with infinite security can walk over the most perilous places, but when one calls his name he plunges down. . . . And now I invert everything and say: the aesthetic does not lie in the immediate but in the acquired—but marriage is precisely the immediacy which has mediacy in itself, the infinity which has finiteness in itself, the eternal which has the temporal in itself. (*O*, 96)

The somnambulism of first love, a category common to both esthetical and ethical modes, terminates in the paradoxes of marriage. In this gesture of inversion, the judge displaces the self-contradiction of ironic language to the serene hearth of marriage. As a paradoxical mode, marriage acquires the ironic qualities attributed in the esthetic papers to seduction. With justification the judge describes this rhetorical gesture on his part as an inversion: he reverses the placement of the apprehension of the articulation, the linguistic basis of all experience, from the domain of art to that of marriage. Marriage is now as ambiguous, paradoxical, and unpredictable as seduction ever was.

The residence of reflection and articulation on both sides of the metaphysical watershed dividing the esthetic from the ethical is of profound consequence for the dialectical framework of *Either/Or* and for any notion of progress that we may ascribe to Kierkegaard's work. If marriage is as self-contradictory as seduction, the apprehension of the linguistic constitution of experience and reality is as fundamental to the ethical order as it is to art. The judge confesses this in so many words. "The same aesthetic quality which was found in first love must, therefore, also be found in marriage, since the former is combined in the latter" (*O*, 61). The self-contradiction of marriage becomes the medium for change and personal growth. The possibility for change has migrated to marriage from the chain of seductions. With this formulation, the esthetic and the ethical move into a final deadlock. No longer ascribing the naive ideals of immediacy and nonreflection to each other, the esthetic and the ethical admit that they are both articulate and ultimately ironic modes.

More than merely intimating a stage, *Either/Or* is a stage in its own right, a theater for the multifaceted linguistic capabilities that Kierkegaard groups under the rubric irony. The work runs the complete ironic course rehearsed in *The Concept of Irony*. Beginning with an enunciation of esthetic divergences from ideational and deterministic thought, an exploration of the particular types of negativity, ambiguity, freedom, and subjectivity comprising the complex of irony, the work culminates in the dramatic and feigned capitulation to a system that has already been dismantled. Ironically, the work is never more ironic than in its straight-faced codification of the metaphysical and teleological system that the language-based economy of art undermines.

In the wake of such a strategy, in which the symmetrical equilibrium of the esthetic and the ethical is itself a ruse camouflaging the unlimited extension of irony, the somber tone that colors much of Kierkegaard's later writing is not to be taken at face value. It might seem that Kierkegaard's later works comprise a retreat, a step backwards from esthetic excess into a utopia of religious fervency and reverence. From this point of view, the existential pathos elaborated in the *Concluding Unscientific Postscript* might seem a concluding positivistic tack in Kierkegaard's work, a consummate recuperation and sublimation of ironic negativity. Yet the conceptual framework surrounding religiosity and existential pathos, the philosophical buttresses of their cathedral, are terms that have all been rendered hopelessly problematical and ambiguous by such works as those that we have examined. Religious experience and the existential pathos that will not allow any particular mode of thought to offer a definitive solution to life's enigmas arise in the context of Kierkegaardian terms whose ambiguity, and hence irony, are well established. The religious domain at which Kierkegaard's thought may seem to terminate is conditioned, qualified, and ultimately ironized by notions of subjectivity, freedom, and history that are themselves self-contradictory. The *Concluding Unscientific Postscript,* which culminates in a "subjective Christianity" that corrects the arbitrary orthodoxy of "childish Christianity," is attributed to one "Johannes Climacus." Even at its "Climacus," its high point, Kierkegaard's religious discourse is rendered unreliable by the stage machinery of narrative surrogation; and by name at least, the Johannes who is its author belongs to the lineage of Don Juan and the seducer. The ironic cycle rehearsed in *The Concept of Irony* and repeated at the level of performance in *Either/Or* thus qualifies all appeals to idealism and religiosity that emerge in Kierkegaard's subsequent work. The wake left by Kierkegaardian irony, articulated through the medium of aphoristic utterance, is ultimately irreversible.

[IV]

HEGEL AND KIERKEGAARD

As we have intimated from the outset, our verdict in assessing any progression that may transpire from Hegel to Kierkegaard is hopelessly split. In certain senses, to be sure, Kierkegaard is *beyond* Hegel, specifically beyond the mechanistic formalism into which the Hegelian discourse occasionally lapses. Yet equally inescapable is the observation that in other regards, specifically where he misreads Hegel by overlooking the Hegelian capacity for irony, Kierkegaard takes a *step backwards* from his predecessor.

Our earlier discussion unavoidably touched upon several of the ways that Kierkegaard reacts to the oppressive qualities of the Hegelian discourse with some violence. We have observed how both the involuted narrative structures that Kierkegaard constructs for his works and the intimate stance assumed by his narrators toward the reader inject an element of unreliability into a philosophical discourse that in Hegel's style often claims the objectivity of a universal knowledge. Otherwise put, by means of narrative complexity and by allowing an intimate approach to enter philosophy, Kierkegaard goes far beyond Hegel in acknowledging the fictionality that characterizes all discursive modes, including philosophy. The fullest extension of Kierkegaard's disclosure of the fictional potential of philosophical discourse is evident in the manner in which certain of his works allegorize the interaction between the reader and the writer. While the Hegelian discourse does divide into several strands, or voices, expressive of different perspectives or points of view, it never goes so far as to stage specifically the readerly-writerly interaction.

We have also had occasion to observe how Kierkegaard attacks Hegelian claims of a progression or consummation of consciousness by paralyzing the at times mechanistic movements of dialectical operations. Kierkegaard halts dialectical progress by confining it to the space of a single dialectical stage or cell, the scene of a single Either/Or. He parodies Hegelian procedures, in other words, by arresting their ostensible movement. The denial of motion became a leitmotif of his early work.

Yet in the ironic model of literary history that emerges from the Hegel-Kierkegaard confrontation, Kierkegaard's seeming "advances" beyond Hegel themselves constitute evidence of his misreading his forerunner. In the context of Kierkegaard's fictionalization of philosophical discourse, such an undecidable allegory of reading and writing as the one staged in the "Diary of the Seducer" comprises a clear progress beyond the neutrality of the omniscient Hegelian voice. Yet the exchange of ruses and, eventually, positions that takes place between Johannes and Cordelia in the "Diary" is a quite concrete application of the reciprocal play of forces in Hegel's "Force and the Understanding." Stylistically, Kierkegaard's allegory of fictive and erotic deceit may comprise an innovation, but the mechanics of infinite reversal derives from the heart of the Hegelian formal operations. By implication, all of the scenarios of two-sided symmetry and reversal in Kierkegaard's work, including the consummate Either/Or coupling the esthetic and ethical modes, belong to the Hegelian logic before they supersede it.

Kierkegaardian repetition finds itself in a similarly ambivalent position. On the one hand, the fictive quality of the situations in which Kierkegaardian repetition appears and the playful metaphors that Kierkegaard invokes to describe it bespeak a poetic license far beyond the tolerances of the Hegelian discourse. Yet the circularity, autonomy, and unpredictability of Kierkegaardian repetition have all been rehearsed in the infinite cycles to which the Hegelian text occasionally—and quite literally—reverts.

There are even certain regards in which Kierkegaard's "advances beyond" Hegel are more retrograde than the comparable aspects of Hegel's system. Kierkegaard takes issue with the compulsive progressiveness of the Hegelian dialectic. But the fictive genealogical framework organizing the *Phenomenology*, the *Aesthetics*, and other works affords Hegel the possibility of applying the *same procedures* to an extraordinarily *wide range* of themes, institutions, and ages. The temporalization or suspension of time in the *Phenomenology* enables

Hegel to consider material as diverse as electricity and animal gods. Kierkegaard's self-imposed confinement to a single dialectical stage may unmask the naiveté of Hegel's insistence on development, but it also tends to limit the areas of inquiry that he explores. Kierkegaard seems never to be able to escape the domain defined by esthetic excess and its implications for the subjective theater of choice. In other words, Hegel's discourse does include an omniscient narrative voice whose neutrality is particularly suspect. But this is merely one voice entertained by the Hegelian perspectivism, which vacillates from inside to outside as from generality to particularity. Ironically, at least in one sense, Kierkegaard's counterpoint of two voices, even if they are self-contradictory, may be a poorer arrangement than Hegel's orchestration of five perspectives.[34]

The "mischievous face of irony" at the heart of the Kierkegaardian esthetics "peeps out" through the solemnity of his teleological and theological speculations well into the twentieth century. In both theoretical and fictive terms, a writer such as Franz Kafka found no more formidable a model than Kierkegaard. Kafka's scenarios of opposed characters, who may be double elements of the same personality, in such works as "Description of a Struggle" and "First Sorrow" are strongly indebted to Kierkegaard's ambiguous oppositions and triangular arrangements in *Repetition* and the "Diary of the Seducer." Kafka endows his briefest works of fiction, his parables and meditations, with the arbitrariness and finality that Kierkegaard achieves in his aphorisms. And at certain moments in his narratives Kafka simply turns to Kierkegaard for a guidance consisting in phrases and sequences.[35] In a similar fashion, the interaction between Bloom and Stephen Dedalus in Joyce's *Ulysses,* and the potential triangular liaison linking them to Molly, owes much to the Kierkegaardian configurations, possibly through the intermediacy of Ibsen.[36] And yet those aspects by which Kierkegaard is most germane to the twentieth century turn out to be his points of closest contact to Hegel. Kierkegaard's sudden reversals of perspective and allegiance, the endless suspense of his conflicts, both internal and external, and the arbitrariness of the coincidences that he terms repetitions all have roots in the Hegelian poetics.

Kierkegaard himself thus remains split between his uncanny anticipation of the characteristic features of modern esthetics and a far more primitive, pre-Romantic age. In his experimentation with the formal procedures of philosophy, he opened up the no man's land between philosophy and literature, which he transformed into a garden flowering with a hybrid critical discourse possibly more suggestive than either of its constituents. The creativity of the narrative unreliability that he introduced into philosophical discourse and of the allegories of reading and writing that he staged there is equaled by the attentiveness with which he pursued the implications of a language-based rather than an ideal-based reality. Sundered between his analytical rigor and his fictive invention, Kierkegaard forged a link between Romanticism and the twentieth century, where his writing is still at home.

FOUR

The Subject of the Nerves: Philosophy and Freud

[I]

THE SOUR TURN

Ladies and Gentlemen,

The focus of the following analysis will be none other than Sigmund Freud.[1] If such a subject proves as exasperating as rewarding, it is by virtue of an enigmatic turn in his career. It was the great contribution of our patient to have opened the hygienic space of the clinic to the esthetic intuitions of Romantic literature and theory. We remain in his debt because he took on the formidable task of characterizing human consciousness by formulating a grammar of psychological drives and operations whose terms derive primarily, not from medicine, but from esthetic, mythological, and religious *texts*. Like Saussure, Freud opened the twentieth century with a declaration of the primacy of linguistic functions within the subjective and social spheres. The great laws of the Freudian unconscious are, like the relations between Saussurian signifiers, *differential*.[2] Dreams become intelligible not through the application of a fixed key to their code but through the negative relations that define the great laws of the unconscious: repression, displacement, condensation, substitution, regression, and deferral. As he progresses from the *Studies On Hysteria,* with its rather schematic program, to the groundbreaking formulations of *The Interpretation of Dreams* and *Jokes and Their Relation to the Unconscious,* Freud affords his reader a sense of discovery rare in modern theory or literature. The pleasure deriving from such works is primarily a linguistic one. If dreams, jokes, and the unconscious comprise a hitherto submerged and despised facet of humanity, Freud makes them accessible to a lexicon whose terms themselves carry out linguistic functions. The joy of reading Freud is the exuberance of witnessing the secrets of consciousness unfold to the sensibility of language.

If there is a dark side to our subject, it is the extent to which he succumbed to the trying and ultimately stultifying competitiveness inscribed within his own notion of the Oedipus complex. If we may postulate that the expansiveness of the first great works of maturity (generally but not systematically) gives way in later treatises to a certain defensiveness, self-righteousness, and pedantry, this is the result not so much of a turning away from earlier insights as of a confusion of roles. For all the creative power that Freud released when he applied nineteenth-century esthetic principles to the clinical subject, he hardly ignored the privileges, material and strategic as well as intellectual, accruing from his placement within a scientific superstructure. Posterity records Freud's discouragement of innovation within his circle,[3] the fainting fits that accompanied his disputes with Jung,[4] the rings that Freud bestowed upon his closest and most loyal disciples, making them the bishops in an expanding, global church.[5] One of the most striking aspects of Freud's writings is their circular nature, the manner in which they lend themselves to the constructs that they themselves generate. Freud imposed upon psychoanalysis the repression that he attributed to civilization; he became the intolerable chieftain of his own primal hoard. In stepping back from the unlimited possibilities generated by interpretation and association, he entered the backwaters of regression; he thus submitted to the theoretical equivalent of the death instinct.

Half a century intervened between the excruciating deadlocks explored in Kierkegaard's works and Freud's early psychoanalytical publications. Yet in Freud's career not only the conflict between linguistic apprehensions and dialectical operations but the structure of conflict itself remains intact. For all the play accommodated by the grammar of distortion that Freud applied to human consciousness, his findings were always adapted to the procedures and aspirations of science. In the case of Kierkegaard, the structures of opposition and negation continue even when the ethical has been ironized. By the same token, Freud's scientific and Messianic missions reinstate the imperatives of clinical order even when they have been hopelessly disqualified by an esthetic lexicon of distortion.

The writings of Freud represent the culmination of a theme that, although enunciated only fragmentarily by Kierkegaard and Nietzsche, became an insignia of modernity. The subject of the nerves is a touchy one, placed halfway between intellectual virtuosity and forces beyond control. Freud's clinical role put him in a position to supply an empirical referent for the quakings and paralyses that Kierkegaard and Nietzsche[6] introjected into dialectical reasoning. In

Freud's work the nerves, which earlier served as a mere example of the violence repressed in systematic thought, stand out in full relief and become tantamount to a central character.

It was to Freud that Walter Benjamin was turning when he identified the hallmark of modernity as shock. In his seminal essay "On Some Motifs in Baudelaire," Benjamin explored the traumas undergone by the masses in advanced Western societies since the industrial revolution. As the mass-psychological symptoms of an age dominated by sensory overload and repetitive activities, Benjamin cites the jumbled space of the modern city, the frenetic pace of a calendar devoid of ritual markers, an eroticism of encounters rather than attachments, and games that continue rather than diffuse the mechanical tasks of the workplace.[7] More important than the specific aetiological role played by any of these factors in a mass pathology is that for Benjamin too, addressing problems, an audience, and a scale markedly different from Freud's, the changes of modernity initiated a crisis of the nerves.

For all its centrality to modern literature and theory, however, the figure of the nervous system does not elude the inherited impasse that delimits the Freudian enterprise. On the one hand, the nerves constitute the system of transmission and reception that define sensibility itself. The nervous system is the *media,* as it were, of subjectivity. It communicates the information and impulses at the basis of the higher productions of human activity. Yet the form of the nerves is no less significant: a complex, intertwined latticework, folded over on itself and interrupted countless times. In the lineaments of its form, the nervous system comprises the open combinatorial matrix that we know as the literary text, nonlinear in its evolution and operation, irrational in its associations, multiple in its structuration.[8] As a text, an open network, the nervous system undermines the very human subjectivity that it defines. This explains how Benjamin could characterize the citizen of the Modern age through metaphors of violence and irrationality. A creature of overload, the person of the crowd is a *subject* only to the extent that he or she undergoes the textual bewilderment of urban space and time, erotic cruising, and gambling.

Yet whether on the basis of scientific commitment, moral scruples, strategic circumspection, or personal ambition, Freud repeatedly subjected the textual configuration of the nerves to a characterization in terms of the rhetorics of mechanics, electrical charge, and inherent evolution. Although scholars describe Freud's "abandoning," near the turn of the century, his project of describing consciousness in "neurological" terms,[9] throughout the duration of his career he characterized a multitude of psychological functions in terms of neurological "paths," "levels of excitation," and dammings or blockages of energy. In Freud, the nervous system constitutes both a textual fabric of near-infinite complexity and a machine obeying the least subtle laws of physics.

Already I have suggested two ways of formulating a fundamental Freudian impasse: either as a modal shift in Freud's career between improvisation and earnestness or as a confusion of linguistic and scientific interests. Yet at the widest perimeter this watershed, however articulated, is an instance of a supplemental relation characterizing all systems of postulation and signification. As Samuel Weber has so eloquently stated, Freud's career, like his notion of the joke, *straddles* the interstice between a systematic theory of human subjectivity and the associative convulsions upon which systems and subjects founder.[10] The following reading of Freud is an attempt to account for the coexistence and fate of the two modes that organize his work, although they do so in no definitive logical or temporal order.

Our first step is to return to an initial but as yet unsubstantiated assertion that the great breakthroughs in Freud's early work arise from a decoding of dreams, jokes, and other manifestations of the unconscious by means of a grammar whose terms consist in *poetic* distortions. On a manifest level, the outrage that Freud's early investigations evoked resulted from the sensitive areas that he touched: incest, sexuality in general, and authoritarian repression. Yet from the perspective of intellectual history, the Freudian scandal consisted no less in his introduction of linguistic principles within the controlled environment of the clinic.

Goethe belongs to a select coterie of historical and cultural personages, including Leonardo da Vinci and Shakespeare, that Freud intensely admired and with whom he identified. In substantiating my rather large first premise, that Freud derived his initial conceptions of repression, displacement, condensation, and regression from nineteenth-century esthetics, I will refer to Goethe's *Faust* as a work in which many of these movements are dramatized. Of all the artifacts that appear in Freud's writings, none is cited as frequently or significantly as *Faust*.[11] Like much of Freud's work, *Faust* is informed by concerns of a subjective and highly metaphysical nature. I will argue nonetheless that *Faust* combines many of the varieties of poetic distortion that became the distinctive features of the unconscious, in "normal" people as well as neurotics. Certain of these distortions belong to a negativity contained and sanctioned by the play's wider metaphysical aspirations; others demonstrate a pure and nonrecuperable play of signifiers that surfaces in such Freudian instances as the condensation of the joke and the scenic overlays that take place in certain dreams (for example, the "Wolf Man"'s tree dream).[12] *Faust* is not the only instance of a Romantic artifact that could be cited as a precursor of Freud's cognitive grammar, yet in its markedly dialectical framework it serves as a dramatic counterinstance of the Hegelian tropes, setting the stage for Freud's (and Yeats's) appearance within the Hegelian aftermath.

If the joyous linguistic discovery of Freud's early work prompts an appeal to proper works of art, his lugubrious mood demands an inquest into the most concrete relations of power and intersubjectivity predicated by psychoanalysis. Only in the *Three Essays on the Theory of Sexuality* (1905) does Freud complete the application of the fundamentally linguistic processes that characterize dreams and jokes to a homogeneous and evolutionary model of subjectivity. Once there is a subject, however infantile, there is a space permitting the observation of the procedures of (un)consciousness, whether normal or neurotic, whether by the analyst alone or in conjunction with the patient. It is in formulating a model of subjectivity that Freud's scientific program owes its greatest debt to the Hegelian formal tropes, and my second major undertaking will be to assess this indebtedness.[13] The Freudian subject, and particularly the neurotic, is the agent in whom the distinctively Hegelian operations of internalization and externalization, bifurcation, and circularization have gone awry. Far from the antithesis of the philosopher, the neurotic is a thinking subject in whom the characteristic gestures of speculation have gotten slightly out of control. The neurotic is not an outlandish mutation of the philosopher but rather an intimate relative, separated only by a single qualification: that what is normative for the Hegelian speculator is pathogenic for the neurotic. Despite Freud's occasional dismissals of philosophy,[14] the cure of the neurotic involves a restoration of philosophical efficacy.

Yet at the same time that a tradition of philosophical rectitude prevails within psychoanalysis, above all on the side of the investigator, all the personae in the act are readers: Freud, analyzing and preserving for posterity the first patients; the analyst, critically examining the neurotic; and the patient, seeking to overcome certain dysfunctions. By their involvement in the interpretative process, the participants tend to lose the clarity that might once have attached to their roles. That deranged philosopher the neurotic occupies the privileged relation to the nervous system as a textual configuration (just as Block, the most shattered character in Kafka's *The Trial*, is most intimately familiar with the manifold controls exercised by the court).[15] While perhaps an aberrant in comparison with the analyst, the neurotic becomes the critic *par excellence*. The critical function resides within the textual complications of neurosis. In maintaining merely a secondhand relation to the text of the nerves, the analyst becomes at best an archivist, a literary historian. The analyst maintains a critical function only to the extent that he or she remains neurotic. And as founder, impressario, and historian of the psychoanalytical movement, Sigmund Freud remains at the farthest possible extreme from the function of criticism.

By virtue of its readerly and writerly dimensions, psychoanalysis finds its philosophical line of descent folded back on itself. In terms of the textual economy operating in psychoanalysis since its emergence from linguistic apprehensions, the neurotics are invested with all of the intensity. This is the case with Hoffmann's Nathanael, who, as the inspiration for the Freudian notion of the uncanny, stands at the Romantic horizon of this historical movement.[16] The inherent critical economy of psychoanalysis, situating the neurotic at the locus of the text, thus undermines the hierarchy proceeding downward from Freud to the actual analyst and the patient.

Even where it is most speculative, then, in its formation and characterization of a psychoanalytical subject, the Freudian enterprise implies an interpretative division of labor. My final task in tracing the counter textual and speculative configurations in Freud's work will be to account for a curious tendency. The consummating statements of Freud's later treatises are extreme both in their dialectical economy and in their textual indeterminacy. It is as if the opposed enterprises of linguistics and logic declare an armistice and encourage maximal development on the part of each other. Having relied heavily on the structure of opposition itself, toward the end of his writings Freud renounces this procedure and metaphysical attitude. A conflict between linguistic play and scientific insemination terminates in a joining of the ways, a gesture which might seem more uncanny did it not also conclude Proust's *Recherche,* thus furnishing a legend for the predicament of modernity.[17]

[II]

CLINICIAN AT THE WITCH'S KITCHEN: FREUD THE GRAMMARIAN

There's still the doctor in your system

Goethe, *Faust*

I begin with the outrageous pronouncement that in order to formulate a grammar of dreams, jokes, and the unconscious, Freud needed little more than to be an astute reader of literature, and specifically of Goethe's *Faust*. Yet before demonstrating that this theater piece is a virtual source book of psychoanalytical structures and acts, I would like to outline the grammatical project that absorbs Freud's early works. Freud, in characterizing the process known as "secondary revision," sets up an opposition between "dream-thoughts" (*Traumgedanken*) and the "content of the dream" (*Trauminhalt*) worthy of the ponderous conflicts that proliferate in *Faust*. According to Freud's scenario, the "dream-thoughts," those only too human wishes and conjectures drawn from everyday experience and disfigured by the dream-work in the interest of evading conscious censorship, are "entirely rational" (*völlig korrekt*). It is not the impulse or motive for dreams that is lacking in logic or propriety in any way, but the dream itself as an autonomous mechanism. The dream constructs itself around, in opposition to, and in spite of the rational control that would inhibit the indiscretions urged and constituted by the wish.

> On the other hand, the second function of mental activity during dream-construction [*jenes andere Stück Arbeit*], the transformation of the unconscious thoughts into the content of the dream, is peculiar to dream-life and characteristic of it. This dream-work proper diverges further from our picture of waking thought than has been supposed. . . . The dream-work is not simply more careless [*etwa nachlässiger*], more irrational [*inkorrekter*], more forgetful [*verßeblicher*] and more incomplete [*unvollständiger*] than waking thought; it is completely different from it qualitatively and for that reason not immediately comparable with it. It does not think [*denkt*], calculate [*rechnet*] or judge [*urteilt*] in any way at all; it restricts itself to giving things a new form [*umzuformen*]. It is exhaustively described by an enumeration of the conditions which it has to satisfy in producing its result. That product, the dream, has above all to evade the censorship [*Zensur*], and with that end in view the dream-work makes use of a *displacement [Verschiebung] of psychical intensities [Intensitäten]* to the point of a transvaluation of all psychical values [*Umwertung aller psychischen Werte*]. The thoughts have to be reproduced [*wiedergegeben*] exclusively or predominantly in the material of visual and acoustic memory-traces [*Erinnerungsspuren*], and this necessity imposes upon the dream-work *considerations of representability [die Rücksicht auf Darstellbarkeit]* which it meets by carrying out fresh displacements. Greater intensities have probably to be produced than are available in the dream-thoughts at night, and this purpose [*diese Zwecke*] is served by the extensive *condensation [die ausgiebige Verdichtung]* which is carried out with the constituents of the dream-thoughts. Little attention is paid to the logical relations between the thoughts; those relations are ultimately given a disguised representation [*versteckte Darstellung*] in certain *formal* characteristics of dreams. (*S.E.*, V, 506–7)

If I quote this passage, which concludes the section on secondary revision (*sekundäre Bearbeitung*) in *The Interpretation of Dreams,* at length, it is because it encompasses so many of the divergent and at times conflictive activities combined in the Freudian agenda.

In miniature, this passage spans the tortuous path that leads from dialectical logic to the problematic of representation and back to a certain formalism. At the beginning of the passage, the dream-work is contrasted, by dualistic opposition,[18] to the rationality of conscious thought, including that which prompts dreams. The irrationality, carelessness, and fragmentation that Freud attributes here to the dream-work are strongly reminiscent of the excesses that Kierkegaard ascribed to the esthetic mode. In stressing the topsy-turvy quality of the dream-work, Freud emphasizes its transformational activity. The dream-work displaces, not thoughts or structures, but "intensities," a marginal term at the interstice between quantity and quality. Freud describes the dream-work's revolutionary potential as a Nietzschean transfiguration of values.

The *suspension* of logical and, by implication, moral constraints in the dream-work does not, however, liberate this distortion from its placement within a binary framework. The dream-work plays cat-and-mouse games with the conscious. By means of its tricks, it conveys the ultimately concrete and sensible dream-thought past the pitfalls of censorship. This oppositional relationship between an agent of rational positivity and a negative defined as the release of limit constitutes Freud's major structural debt to a Romantic work such as *Faust,* whose action is largely powered by the extension of such conflict into virtually every dimension of the stage machinery.

For all its reveling in the constraints lifted by the dream-work, the above passage never repudiates the imperatives of logic and form. Yet there is a moment when the passage's dialectical underpinnings seem abandoned, when it considers the problems of representation and misrepresentation involved in transporting the controversial dream-thought past the censors of propriety. It might seem at this point that in conjunction with the dream's declaration of logical independence, Freud undertakes an analysis of mental representation on its own terms. A decisive shift in Freud's emphasis from psychology to the problematic of language seems assured when in taking up the "considerations of representability" by which the dream-work camouflages the dream-thought, he deploys a rhetoric of "visual and acoustic memory-traces" reminiscent of Saussure. Such future stocks-in-trade of unconscious activity as displacement (*Verschiebung*) and condensation enter Freud's discourse as agents of the distorted representation by which the dream-thought is metamorphosed into the dream.

Yet the Freudian problematic of representation is in the service of an inductive logic that insinuates itself into the passage, temporarily supplanting the oppositional one. The dream-work is "exhaustively described by an enumeration of the conditions which it has to satisfy in producing its result." For all its excess, in other words, the dream-work is exhaustively accountable, both quantitatively and logically, as the contrary of the demands of logic. The dream-work is to be inferred from, or is determined by, the commands of the conscious, which was earlier defined as the etiquette of logic itself. It may very well be that the particular measures taken by the dream-work in order to evade censorship are of great linguistic moment and ultimately undermine the considerations of logic and representation that they ostensibly serve. As this passage dramatizes, however, whatever violence is ascribed to the distortions composed by the dream-work, the dream-economy may never be divorced from the calculi of opposition and inference.

It is not by accident that in addition to the protean rubric displacement, which is applied in so many contexts that it defies any single definition, the single element in Freud's grammar of the unconscious appearing in the above passage is condensation. Apart from certain instances of displacement, condensation (*Ver-dichten*) is the only element in the Freudian grammar to live up to its German name, that is, to characterize linguistic processes in fully poetic or linguistic terms.[19] The linguistic grafts and abbreviations populating our jokes and dreams with a menagerie of hieroglyphs are poetic objects whose wonder is not derived from any metaphysical or, for that matter, psychoanalytical superstructure. Repression and regression, on the other hand, bear entire metaphysical complexes with them. In exhaustively accounting for the manner in which the dream-work circumvents the interdicts of rationality, Freud fashions a vocabulary of distortional terms, which he then applies iterably to normal and pathogenic conditions, from disease to disease and from case to case. These elements, which include displacement, repression, regression, the combination of opposites, and condensation, become what Freud describes at the end of the passage as "certain *formal* characteristics of dreams." Freud's lexicographical enterprise thus becomes, by virtue of the logics that it never abandons, a *formalism*, that is, a mode of description based on persistent repetitive analogies. Not only all its constitutive elements (save condensation) but this formalism as a method itself carries with it metaphysical valences in conflict with Freud's linguistic interest. The distillation of the formal characteristics of dreams fills consciousness with structures instead of substances; it privileges form over content. The volatile representational and distortional activities of dreams ultimately result in formal characteristics that are definable, quantifiable, and inert, however broad their application may be. As a microcosm of the trajectory pursued by Freud's career, the above passage predicts as much as it summarizes. The great liberations announced by the uncovering of the unconscious amount to little more than flirtations. The necessities of logic and the mores of science persist even through the upheaval attributed to dreams and the unconscious.

That Freud's approach to the unconscious and its manifestations assumed the form of a lexicon is highly significant, however formalistic the elements in the Freudian grammar became, however much the relapse into metaphysical attitudes approached repression. The major categories in the lexicon of the unconscious may vary in the degree of their generality, yet each is in itself a complex trope, encompassing subtle variations of nuance and activity. The most compelling demonstration of the grammatical dimension of Freud's writing may well consist in pursuing the vicissitudes of a number of the key terms through the early works. Freud is to be admired for the specificity and variety with which he coined terms. In the interest of our own economy, our discussion will be limited to four categories—repression, regression, displacement, and condensation—although these exhaust neither the Freudian lexicon nor the confusion between Freud's linguistic and scientific projects. Freud treats all of these terms as figural tropes or grammatical rules, yet three of them—displacement, repression, and regression—merely extend the metaphysical battle between positivity and negativity, and only condensation fulfills the grammatical or semiological status ascribed to all four terms.

The single most dominant metaphor throughout Freud's writings is that of the river or stream whose current, free to pursue its course, leads to fulfillment and satisfaction but whose blockages are the image of frustration and the root of all neurosis.[20] The current running through Freud's work is "only" a metaphor, yet the impact of this figural flow upon major psychoanalytical attitudes and diagnoses is quite literal. In its capacities for twisting and branching, the Freudian river holds in reserve some potential for textual involution. Yet far surpassing the complications of this current's byways is the strength and compulsion of its sheer force. The image of the river is a variation on the organic metaphor of the tree that is so central to the evolutionary idealogy enunciated in the "Preface" to the *Phenomenology of Spirit*. Freud's current has its sources and forerunners in the implicit necessity of the Hegelian dialectic and in the streams and weavings of *Faust*.

The threat posed by the damming up of an otherwise free flow is never more pernicious than in relation to sexual energy, so it is fitting that we should find one of Freud's most fully elaborated stream images in the first of the *Three Essays on the Theory of Sexuality* (1905). In explaining the "Apparent Preponderance of Perverse Sexuality in the Psychoneuroses," Freud writes,

> Most psychoneurotics only fall ill after the age of puberty as a result of the demands made upon them by normal sexual life. (It is most particularly against the latter that repression [*Verdrängung*] is directed.) Or else illnesses of this kind set in later, when the libido fails to obtain satisfaction on sexual lines. In both these cases the libido behaves like a stream [*Strom*] whose main bed has become blocked [*dessen Hauptbett verlegt wird*]. It proceeds to fill up collateral channels which may hitherto have been empty. (*S.E.*, VII, 170)

Although the blocked libido may be diverted into collateral channels, the explicitly sexual nature of the problem in Freud's language is not. The bed of the dammed libido stream is a quite literal one, yet the verb applied to the blockage, *verlegen*, also signifies publication. The stream and marriage bed of sexual frustration are thus exposed to public scrutiny and sanction.

The optimally free-flowing stream, whose diversions as well as dams spell danger, rushes into an enormously wide range of psychological and psychoanalytical situations. The metaphoric river in Freud flows from the early *Studies on Hysteria* (1893–95), where "the sum of excitation, being cut off from psychical association, finds itself all the more easily along the wrong path to a somatic innervation" (*S.E.*, II, 116), to "the homosexual current of feeling" in a woman's development, which "in favorable circumstances . . . often runs dry," elicited in explanation of Dora's *Case of Hysteria* (1907). Even during the period around 1915, when Freud wrote his *Metapsychological Papers,* a "damming-up of the libido in the ego" served to explain the phenomenon of narcissism (*S.E.*, XIV, 85).

Yet far more crucial than the *extent* of the metaphorical stream's meanderings is its place within the economies of repression and regression. The metamorphosis from wishes and perceptions to dreams is formidable. In a consummating passage from *The Interpretation of Dreams,* Freud characterizes this transformation in the following manner.

> The unconscious wish links itself up with the day's residues and effects a transference [*Übertragung*] on to them; this may happen either in the course of the day or not until a state of sleep has been established. A wish now arises which has been transferred on to the recent material; or a recent wish [*unterdrückte rezent Wunsch*] having been suppressed, gains

fresh life by being reinforced from the unconscious. This wish seeks to force its way along the normal path taken by thought-processes [*auf dem normalen Wege der Gedankenvorgänge*], through the Pcs. (to which, indeed, it in part belongs) to consciousness. But it comes up against the censorship. . . . At this point it takes on the distortion for which the way has already been paved by the transference of the wish on to the recent material. . . . Its further advance is halted, however, by the sleeping state of the preconscious. (The probability is that the system has protected itself against the invasion by diminishing its own excitations.) The dream-process [*Traumvorgang*] consequently enters on a regressive path, which lies open to it precisely owing to the peculiar nature of the state of sleep, and is led along that path by the attraction exercised on it by groups of memories. . . . In the course of its regressive path the dream-process acquires the attribute of representability. (*S.E.*, V, 573–74)

The trajectory leading from perceptions and wishes to dreams is indeed, as Freud specifies, a "zigzag journey" (*seines mehrmals geknickten Verlaufes*). Soon after this passage, Freud offers the qualification that the steps here described sequentially may actually take place simultaneously (*S.E.*, V, 576). The topographical areas of consciousness implicit in this blow-by-blow description (the primitive emanations of the id, the ego, and the superego) thus behave like excitable and possessive warlords. For each thrust of the repressed material toward consciousness, another stage (or agency) is ready with a parry.

This passage encompasses no less than three of the major mechanisms or strategies available to the unconscious. The potentially damaging wish advances itself by hiding among the subject's freshest experiences and associations. In the above passage this fundamentally metaphoric link is described as a transference (literally, *Übertragung* is a carrying-over), but in the wider Freudian parlance this dissimulation is an instance of displacement. No sooner is the displacement from wish to readily available material effected than it is opposed by a censorship that embodies the structure of opposition itself. Not content with the shift sideways in transference and the head-on collision of censorship, however, the scenario outlined in the above passage offers yet a third variety of action: movement backwards. The compromising wish, having been *displaced* to the misleading realm of ready-made associations and *blocked* in the interest of etiquette, "enters the regressive path" afforded by the dream.

Displacement, repression (censorship), and regression are thus the conceptual correlatives to the directional possibilities of movement: sideways, in opposition, and backwards. If displacement effects a metaphoric shift, repression and regression arise from the domain of dialectical logic. The deadlock resulting from repression is no less logical than libidinal. Repression merely actualizes the reverse movement implicit in any progressive scenario. Given the metaphoric dominance attached to the image of streams in Freud's work, it is highly paradoxical that one of the liberties ascribed to the dreamwork should be a systematic retraction of progress.

In its variegated usages, displacement incorporates the very lateral shifts that it denotes. As suggested in the first lengthy Freudian passage that we considered, displacement's primary function in *The Interpretation of Dreams* and the early works is as a shifter of values. By means of under- and overvaluation, the displacement of the dreamwork shields the disconcerting aspect of the dream-thought from detection by the censor (*S.E.*, IV, 307–8; V, 531). By the time of the *Metapsychological Papers,* displacement has increased its conceptual range in becoming the *substitutive* mechanism within a hypothetically unlimited matrix of associations.

> As a substitute for him [the father] we find in a corresponding place some animal which is more or less fitted to be an object of anxiety. The formation of the substitute for the ideational portion . . . has come about by *displacement* along a chain of associations which is determined in a particular way. The quantitative portion has not vanished, but has been transformed into anxiety. The result is fear of a wolf, instead of a demand of love from the father. ("Repression," *S.E.*, XIV, 155)

If this is a wider notion of displacement than prevails in *The Interpretation of Dreams,* this is not so merely because there are more potential substitutes than intensities but because the revised version has broken with the notion of quantity in general. In *The Interpretation of Dreams,* "displacement" is above all a quantitative term, regulating the measure of psychic intensity. The displacement by which a father becomes a wolf, by which the *love demanded* from the father becomes the *fear evoked by* the wolf, takes place on the organizational and structural, rather than the quantitative, level. It is only a stone's throw from the general substitutive economy of displacement in Freud's later works to the notion of deferred affect and the repetition of the primal scene. The conception of displacement as the general principle of substitution for objects, impulses, and, for that matter, quantities is merely a spatialized version of a displacement—or deferral—that "takes place" in time. Already in *The Interpretation of Dreams* Freud specifies that "a humiliation that was experienced thirty years ago acts exactly like a fresh one throughout the thirty years, as soon as it has obtained access to the unconscious sources of emotion" (*S.E.*, V. 578)—and this is merely a primitive forerunner of the mechanisms of deferral worked out in the analysis of the "Wolf Man" case (*S.E.*, XVII, 43–45, 57, 58, 107–9, 112). One could argue, then, that in the course of its internal metamorphosis, Freudian displacement approaches the general exchange characterized by Saussurian signification.[21]

To lay such stress upon an apparent broadening within displacement overlooks, however, a curious coincidence, that for Freud in 1915 as well as ten years earlier the tactics of displacement are integrally linked to the scenario of repression. In the case of repression, the peculiar literality that images and associations attain in dreams extends to the Freudian terminology. The psychoanalytical term "repression" seldom ranges far from the figure of the censor which Freud has summoned as an illuminating example. On the manifest level, repression seems to oppose displacement: displacement defends by camouflage what repression would squelch or efface. Yet tactically, repression and displacement are on the intimate terms that prevail between organized crime and the police. It is no accident that metaphors of political and mythical upheaval surface when Freud characterizes repression. The unconscious wishes that activate the dream-work, "held under repression" (*Verdrängung*), "remind one of the legendary Titans, weighed down since primaeval ages by the massive bulk of the mountains which were hurled upon them by the victorious gods and which are still shaken from time to time by the convulsions of their limbs" (*S.E.*, V. 553). Only a few belated and uncanny twitches escape the control of repression.

In comparison with repression, displacement might seem one endless and uncontrollable convulsion, but Freud makes no effort to conceal the collusion between the terms. Another of the political similes from *The Interpretation of Dreams* has repression assuming the basic function assigned to displacement at this stage of Freud's work. In describing the aura of uncertainty in which the dream is often retrospectively enshrouded, Freud compares this mode of repression to "the state of things . . . after some sweeping revolution in one of the republics of antiquity or of the Renaissance."

> The noble and powerful families which had previously dominated the scene were sent into exile and all the high offices were filled by newcomers. Only the most impoverished and powerless members of the vanquished families, or their remote dependents, were allowed to remain in the city; and even so they did not enjoy full civic rights and were viewed with mistrust. (*S.E.*, V, 516)

In this instance, the exile of compromising thoughts is in the service of repression, but the form of this tyranny is precisely the misvaluation previously attributed to displacement. The survival of the meanest relatives in the dream, as in the city, belongs to the quantitative accounting of displacement.

The location of the bizarre distortions of displacement within the domain of repressive control is nowhere more explicit than in *Jokes and Their Relation to the Unconscious* (1905). In this text, the cooperation between displacement and repression in dreams is so strong that Freud must sever jokes from dreams altogether. "As we know, the displacements in the dream-work point to the operation of the censorship of conscious thinking, and accordingly, when we come across displacement among the techniques of jokes, we shall be inclined to suppose that an inhibitory force plays a part in the formation of jokes as well" (*S.E.*, VIII, 171). In this formula, the relation between displacement and repression is so direct (pointing) that we can scarcely imagine any conflict between them. In the joke-work, on the other hand, displacements are relegated to a "subordinate place." "For jokes do not, like dreams, create compromises; they do not evade the inhibition, but they insist on maintaining play with words or with nonsense unaltered" (*S.E.*, VIII, 172). Even for Freud, then, the "relief" and economy achieved by the joke-technique are of a radically different order from the joint cooperation between displacement and repression. What liberates the joke from the displacement and censorship of the dream is precisely condensation, the undirected play of words and "unaltered" nonsense that are autonomous from subjective intentions and aims.

Our discussion to this point suggests that our first two entries in the Freudian grammar, displacement and repression, are inextricably bound to a dualistic scenario in which certain energies attempt to circumvent the control of a censor. It is significant that the agent of repression is a censor, whose official function within the state of the mind is readership, but only in the interest of authoritarian control. The role of the censor within Freud's intrapsychic elements is that of a subject before the subject. The censor is a mentalistic homunculus, exhibiting the characteristics of subjectivity in advance of subject formation.[22] The potentially unlimited range of displacement in Freud's early work is held in check by a preexisting mental scenario of repression. Ultimately, in the alternation of surveillance and ruse, displacement and repression cancel each other out.

Blocked in an oppositional stalemate, the Freudian current of psychic energy revives its flow by reversing direction and flowing backwards, where the past is ostensibly located. This retrograde movement is at once a release and a defeat, an escape from stasis and a retreat.

The only way in which we can describe what happens in hallucinatory dreams is by saying that the excitation moves in a *backward* direction. Instead of being transmitted towards the *motor* end of the apparatus it moves towards the *sensory* end and finally reaches the perceptual system. If we describe as 'progressive' the direction taken by psychical processes arising from the unconscious during waking life, then we may speak of dreams as having a 'regressive' character. (*S.E.*, V, 542)

Instead of flowing *away* from the unconscious, nervous energy in regression flows backwards through the systems of perception and memory *toward* it.

Like displacement, regression is a multivalent term. Just as displacement tampered with the intensity with which impressions are endowed in dream-representation, regression is a shifter between ideas and sensory images. "We call it 'regression' when in a dream an idea is turned back into the sensory image from which it was originally derived. . . . *In regression the fabric of the dream-thoughts is resolved into its raw material*" (*S.E.*, V, 543). Regression transforms ideas, abstract constructions, into the "raw material" of sense data, from which they were *derived*. Implicit in this scenario is not only an *evolution*, from the sensory to the cognitive, but a morality. In the mind's normative state, its neurological paths are *unidirectional*. "Regression, wherever it may occur, is an effect of a resistance opposing the progress of a thought into consciousness along the normal path, and of a simultaneous attraction exercised upon the thought by the presence of memories possessing great sensory force" (*S.E.*, V, 547).

In this latter formulation, the constellation of mechanical, logical, and normative presuppositions surrounding repression converge. In its mechanics, the mind corresponds to a circuit of electromagnetic charges and attractions. That regression occurs in the aftermath of an obstruction and is therefore a last resort endows it with a necessity equal to that of forward progress. The regressive pathway owes its form to the inhibited progression: it duplicates the narrative sequence, only in reverse order. The product of this negative evolution is a substance more primal and reliable than the abstract component of dreams. If not in the service of the censor, regression is oriented toward an entity no less primordial: the essence of sensation. Freudian regression thus entertains a Sense-Certainty that Hegel merely posits.

If displacement and repression establish a basis for logical negation within the grammar of consciousness, regression is Freud's primary vehicle for a temporal metaphysics of progress, evolution, and recurrence. Implicit in this scenario is the existence of aboriginal mental strata and structures. This capacity to revert toward the unconscious through the dreams and memories constitutes the very possibility for the repetition of (primal) scenes and justifies the use of the scene as a cognitive unit.

Each in a different way, then, our first three entries in the Freudian grammar of consciousness reinstate the authority and metaphysical aspirations ostensibly suspended by the dream-work. The fundamental discrepancy between the grammatical claims and the metaphysical residue of these terms explains why *Jokes and Their Relation to the Unconscious* occupies a unique position among all of Freud's writings, not merely among his early works. This is the only work dominated by the economy of condensation, which is the single Freudian trope that resists a regression into metaphysical terms. To be sure, condensation is merely one joke-technique alongside an ample list of others. But in *Jokes and Their Relation to the Unconscious* the remaining joke-techniques are predicated on the verbal distortions exemplified by condensation, whereas in Freud's contemporary writings condensation is merely one minor figure challenging repression. Freud repeatedly characterizes the order of condensation as an economy, as an ellipsis or pooling of resources whose concentration permits a sudden release of energy. As we will observe, however, the domain of condensation could just as well be described as a poetics, for the hybrids effected by this trope perform a variety of figurative functions. *Jokes and Their Relation to the Unconscious* opens a new and perhaps singular qualitative horizon in Freud's work not only because of its sustained wit but because it does not compromise the grammatical and linguistic bent of condensation. Both an exception to the direction pursued by Freud's other works and an exemplification of how psychoanalysis arose within a clinical setting, this work declares and forges its own genre.

Because the "relief" provided by the joke is always in opposition to something, *Jokes and Their Relation to the Unconscious* cannot be characterized as completely evading the scenario of repression. Nevertheless, even if the subcategory of joking ultimately capitulates to a wider model of subjectivity, this in no way denies the dominance of verbal play within the joke itself. In summarizing the techniques accessible to the joke-work in a manner consistent with his self-avowed formalism, Freud composes what is in effect a catalogue of poetic figures of speech:

> Let us therefore try to summarize them [joke-techniques]:
> I. Condensation:
>   (*a*) with formation of composite word,
>   (*b*) with modification.

II. Multiple use of the same material:
    (*c*) as a whole and in parts,
    (*d*) in a different order,
    (*e*) with slight modification,
    (*f*) of the same words full and empty.
III. Double meaning:
    (*g*) meaning as a name and thing,
    (*h*) metaphorical and literal meanings,
    (*i*) double meaning proper (play upon words),
    (*j*) *double entendre*,
    (*k*) double meaning with an allusion. (*S.E.*, VIII, 41–42)

Although endowed with the simplistic organization of a list, this miniature poetics of the joke is a complex machine, with several conflicting lines of subordination. The fundamental unit of the joke (and therefore of the entire linguistic facet of Freud's writings) is the composite word (*Mischwort*) made possible by condensation. Double meaning (*Doppelsinn*) and multiple use (*Verwendung des nämlichen Materials*), while ostensibly of the same order as condensation, merely elaborate the poetic potentials of the composite word.

The composite word that is the product of condensation is itself a metaphor. The joke is above all a metaphor whose outlines emerge through the free play of language. The marginal economy of verbal play in Freud's work is dominated by this figure. The variations on the joke for which Freud's catalogue also provides are supplemental to metaphor. As a combiner of opposites, the joke completes the task of oxymoron; as a scrambler of sequences, it effects hysteron proteron; the joke's counterprocesses of fragmentation and unification perform oxymoron; the unanticipated substitutions that the joke offers are metonymic. Yet all these tropes are addenda to the fundamentally metaphoric base of the joke-work. One category of joke ostensibly kills the metaphor by literalizing it; but this assault, which confuses the vehicle for the tenor, merely emphasizes the metaphoricity not only of the joke but of Freud's entire grammatical enterprise.

Jokes are akin to such other manifestations of the unconscious as dreams and slips in the sense that they arise within an unlimited latticework of associations. Yet of all the products of the unconscious, the joke is the only one that does not submit to diagnosis and is irreducible to pathology. Dreams, for all their associative complexity, ultimately yield themselves to an interpretation whose coordinates derive from a predetermined model of the subject and from preconceptions of subjective efficiency. To be sure, Freud *records* jokes with great dexterity: he infers their submerged sexual content and

extrapolates their wider social purposes. Yet jokes resist interpretation in the sense that the term is applied to dreams because even by
Freud's admission, they are not subjective in the same personal way.
Jokes are depersonalized because they inhabit a domain where linguistic processes ignore the imperatives of volition. Freud places jokes
in a socio-psychological sphere quite alien to the melodramatic setting
of hysterical episodes and dreams because they function as amend-
ments to the linguistic social contract described by Saussure.[23]
Dreams recur and evolve, but the modes of their conscious rationalization are quite finite. There is no horizon for the proliferation of
jokes because the key to their signification is by definition uncodified.
A sibling of metaphor, the joke inhabits the only realm of undirected
condensation charted by Freud.

Our preliminary examination of the strategically self-defeating linguistic project in Freud places us in a position to assess the indebtedness of Freud's grammar of jokes, dreams, and the unconscious to a
particularly close reading of Goethe's *Faust*. If the categories of displacement, repression, regression, and condensation may be taken as
a blueprint for the initial design of the Freudian project, *Faust* serves
as a veritable textbook for these activities. In relation to an exemplary
Romantic artifact such as *Faust*, Freudian approaches that were by
clinical standards inconceivable become, if not predictable, less mirac-
ulous. In its tortured attitude toward language, *Faust* serves as an
antecedent to Freudian strategies in another sense. Within Goethe's
drama, language is both the form of all desire and the nature of
everything contemptible and suspicious. So self-contradictory is the
attitude toward language in this text that its trajectory runs the full
circle from seduction to the aversion of reaction-formation. If the
Freudian grammar of consciousness becomes a subjective metaphysics with a linguistic margin under the rubric of condensation, this
development has a precedent in the Faustian allures and threats of
language.

In its widest dimensions and structures, *Faust* rehearses the oppositions that become so crucial to the Freudian topography and to the
interaction between the conscious and the unconscious.[24] *Faust I* is an
existential melodrama that plays itself out within the medium of the
passive feminine subjectivity ascribed to Margaret. The drama's first
half measures, in existential terms, in terms of the metaphysical conceptions attending Christian existence, the impact of the negativity
for which Faust yearns and which Mephistopheles personifies. As the
text specifies, this negativity has two forms, one of moral anomie and
one of textual involution. The initial theater for the opposition be-

tween, on the one hand, reason, morality, and divine grace and, on the other, confusion and depravity is Faust's study. At stake are the conditions of the pact by which Faust assumes, as in the sense of a debt, Mephistopheles' negativity.

This opposition reiterates itself not only in the moral conflict faced by Margaret (and secondarily by Marthe) but also within the drama's stage machinery. The topsy-turvy world represented in the Witches' Kitchen and *Walpurgisnacht* scenes is a dramatic correlative to Mephistophelean negativity. *Faust I* is dominated by an economy of opposition whose atmospheric details lend themselves remarkably easily to the Freudian split between the conscious and unconscious levels. What I am suggesting is that in *Faust,* as in Kierkegaard's writings, the structure of opposition and the existential sphere go hand in hand. Internal conflict is the essence of the existential limits portrayed so poignantly by Gretchen. It comes as no surprise, then, that as the tableaux of *Faust II* move away from the domain of existential melodrama, the role of oppositions, figural as well as dramatic, diminishes markedly. In the wake of *Faust I,* for example, Faust and Mephistopheles become fellow travelers rather than adversaries in a highly pitched battle over the soul.

In its suspension of specific conflicts and the dramatic unities, *Faust II* may be said to relate to *Faust I* as the dream-work does to waking activity. *Faust II* places in a dominant position the forms of anomie and confusion that in *Faust I* were granted exceptional status, that is, were confined to incidental scenes of negativity. Indeed, the scenic progression in both parts of *Faust* has the disjointed quality that Freud assigns to dreams. Yet in *Faust II* not only the format but the ideology of enlightenment is relegated to a subordinate status.

In its basic dramatic interactions, its *mise en scène,* and in the connections between its structural units, *Faust* belongs to the scenario of repression, with its implicit attempt to befuddle the censor by displacement. The two climactic events within a dramatic framework that may well encompass only *Faust I* are seductions. As Kierkegaardian seducers, Mephistopheles in relation to Faust and Faust in relation to Margaret play at liberating their quarry from their predetermined scruples and inhibitions. This repressive conflict between a certain idealism and anomie takes place both within the minutiae of the play's imagery and on the widest level. This opposition displaces itself freely from setting to setting and from level to level of generality. We have already observed a recurrence of Mephistophelean negativity in various settings in *Faust I.* Similarly, certain of the decisive events of *Faust I* receive phantasmatic treatments in *Faust II:* Faust's initial contract with Mephistopheles becomes the emperor's instituting a paper-based economy; the seduction and abandonment of Gretchen is metamorphosed into a mythopoetic union between Faust and Helen of Troy.

The repression making *Faust* a prototype for the Freudian enterprise takes place on a level even more specific and persistent than that of the play's structural units. Throughout the duration of the play, the metaphors of weaving, plaiting, and braiding dramatize a certain negative capability harbored by the play as a text. While *Faust* suffers from little ambiguity in representing the existential threat posed by moral and theological anomie, its ambivalence toward its own linguistic capabilities is severe. *Faust* transpires from text to text. The curtain rises on a hero stultified from a lifetime spent among books, in the pursuit of learned disciplines. The Faust who yearns for an escape from the self-enclosed textual domain of his study has adopted an attitude that, as Jacques Derrida has demonstrated, is ingrained in the Western tradition whose depths he will plumb.[25] Not merely a repository of writing, Faust's library is a dungeon, a tomb, a charnel house of morbidity. Paradoxically, however, when in the course of the play Faust confronts the dynamic activity for which he longed from the prison of his library, this ferment is couched in terms of a rhetoric of textual activity: weaving, spinning, and knotting. The play's relation to its own language is thus repressive. Linguistic activity is both a form of death and an allure, as fundamental as the geology of Greece, as beautiful as Helen of Troy. This markedly ambivalent attitude toward language is the most emotional interest that Goethe and Freud share.

The single most dominant gesture performed by the text of *Faust* is an exploitation for spiritual purposes of activities couched in the specifically nonmetaphysical terms of inscription and involution. The play's textual metaphors arise in opposition to an economy of divine reason, volition, and illumination based on the figure of the sun. Barely do these nonteleological figures enter the action, however, when they are assigned a spiritual meaning and purpose.

For Goethe as well as Freud, the optimal condition for physical and mental well-being is an unobstructed flow of force. In Goethe, the primal energy issues from a divine source, but its qualities have a distinctly Freudian ring.

> Freed from the ice are brooks [*Strom*] and rivers
> By spring's enchanting, enlivening gaze;
> The valley is blithe with hope's green haze;
> Hoary winter with senile shivers
> Back to his mountain lair withdrew.
> Thence he flings, shorn of his powers
> Granules of ice. . . .

The sun, however, allows no white,
All is astir with shaping and striving [*Bildung und Streben*],
All he would dower with hues and enliven. . . .

See how the gate's dark cave exudes
Teeming colorful multitudes.
All seek the sun with glad accord,
They exult in the rising of the Lord [*die Auferstehung des Herrn*];
For they are resurrected themselves,
Freed from the shackles of shops and crafts,
From shifty dwellings like narrow shelves,
From smothering roofs and gable lofts,
From the city streets with their smothering press . . .
They have all been raised to light.
Look, look, how nimbly the human crest
Breaks and surges [*wie behend sich die Menge*
Durch die Garten und Felder zerschlagt,
Wie der Fluß . . .] (*Faust*, ll. 902–31)

This famous speech by Faust introduces the theme of the relentless movement that spells the play's existential tragedy. The single term specified by Mephistopheles in the pact, an acceptance of this indifferent motion, is, of course, the crushing outcome that Faust must confront as he abandons Gretchen in all her human vulnerability. The above lyric is also notable as the play's most powerful and specific articulation of its economy of the sun.[26] Within these lines, God and nature are coordinated. The solar heat and illumination that cause the spring and motivate nature also describe the spiritual destiny of mankind. There is a direct correlation between the freeing of the frozen brooks and the teleological fulfillment of men, whose collectivity also forms the image of a current or flow.

The positive forces that will be diverted, displaced, and perverted by a combination of moral depravity and textual involution are concentrated in the economy of the sun. As the matrix of an inherently salutary shaping and striving, the economy of the sun occupies a place analogous to that held by the Freudian instincts. In Faust's lines, the tide of humanity emerges from a restraint and sterility that are quite similar to his own predicament. Faust's vision of the hoard of rejuvenated believers redeems the limits of his own situation and describes a reconciliation from which he is excluded. In the above passage, the conditions of urban life are the whipping boy for the order and expectations maintained by the economy of the sun, but in the play's first lines Faust's imprisonment is that of a jaded reader.

The drama's chief paradox is that in order to characterize the diabolical forces in conflict with the economy of the sun, Goethe repeatedly resorts to a textual rhetoric of weaving. No sooner does he deploy this metaphoric, however, than he places it at the disposal of the ideology of divine purpose and redemption. Images of complication and involution enter the discourse as an appealing but forbidden fruit, only to be reinvested with spiritual meaning. This occurs twice in the play's opening lines. Contemplating the design (*Zeichen*) of the Macrocosm, Faust describes his body and soul as textual networks of energy. A "reincandescent" life joy (*Lebensglück*) courses "through vein and nerve." For all the passage's references to communicative as well as organic networks, however, the sign grounds a unity of action and life: "Wie alles sich zum Ganzen webt,/Eins in dem andern wirkt und lebt" (11. 430–48). Similarly, the spirit who speaks only a few lines later characterizes its own activity in explicitly textual terms.

> In tides of living, in doing's storm,
> Up and down I wave [*walle*],
> Waft to and fro [*webe*],
> Birth and grave,
> An endless flow [*Meer*],
> A changeful plaiting [*Weben*]. (11. 501–6)

No sooner is this uniquely poetic tumult presented, however, than it is historicized and theologized: "Thus at Time's scurrying loom I weave and warp/ And broider at the Godhead's living garb" (11. 509–10). Threatening in its own right, the textual play of weaving must be rehabilitated. It redeems itself by serving as the origin of time and by producing the garments of a God alive with presence. In complete contrast, the devil (or the unconscious) succeeds by seduction; it exercises the force and dynamics of language; it assumes the form of a book. Again and again, however, this restricted but irresistible book, this inevitable pornographic interlude in the life of the spirit, is fitted to a spiritual use. The rhetoric of textual weaving dominates the supernatural settings and Mephistophelean exhibitions of both segments of the play. The ultimate harnassing of this dramatized textual process implies that even the most diabolical (or in *Faust II*, diffuse) scenes belong to the economy of the sun.

It is with regard to the various activities of condensation that we can best gauge Freud's contribution not only to the history of medicine but also to the realm of letters. Although joke-condensation delineates a space in which linguistic processes resist reflexive assumptions and configurations, those activities in *Faust* that approximate condensation participate fully within the play's historical and teleological programs. In a passage from *Jokes and Their Relation to the Unconscious* already cited (pp. 175–76), Freud lists the metaphoric, metonymic, oxymoronic, and synecdochical qualities of the joke. If *Faust* is anything, it is a work keyed to certain powerful metaphors, notably of the sun, streams, and weaving. Yet the sun, as has been noted, comprises not merely a figure of speech but an entire metaphysical order, while the image of the text-within-the-text is compulsively bound to the drama of the redemption of the soul. Even the metonymic displacement of these metaphors to wildly divergent settings enforces the dominance of a ubiquitous subject (or subject matter) in the play.

As a reader of *Faust,* Freud could well have found a precedent for the synecdochical distortions of jokes in the play's repeated contrasts between the Microcosm and the Macrocosm. In the desperation of his self-enclosed textual existence Faust consults the sign of the Macrocosm (11. 447–53), and Mephistopheles disdainfully places humanity on the scale of the Microcosm (11. 1349, 1780). But for all the play's concern for the interaction between the part and the whole, both as a theoretical problem and within its own construction, it never relinquishes its orientation toward a coordinated and organic totality. It is in this sense that the world, for all the disparate fragments woven under the sign of the Macrocosm, is filled with "harmonies" (11. 450–53).

The play's macrocosmic totality similarly prohibits its oppositions from ever becoming the composite words, often linking opposites, produced by the joke-work. While jokes whimsically bond opposites, *Faust* never abandons a program of unity-in-opposition. Mephistophelean irreverence is symmetrically coordinated to the assertions that power the economy of the sun. Desire is systematically distributed to matched pairs. The pairing of Mephistopheles and Marthe parodically reiterates the seduction scene between Faust and Gretchen. The union of Faust and Helena is a phantasmatic comment upon the same love story. Like the primal monsters that fill the *Walpurgisnachtstraum,* opposition in *Faust* never matures; it never explores the potentials of asymmetrical oxymoron.

Faust thus offers us a rare view of what Freud *took over* from Romantic literature and what he contributed. The play seems to predicate the psychosexual division of labor between ego, id, and superego, but doesn't quite. To be sure, a primal force underlying all growth and activity operates in the work, but the solar energy corresponding to the id also has divine sanction, that is, it is already subordinate to the superego. Generically, the detached lyric, often appearing at the beginning of the scene, is Goethe's medium for this primal but also divine force. The play's dramatic interaction, on the other hand, belongs to the sphere of the ego, the arena and arbiter of opposition. If the economy of the sun is a monument to the control and rectitude of the superego, the play's representations of negation and play occupy the domain of the ego. The personal temptations confronted by Faust, Gretchen, and Marthe in *Faust I*, and on a societal level by the general audience in *Faust II*, parallel egoistic conflicts. Yet the work's representations of play also share the characteristics of the limited satisfaction that the ego affords.

Play is invariably sanctioned in *Faust*, that is, it is calibrated according to the interests of a wider system. If ethereal lyrics, spoken from a perspective of broad generality, comprise an exemplary medium for the interests of the superego, doggerel and naively allegorical insertions satisfy the conditions for a play sanctioned but limited by an overall control. The *Walpurgisnachtstraum* may consist of pointed and often witty fragments whose sequence is often alogical or arbitrary, but Goethe rigorously maintains the metrical and rhythmical schemes of the four-line stanzas into which the speeches are divided. Similarly, the songs inserted into *Faust I* seem to offer whimsical diversions from the dramatic action both generically and in terms of the subject matter that they introduce. Yet these songs (the "rat" and "flea" songs in Auerbach's tavern and Gretchen's lament of the cup are good examples)[27] invariably allegorize, in a straightforward manner, the events and predicaments of the driving "action."

If repression is the primary activity of the superego, then displacement, regression, and condensation belong to the egoistic sphere of *Faust*. Freud diverges from the primitive blueprint of his system sketched in *Faust* because he frees the activities of condensation from the interests of control, measure, or compromise. There is no place for the id in *Faust*: in the economy of the sun the id is conflated with the superego. Freud provides for a play activity that breaks the gravitational field exerted by the spirit or psyche. The joke is precisely the Freudian mechanism that gives access to the energies of the id. The joke is Freud's monument to the play of the id, a revelry extricated from *Faust*'s margins, despite Goethe's numerous attempts to represent counterfeit, that is, controlled, varieties of play. As a counterfeiter of play, Goethe is the dramatic equivalent of his own uncircumspect emperor.

Freud violated the clinic because he lavished upon it the fruits of nineteenth-century esthetics. Not only did Freud *import* esthetic considerations but, by means of the joke, he isolated linguistic terms from their place within a subjective economy. He thus tested the limits of Romantic coordination, even if he never definitively superseded them.

[III]

THE NEUROTIC AS DERANGED PHILOSOPHER

Circle of fire! Whirl round, circle of fire! Whirl round!
                    E.T.A. Hoffmann, "The Sandman"

The only subject present in Freud's grammatical enterprise is a residue of personality attached to a metaphor, a subject implicitly inhabiting a figural stream. The birth of the Freudian subject, the literalization of a figurative potential for subjectivity, and the delineation of an identifiable subjective sphere still take place during the breakthroughs of the great early works. But once these advances have occurred, the grammar of consciousness and its key trope, condensation, are fated to a tangential role within the Freudian enterprise, effaced by the regulated operation of a subject machine.

It is in the *Three Essays on the Theory of Sexuality* (1905) that a sequence of psychosexual developments is superimposed upon the fundamentally spatial and synchronic grammar of cognition. The child is the offspring of this merger, the first Freudian entity both functionally articulated and equipped to develop in the stream of time. But what is asserted at the outset of Wordsworth's *Ode on Intimations of Immortality* only bears more weight in the Freudian system. The child of the *Three Essays* is not only the father but also the first draft of the Freudian adult. As characterized in the *Three Essays*, childhood is a normative category, consisting in a sequence of exemplary stages in the management of sexual energy.[28] Childhood defines the nature, physiological loci, and fate of erotogenic impulses. As opposed to adulthood, where many variables enter, childhood is reducible to a sequence of optimal moments in the evolution of the sexual force, including orality, anal-sadism, latency, and the object-choice following puberty.

The adult, in both the general and most specific senses, is the result of the problem in energy management faced by the child. As Freud freely admits, the path of optimal development is a narrow one, so inaccessible that it exists more as a logical extreme than as an available alternative. "Neurosis" is Freud's blanket term for the dysfunctions that emanate from the matrix of childhood. The malfunctions of neurosis occur both internally, within the coordination of the various mental operations comprising the subject, and sequentially, in deviating from the optimal train of events. In almost necessarily violating the exemplary coordination of functions and trajectory of steps defined by childhood, the Freudian adult is condemned to a life of neurosis. The virtually unavoidable necessity of neurosis brings Freud close to the sense of degradation, prior loss, and belatedness that colors so many of the major projects of modernism from Yeats to Eliot and Pound.

It is hoped that our exploration into the grammatical organization of Freud's early works has shed some illumination upon the constituents of Freudian subjectivity. Our concern now shifts to the *derivation* of the properties of the neuroses, which in turn determine the course of adult experience. Our direction of pursuit is analogous to the one followed in the preceding section: just as in synthesizing a cognitive grammar Freud needed little more than to import certain scenarios from Romantic literature, in elaborating the neuroses he appealed to standard procedures of philosophical speculation, as they were assembled and formalized by such a writer as Hegel. As malfunctions or derangements, the neuroses play upon and adjust the normative procedures of bifurcation, reciprocity, internalization, externalization, and circularization. The neuroses register themselves as black marks upon the virginally white curtain issuing from these time-honored philosophical conventions. The neurotic is a deranged philosopher because his or her delusions, tricks, and sufferings consist of standard philosophical procedures imported to the subjective sphere, where they are carried just a bit too far. It is, as we shall see, in the nature of both subjectivity and philosophy that this simple process of application should invariably result in a disaster, and one on a minor or domestic scale.

The close affinity between the norms of philosophy as codified by Hegel and the neuroses suggests that what is useful for the philosopher is unhealthy for the subject; that what is reassuring for the subject stifles the philosopher. The relation between philosophy and psychoanalysis might be simply adversarial were it not for the bizarre appetite of a third party, the critic. From Nietzsche to Heidegger and Derrida, the occupier of the critical position assimilates the poisonous by-products of both systems and makes sense of an intolerable impasse. Underlying the refinement of philosophy, the critic is willing to intuit irony and rage; in the pain of the personal agony familiar to us all the critic discerns the lineaments of systematic speculation. In mixing poisons the critic only increases uncertainty, but it is in this toxic environment that neurosis and philosophical procedure enter communication.

It is precisely in the figure of the child that the neurotic traits which in the *Studies on Hysteria* and *The Interpretation of Dreams* are arranged spatially and lexicographically intersect with an evolutionary model of development. By positing an exemplary sequence of developments in the child and adolescent, Freud is able to locate the genesis of neurosis at specific strategic moments. In the *Studies on Hysteria*, what Breuer terms "splitting of the mind" (*S.E.*, II, 222–39), a simple extension of the Hegelian bifurcation, functions as an inevitable landmark upon the mental topology of neurotics. "*The splitting of consciousness which is so striking in the well-known cases under the form of 'double conscience' is present to a rudimentary degree in every hysteria*," write Freud and Breuer jointly in their "Preliminary Communication" (*S.E.*, II, 12). The splitting of consciousness is a convenient mechanism for characterizing the mind's aversion to "incompatible" ideas. A wide range of symptoms, whether amnesia, "hypnotic states," or anxiety, can all be explained by the mind's splitting itself off from, repressing, or excluding what is unconscionable to it (*S.E.*, II, 167; III, 46–47). Hysterical conversion constitutes a *symbolically determined* shift of the traumatic origin to "abnormal" reflexes or somatic phenomena (*S.E.*, II, 206, 209).

The formal process of bifurcation exists in the *Studies on Hysteria* as a "rudiment," a static trait applicable to every case. But by the *Three Essays on the Theory of Sexuality*, the logic of bifurcation has been incorporated into an evolutionary framework. In their new emanations, opposition and splitting are not simply taken as givens; they accompany the decisive post-puberty crisis centered on the choice of a sexual object. The split mind is not an ongoing fact but a phenomenon brought into play by a choice-situation itself involving discriminations of identity and difference. Freud's positing a sexual choice-situation continues a line running from Hegel's Antigone through Kierkegaard's "Judge William." The choice of a sexual object is both *reflexive* and *deterministic:* it reflects the primal configuration of the family and determines the sexual courses of action open to the subject. The decisive moment of object-choice is both born in and fated to opposition. It arises out of the logic of bifurcation, the epistemological division between the subject and the object, and the physics of the attraction and revulsion. Yet this crucial act gives rise to a range of diseases and dysfunctions—for example, hysteria, obsessional neuroses, paranoia—that are themselves to be diagnosed according to logical and subjective affinity and incompatibility.

Dualism, the logic of bifurcation, thus runs a full course in Freud's work. At the beginning, it is the very nature of consciousness. As

Freud moves toward conceptual frameworks that are not only more dynamic but also more subject-oriented, he marshals entire sets of instincts in opposition to one another. "The conflicts of feeling in our patient [the "Rat Man"] which we have here enumerated separately were not independent of each other, but were bound together in pairs" (*S.E.*, X, 238). Yet in the overall trajectory of Freud's writing, any neatness of opposition breaks down. Both in the topographical scheme, where the superego precipitates out of the stand-off between the ego and the id, and in the life of the instincts, where, finally, the death instinct and the repetition-compulsion qualify the conflict between the reality and pleasure principles, a factor of asymmetry eradicates the possibility of ongoing dualism. We will have the occasion to observe a final, even consummate dualism in Freud's work: in *Beyond the Pleasure Principle* the dialectical tendencies in Freud's writing join his widest linguistic apprehensions. But even this merger is achieved only by expanding the matrix of dialectics beyond the point of recognition.

We witness the transformation in Freud's work from a tabulated[29] to an internal subjective space at a point in the *Three Essays on the Theory of Sexuality* when infantile sexuality and hysteria are arranged in a parallel configuration.

> The character of erotogenicity can be attached to some parts of the body in a particularly marked way.. . . . The same example [sucking], however, also shows us that any other part of the skin or mucous membrane can take over the functions of an erotogenic zone, and must therefore have some aptitude in that direction. Thus the quality of the stimulus has more to do with producing the pleasurable feeling than has the nature of the part of the body concerned. . . . A precisely analogous tendency to displacement is also found in the symptomology of hysteria. In that neurosis repression affects most of all the actual genital zones and these submit their susceptibility to stimulation to other erotogenic zones (normally neglected in adult life), which then behave exactly like genitals. . . . Erotogenic and hysterogenic zones show the same characteristics. (*S.E.*, VII, 183–84)

In this passage, displacement, which has hitherto functioned as a grammatical heading, steps beyond the frame of a lexicon and enters the human body. Erotic nerve impulses, the raw stuff of sensation, now move through the bodily tissue the way ideas did, in the early works, through the mind. The body thus inherits, in these lines, the subjective qualities of association previously reserved for consciousness. As opposed to the lexicon of hysteria, the body endures in time. The birth of the Freudian subject takes place when the machinery of mentalism is installed in the space of the body, which henceforth houses an evolving consciousness. In a literal sense, the subjectivity made possible by the transfer of mental paths to the body works like a *vehicle:* it moves through time en masse; its internal operations are determined by the grammar of dreams and hysteria.

The decisive events in the temporal development of the Freudian subject are biological: birth, weaning (though rarely explicit in the Freudian parlance, this colors the Oedipal crisis heavily), and puberty. The internal operating principles of the subjective vehicle as it negotiates these great twists of life, are, however, Hegelian in a sense by now familiar. If the Freudian instincts are the great, all-motivating force behind human development, occupying a position analogous to that of Goethe's sun, they are articulated by Hegelian operations as soon as they occupy a corporeal space.

No sooner does a subject known as the child exist than it must choose an object. The finding of an object is endowed with a teleological necessity: it represents the consummation of the preexisting instinctual Force in the subject. Even this inevitable choice is bifurcated:

> It occurs in two waves. The first of these begins between the ages of two and five, and is brought to halt by the latency period; it is characterized by the infantile nature of the sexual aims. The second wave sets in with puberty and determines the final outcome of sexual life.
>
> Although the diphasic nature of object-choice comes down in essentials to no more than the operation of the latency period, it is of the highest importance in regard to disturbances of that final outcome. The resultants of infantile object-choice are carried over into the later period. . . . Their sexual aims have become mitigated and they now represent what may be described as the 'affectionate current' of sexual life. Only psycho-analytic investigation can show that behind this affection, admiration and respect there lie concealed the old sexual longings of the infantile component instincts which have now become unserviceable. The object-choice of the pubertal period is obliged to dispense with the objects of childhood and start afresh as a 'sensual current'. Should these two currents fail to converge, the focusing of all desires upon a single object, will be unattainable. (*S.E.*, VII, 200)

This passage may be read as a thinly disguised Hegelian machine, replete with not only dualistic oppositions but also temporal stages of instinctual assertion, remission, and synthesis. The imperative to choose, one strongly reminiscent of "Judge William"'s ultimatum in the *Or,* imposes an epistemological division of labor upon the new-born subject. Not only is the decision necessary, the correct option is already predetermined. Superimposed upon the epistemology installed within the child is a physics of identity and difference close to the one dominating Hegel's "Force and the Understanding" and ultimately deriving from Plato.[30] As Freud's diagnoses of paranoia will demonstrate, not only must the nascent subject choose, but he or she must choose the object of the opposite gender. Opposition thus decides the "vicissitudes" of the instincts, as well as the *structure* of consciousness.

Not only does the newborn, before awakening, as it were, inherit a logic, an epistemology, and an other-oriented teleology but the stages of its development are arranged in a dialectical sequence. The primacy of the experiences and bondings of early childhood is interrupted by a latency, a negation of desire, allowing some limited scope for realignment. Puberty brings about an *Aufhebung*, a *relève* of this initial passion, but one endowed with the solemnity of a final orientation. Augmented both in specificity and in sense of mission, the consummate sexuality of biological maturity determines the adult's state of being. The passage only underscores the Force of a certain biological triumph when it frames "the focusing of all desires upon a single object," the epitome of fulfillment, amid a synthetic confluence of affection and carnal love.

In ways suggested by the above two passages, Freud endows the subject emerging in the transitional essays between his grammar and his psychology with the activities of Hegelian speculation. The psychoanalytical subject will henceforth be a *field* for the operation of bifurcation, opposition, inversion, substitution, and repetition. "Neurosis" will be the term applied to the major categories of malfunctions in these activities. Because Freud's discourse never exceeds the plane in which these activities operate and are in some sense correctable, he never characterizes such conditions as paranoia and schizophrenia in other than neurotic terms. There is little place in Freud for distortions that challenge the existence as well as the details of reality. All disease, according to Freud, psychotic as well as neurotic, is reducible to indiscretions within the various orders demanded by philosophical discourse.

Although Freud reached a high degree of refinement in diagnosing a wide range of psychological maladies, he never deviates from the assertion that neurotics are made and not born. The writings that precede the *Three Essays on the Theory of Sexuality* are to be admired for the comprehensiveness of their schematic aspirations. Within these works, the various psychological dysfunctions are features initiated by a sexual trauma which are applied to an internal subjective space. Yet the various types of neurosis do not merely relate to essential conditions or symptoms; they are coordinated with each other to encom-

pass all variations made possible by the traumatic situation. Freud is
not merely attempting to characterize and remedy specific illnesses;
he is striving to establish an integrally related diagnostic network
reaching all possible variations on the sexual theme. In this sense, one
condition, let us interpose obsessional neurosis, answers to the logical
possibilities left vacant by, say, hysteria. As important as the manifestations that determine two, instead of one, illnesses is the effort to
synthesize the net that will catch all the fish waiting in the neurotic
sea. Even in the later works, the Freudian discourse never abandons
its schematic aspirations.

One is struck, in such early texts as the *Studies on Hysteria*
(1893–95), "Further Remarks on the Neuro-Psychoses of Defence"
(1896), and "Sexuality in the Aetiology of the Neuroses" (1898) by a
Freudian compulsion to posit and establish distinctions. In keeping
with the division of consciousness into overt and inadmissible components, which is the first fact of sexual life, Freud's distinction-making
tends to play categories off against each other in pairs. In the *Studies*
and "The Neuro-Psychoses of Defence," Freud distinguishes hysteria
from obsessional neuroses, obsession from phobia, and (in practice
for the division between primary and secondary process) neurosis
from neurasthenia. The intellectual calisthenics involved in these
qualifications produces its own distinct form of pleasure, one which
surely edified Freud. Yet apart from rigor, this thought-work also
suggests a collusion between the categories in the interest of territorial
control. The obsessional neuroses *complement* hysteria not only on the
basis of the clinical data that faced Freud but because they account for
certain possibilities left open by hysteria.

The strategies employed by Freud in staking the territorial claims
of the various diseases illustrate his application of philosophical procedures to the internal subjective space. If hysteria results from "sexual traumas" occurring "in early childhood (before puberty)" whose
content "must consist of an actual irritation of the genitals" (*S.E.*, III,
163), the obsessional neuroses could not complement these conditions
more perfectly. As opposed to the hysteric's childhood victimization,
the obsessive neurotic suffers the "self-reproaches" accruing from
active behavior. While the origins of hysteria are rooted in childhood
experience, the "chronological circumstances" of obsession are indeterminate. Despite the pains that Freud takes to cite instances of hysteria in males, the general rhetoric that he synthesizes for this disease
implies that its sufferer is a female with some heterosexual attachments. But the subject of obsessional neurosis is a male showing "a
visible preference for the male sex" (*S.E.*, III, 168–69, for all these
distinctions).

Similarly, obsessions replace measures that once offered "relief" or "protection" from an original inadmissible ("incompatible") idea. Obsessions derive from the same common ground of bifurcated consciousness as hysteria (*S.E.*, III, 77). But in the case of the less dysfunctional phobias, "substitution is no longer the predominant feature; psychological analysis reveals no incompatible, replaced idea in them" (*S.E.*, III, 80). Phobias are possessed of a generality and a predictability that are, in contrast with obsessions, almost reassuring. Deep-rootedness and the sexual origin of the symptoms also become the criteria for a much broader distinction, between neurosis and neurasthenia. The latter rubric embraces an entire set of everyday discomforts, including "intracranial pressure, proneness to fatigue, dyspepsia, constipation, spinal irritation, etc.," that do not derive from the archaeological strata of sexual trauma. "In every case of neurosis there is a sexual aetiology; but in neurasthenia it is an aetiology of a present-day kind" (*S.E.*, III, 268).

All of these diagnostic comparisons are made possible by the application of oppositions, many of which harbor major metaphysical concepts, to the subject. Obsessional neurosis appears in the space on the topographical map vacated by the passivity, the femininity, and the deep-rootedness of hysteria. Phobias and neurasthenias comprise the superficial and everyday versions of the neurotic symptoms with which they might otherwise be confused. Freud's initial diseases, in other words, fill out the graph whose coordinates are the oppositions between sexuality and asexuality, passivity and activity, childhood origin and recent origin, and self-orientation and other-orientation. The neurotic suffers at the points of friction in this machine. The events of his or her past do not accept their temporal remoteness, and recur in the disguised form of symptoms. The optimally self-destroying dependence on a loving parent outlives its usefulness (*S.E.*, VII, 223). The male obsessional neurotic was precociously sexually active; the female hysteric was forced into passive submission during a phase of sexual dormancy.

The conditions treated in Freud's early writings are thus articulated as indiscretions or inconsistencies on the graph formed by complementary pairs. The cooperative relationship between the diseases and the partners in the ubiquitous diametric pairs assures the Freudian enterprise of logical as well as clinical comprehensiveness. Freud's diseases fulfilled the prophecies implicit in the metaphysical categories that he applied to the subject. An all-embracing composite profile of mental dysfunctions, Messianic in its breadth, is a fitting culmination to a metaphysics already contained in the distinctions between activity and passivity, orientation to the selfsame and to the other.

Once the Freudian schematism opens an explicit temporal dimension, in the *Three Essays on the Theory of Sexuality,* no event is more telling in terms of the future of psychoanalytic theory than the moment of object-choice. Hysteria and the obsessive neuroses are both fundamentally diseases of repression. The dysfunctional symptoms, whether anxious (in the case of hysteria) or not, constitute, in a disguised form, "the return of the repressed."[31] Paranoia, because predicated on the crisis of object-choice, is a disease of *projection.* The dynamic scenario of object-choice enables such Hegelian operations as internalization, externalization, and reciprocity, which figure in the background of hysteria and the obsessive neuroses, to become explicit. When the psychoanalytical subject aligns himself with an object that may be self-identical or different, he summons into play virtually the entire metaphysical apparatus framing Hegelian "Understanding." As Freud formulates the Oedipus complex and analyzes the "Rat Man," Daniel Paul Schreber, and the "Wolf Man," the psychoanalytical subject evolves from the divided victim of early sexual abuse into a sophisticated speculative robot who projects and internalizes, pursues elaborate chains of affinity and circles of repetitive behavior.

Two texts that exemplify this conceptual stage in Freud's writing are his "Psycho-Analytic Notes on an Autobiographical Account of a Case of Paranoia" (1911), the Schreber case, and "On Narcissism: An Introduction" (1914). The latter text formalizes, consolidates, and extends the application of certain mechanisms observed in the case histories.

The denouement of the Schreber case occurs when Freud interprets the patient's delusions of persecution and megalomaniacal visions as projected distortions of a repressed homoerotic desire. Underlying this analysis of Schreber's particular symptoms is a theory of the evolution of a homosexual orientation, one presupposing the division between ego-libido and object-libido, between self-directed and other-directed love. The homosexual lingers "unusually long" in narcissism, which Freud defines as "a stage in the development of the ego which it passes through on the way from auto-eroticism to object-love."

Stunted in development, the homosexual takes "himself, his own body, as his love object. . . . Persons who are manifest homosexuals in later life have, it may be presumed, never emancipated themselves from the binding condition that the object of their choice must possess genitals like their own" (*S.E.,* XII, 60–61).

The specific delusions composed by Dr. Schreber, then, rest on a highly structured background. The raw material for Schreber's paranoid constructions is a homosexual disposition itself based on epistemological and teleological predetermination. The subject *must* evolve to the stage of object-choice; the optimal object is the other rather than the same. The particular specifications of paranoia are logically consistent with the mechanisms of evolution and other-orientation that surround the scene of object-choice. Paranoia transforms the proposition "I (a man) love him" into "He *hates* (persecutes) me" by means of a double shift: love becomes hate, and "I" becomes "he" (*S.E.*, XII, 63). The first of these transformations takes place by virtue of the process of inversion of value that Freud has long observed in dreams and associates with displacement. The metamorphosis of love into hate is also strongly reminiscent of the inverse relation that prevails between two levels of generality in Hegelian "Understanding" whenever a leap of abstraction is made.[32]

Paranoia, then, is a layering of dialectical patterns over an already dialectical ground of childhood experience, a phantasmagoria of superimposed speculative vistas. Like childhood, paranoia is also articulated temporally, and its stages of "fixation," "repression proper," and "the return of the repressed" are joined by logical negation just as latency separates infancy from adulthood (*S.E.*, XII, 67–68).

Paranoia is also characterized by the interior/exterior shifts that set the stage for reciprocal interplay. It hovers between the externalization of projection and the internalization of "the detachment of the libido." The paranoid "refers" his suppressed homoerotic desire "to the external world" (*S.E.*, XII, 66). But this displacement outward is accompanied by a concurrent withdrawal inward. The sufferer of paranoia is situated in the locus of Hegelian Appearance, at the agonizing threshold where the outside vanishes into the inside and the self is indistinguishable from the other. The grandiose dimensions of megalomaniacal delusions derive not only from inadmissibility of homosexual desire but also from volatility of paranoia's speculative site.

Crucial to the diagnosis of paranoia, then, are three Hegelian operations: dialectical choice, inversion, and withdrawal. Paranoia is predicated on a mistaken affinity, a choice of the same instead of the opposite. Accruing from this climactic moment is a reversal from an innate heterosexual orientation to a homosexual one. The widest impact of this syndrome of acts and dispositions is a "detachment of the libido," an overall retreat *within*, a complete opting out of the economy determined by the assertion of attractions and desires. Yet so many pathological conditions are defined in terms of this indifference to power and appetite that Freud must endow paranoia with a greater specificity. Freud's attempt at clarification is self-defeating; he refers the disease to an even more general category, narcissism, which is a rubric for all forms of arrested development and failures in other-orientation.

> The detachment of libido, therefore, cannot in itself be the pathogenic factor in paranoia; there must be some special characteristic which distinguishes a paranoic detachment of the libido from other kinds. . . .
> In hysteria the liberated libido becomes transformed into somatic innervations or into anxiety. But in paranoia the clinical evidence goes to show that the libido, after it has been withdrawn from the object, is put to a special use. . . . From this [paranoic traces of megalomania] it may be concluded that in paranoia the liberated libido becomes attached to the ego. . . . A return is thus made to the stage of narcissism . . . in which a person's only sexual object is his own ego. (*S.E.*, XII, 72)

The shift from paranoia to narcissism in the above passage represents a major conceptual broadening in Freud's work. Up until the elaboration of narcissism in the 1914 essay, all psychological disturbances in Freud can be traced back to a specifically sexual scene. "On Narcissism" characterizes as a major neurosis, hypochondria, whose sexual aetiology is tangential; it accounts for certain instances of self-absorption, such as the comedian's, that are not pathogenic. Yet as significant as these departures is the fact that "On Narcissism" completes the reassembly of the Hegelian speculative machine in Freud's work.

Oxymoron is the structure of adult narcissism. In adults, narcissism is a coincidence of biological maturation with ego-libido, the distribution of desire around the ego that Freud ascribes to infancy and early childhood. The narcissist is a medium in which the two extremes of the Freudian evolution of the subject have entered a relation of synchronicity. Because narcissism is a spatial arrangement rather than a simple succession, it belongs neither to the camp of pure self-orientation (ego-libido) nor to that of other-orientation (object-libido), but is an organic amalgam of the two. It is in recognition of the mitigating effect that narcissism has on any cut-and-dry genealogy that Freud writes that "we form the idea of there being an original libidinal cathexis of the ego, from which some is later given off to objects, but which fundamentally persists and is related to the object-cathexes much as the body of an amoeba is related to the pseudopodia which it puts out" (*S.E.*, XIV, 75).

In his speculations on narcissism, Freud arrives at a uniquely organic moment in his work. Just as, in narcissism, the primary phase of ego-libido becomes indistinguishable from the advances of adult life, so too is the border of subjectivity blurred by protoplasmic fluidity. Continually demanding the attentions reserved for the sick, the hypochondriac "withdraws his libidinal cathexes back upon his own ego" (*S.E.*, XIV, 82), like the amoeba gathering up its pseudopodia. Under the magnetic attraction of self-love, the narcissist gazes inward when he would be scanning the outside world. Because this solipsism is in violation of an other-directed ethos, narcissism establishes specular reciprocity. The scene of narcissism requires at least two observers, one gazing inward and one spectator. Because the introspection is always a violation, the invert, who has turned in, is always a potential gazer-back. Narcissism, by virtue of its spatial and temporal equilibriums, transforms Freudian subjectivity into a mirror hall of infinite reflexivity.

Physically, the fluid border state of narcissism is expressed by an equilibrium of centrifugal and centripetal force. The allures of self-love give Freud pause to inquire "what makes it necessary at all for our mental life to pass beyond the limits of narcissism and attach the libido to objects." The answer to this query is itself circular, but it relies on the danger posed by a complete capitulation to the centripetal. "We must begin to love in order not to fall ill, and we are bound to fall ill if, in consequence of frustration, we are unable to love" (*S.E.*, XIV, 85).

In its circularity and its scenario of endless reflection, narcissism injects infinity into the Freudian system, the same infinity that was both the highest production and the ceiling of Hegelian "Understanding." The reciprocal interplay implicit in the scene of self-absorption initiates a chain of surveillance with no logical necessity to terminate.

> Women, especially if they grow up with good looks, develop a certain self-contentment which compensates them for the social restrictions that are imposed upon them in their choice of object. . . . Nor does their need lie in the direction of loving, but of being loved; and the man who fulfils this condition is the one who finds favour with them. The importance of this type of woman for the erotic life of mankind is to be rated very high. . . . For it seems very evident that another person's narcissism has a great attraction for those who have renounced a part of their own narcissism and are in search of object love. The charm of a child lies to a great extent in his narcissism, his self-contentment and inaccessibility, just as the charm of certain animals which seem not to concern themselves about us, such as cats and the large beasts of prey. Indeed, even great criminals and humorists, as they are represented in literature, compel our interest by the narcissistic consistency with which they manage to keep away from their ego anything that would diminish it. It is as if we envied them for maintaining a blissful state of mind. . . .
> (*S.E.*, XIV, 88–89)

The bizarre constituency including beautiful women, beasts of prey, criminals, and comedians is formed by the reflexive attitude that they share. This Chinese encyclopaedia of subjects vacillates on the border between familiarity and terror that will later define the ambiguity of *The Uncanny* (1919). In repelling, the gaze inward of the woman, the panther,[33] or the child exerts an attractive force precisely upon those observers that the attention overlooks. Narcissism, the subject's taking of the selfsame within himself, incites its opposite, the quest for object-love, in those who have elected the other. Narcissism implies a potentially endless chain of lovesick observers. No sooner does the other-loving subject succumb to the charms of a narcissist than he or she enters upon an absorption that is at least quasi-narcissistic in its intensity. The self-involvement even on the part of an other-oriented lover becomes grist for the love mill of yet another potential lover, and so on. Freudian narcissism is certainly not alien to this potentially infinite love network, which has organized so many literary works.

Narcissism might seem a one-sided absorption, whether in a lake, a painted surface, or a looking-glass. But unlike the tree that falls in the forest, whose decline may or may not be apprehended, the withdrawal of the narcissist depends upon the scrutiny of an other—to desire and enter an internal space so self-contained and self-satisfied that it would almost seem to beg for violation, were this not a projection. So vital is the capacity of narcissistic love to *draw out* other-directed love that the very genetic future, the "erotic life of mankind," depends on it.

Freud's elaboration of narcissism raises the mechanics of reflection and magnetism above the precedence that has always been granted to the hard facts of sexual interaction. As suggested earlier, narcissism, in reaching non-dysfunctional and asexual behaviors, represents a decentering from the primacy of the erotic scene in Freud's work. Henceforth, the logics of dualism and inversion, which in earlier writings were at the service of, in the quest of, the primal scene, exercise a momentum and a volition of their own. By *Instincts and Their Vicissitudes* (1915), dualism is the very essence of the instincts. No sooner does a desire express itself than it is accompanied by its passive emanation. The Freudian scenario in which opposite wishes, say, sadistic and masochistic, are on such intimate terms that they mutually *imply* each other is an application of narcissistic reciprocity to the widest energy fields motivating the subject.

As if to underscore its own dialectical organization, *Instincts and Their Vicissitudes* is a text in which logically exhaustive lists and schemas abound.

Observation shows us that an instinct may undergo the following vicissitudes:

Reversal into its opposite.
Turning round upon the subject's own self.
Repression.
Sublimation. (*S.E.*, XIV, 126)

So logical is Freud's concern in this first of the *Metapsychological Papers* that in it he focuses only upon the first two entries in the above list, having explored the metaphysics of repression and sublimation elsewhere in his work. The vicissitudes of an instinct are the forms of reciprocal division that it sustains. As Freud specifies, this reversal is both substantive and directional. No sooner than it is articulated, each instinct implies the negative of its valence and its vector (whether it is active or passive). Each particular wish, then, is merely the expression of an ultimately divisible and suspendible instinctual machine.

Freud himself characterizes the double reversibility of each instinct in terms of their *content* and *aim:*

The reversal affects only the *aims* of the instincts. The active aim (to torture, to look at) is replaced by a passive aim (to be tortured, to be looked at). Reversal of *content* is found in the single instance of the transformation of love into hate.

The turning round of an instinct upon the subject's own self is made plausible by the reflection that masochism is actually sadism turned round upon the subject's own ego, and that exhibitionism includes looking at his own body. . . . The essence of the process is thus the change of the *object*, while the aim remains unchanged. (*S.E.*, XIV, 127)

Ever the attentive paterfamilias, Freud attempts here to mediate a sibling rivalry: whether the instinctual shifts in object or in aim (orientation) take precedence. Ostensibly resolving this squabble within the structure of sadomasochism in favor of the instinctual object, Freud actually demonstrates its equivalence to the aim. The ultimate vicissitude of the instincts is a total and systematic symmetry. Even the term "subject" in this passage, which is one of the few times that Freud prefers it to "ego," is divided, in a qualifying footnote: "As a rule 'subject' and 'object' are used respectively for the person in whom an instinct originates, and the person or thing to which it is directed. Here, however, 'subject' seems to be used for the person who plays the active part in the relationship—the agent" (*S.E.*, XIV, 127–28). Subject to the endless divisions and oppositions of the instincts, even the notion of the subject vacillates between passive and active definitions, between serving as a mere boundary of intention and as agency itself.

It is extremely ironic that when treated in their own right the instincts, the prime movers in the Freudian metaphysics, succumb to the paralysis of systematic and potentially endless symmetry. As each instinctual dimension immediately implies its negation, the force of instinct fizzles. All that Freud gains from this entropy is a certain order, the capacity to endow each instinct with a sequence, a chain of events with the force of logical argument if not of passion:

> In the case of the pair of opposites sadism-masochism, the process may be represented as follows:
> (*a*) Sadism consists in the exercise of violence or power upon some other person as object.
> (*b*) This object is given up and replaced by the subject's self. With the turning round upon the self the change from an active to a passive intellectual aim is also effected.
> (*c*) An extraneous person is once more sought as object; this person, in consequence of the alteration which has taken place in the instinctual aim, has to take over the role of the subject. (*S.E.*, XIV, 127)

In its internal organization, this passage represents, in a literal sense, the machine-work that is the final vicissitude of the instincts. An implement of reciprocity, the instinct replaces object for subject, movement backwards for movement toward, and receptivity for action. With only the most minor of modifications, the same stages apply to the scopophilic/exhibitionistic instinct (*S.E.*, XIV, 129). As this model of speculative control to the point of stasis establishes itself in Freud's work, the underpinning of psychoanalytical theory in sexual activity vanishes, surviving only as a repressed memory.

The mechanics of Hegelian reciprocity are not fated, however, to residing at the level of instincts, which are subcomponents of subjectivity. On the widest level, the interaction between the psychoanalytical patient and therapist is a study in reciprocity. Freud's term for the lateral shifts of emotion between the patient and the analyst is "transference" (*Übertragung*). In the early psychoanalytical writings, "transference" refers to any metaphoric displacement that takes place intrapsychically.[34] Even when it is specifically applied to the analyst-analysand interaction, the term never abandons the metaphoric signification of its earliest images.

> In every psycho-analytic treatment of a neurotic patient the strange phenomenon that is known as 'transference' makes its appearance. The patient, that is to say, directs toward the physician a degree of affectionate feeling (mingled, often enough, with hostility) which is based on no real relation between them and . . . can only be traced back to old wish-

ful phantasies of the patient's which have become unconscious . . . it is only this re-experiencing in the 'transference' that convinces him of the existence and of the power of these unconscious sexual impulses. His symptoms, to take an analogy from chemistry, are precipitates of the earlier experiences in the sphere of love . . . and it is only in the raised temperature of his experience of the transference that they can be resolved and reduced to other psychical products. (*Five Lectures on Psychoanalysis* [1910], *S.E.*, XI, 51)

Transference describes the lateral shift of feelings derived from the patient's experience and memory, where they are too threatening to be explicit, onto the person and mind of the analyst. Whether described as a metaphoric vehicle or as a qualitative stimulus (catalyst), the transference performs a mediatory function. In keeping with the reciprocal logic that prevails in psychoanalysis after "On Narcissism," the impetus of transference must be symmetrically countered by "the patient's influence on his [the physician's] unconscious feelings," aptly designated the *counter-transference* (*Gegenübertragung*, "Future Prospects of Psycho-Analysis" [1910], *S.E.*, XI, 144). With the interplay between the patient's transference and the physician's counter-transference, the physics of reciprocity expands beyond the scale of the intrasubjective, encompassing the mechanisms of defense (e.g., repression), as well as the instincts, to the widest intersubjective horizon projected by psychoanalytical theory, a domain not yet fully mapped to this day.[35]

In the above-cited passage on transference, and long before it in Freud's work, is intimated the way out of the oppressive double bind imposed by reciprocal logic, a paralysis that was also familiar to Kierkegaard. Transference stands on the border between reciprocity and repetition. It postulates a symmetry between the patient and the therapist, yet it also facilitates "re-experiencing" of the repressed. Yet if the repetition whose implicit form is the circle is the non-dualistic variable that breaks up the frozen equilibrium of the reciprocal mechanics, this escape route was familiar to Hegel and integral to the speculative system that he synthesized. The movements of circularity, whether in Nietzsche, Kierkegaard, or Freud, are never autonomous from the dialectical reasoning in which they arise as the reserved potential for a resumption of progress.

The mechanism for repetition in psychoanalytical theory, whether the "return of the repressed," which goes as far back in Freud's work as "The Neuro-Psychoses of Defence" (1896),[36] or the more sophisticated refinement of the repetition-compulsion, might seem to dislocate the dualistic logic that organizes the grammar of consciousness, as well as transference and the instincts in general. Yet for Freud as well as Hegel, the circle, for all its apparent roundness, is merely an appendage to a bifurcated subject, a release switch added at the end of an oppositional stalemate. The death instinct postulated in *Beyond the Pleasure Principle* may in fact deviate from the progressive thrust of the Freudian stream and from the dualistic logic organizing the highest and lowest levels of psychoanalytical abstraction. But this possibly alien element within the Freudian system is predicated upon the shape of the circle, the repetition-compulsion, which is no stranger to dialectical thought.

In our survey of the course of Freud's writing, the figure of the neurotic has assumed many emanations. The early papers concur with Hegel that a divided consciousness is inherently unhappy: the first neurotic languishes in the cognitive involution created when one facet of knowledge is inadmissible to another. As Freud matures well into the first decade of this century, the definitions of the neurotic proliferate. The neurotic fails to evolve properly beyond a dependence on parental doting. He or she errs in the choice of a love-object by gravitating toward people of the same gender. Neurotics magnify the uncertainty of life.[37] They overestimate their own impact upon the world.[38] Their emotional reactions are excessive in relation to the events that incite them.[39] All these dysfunctions violate norms, predetermined standards of evolution, proportion, and orientation applied to the domain of the subject. The degree of neurosis is equal to the difference between an exemplary machine-work of subjectivity and an actual person.

The above transgressions may all be gauged according to the dualistic logic encompassing the scenario of the censor, the psychological defenses, and even the instincts. Yet even when we arrive at what is perhaps the final draft of the neurotic, the compulsive repeater of traumas who has developed an appetite for death, the neurotic remains within the compass of philosophical speculation. Yeats, after all, inscribed his model of circularity, the phases of the moon, upon the opposition between what he termed the primary and the antithetical. Nathanael, the tormented hero of E.T.A. Hoffmann's "The Sandman," spans the variations of neurosis from dualistic repression to mad repetitive gyration. As a martyr to virtually any form of neurosis encountered in Freud's discursive texts, Nathanael is an emblem of the personal suffering that prevails throughout the entire Romantic-Modern age initiated by Hegel. As a child, Nathanael witnesses a trauma certainly worthy of suppression. As a young man, he is systematically ambivalent in his relations with the "objects" of his love. Toward Klara, his societally sanctioned and accessible prospective mate, he alternates a stilted admiration with sudden episodes of withdrawal and morbidity, colored by underlying aggression. The instability of Nathanael's "object-choice" is highlighted by the ease with which his hypocritical affection for Klara can be transformed into a far more ardent passion for Olympia, a clockwork woman, a figuration of subjectivity stripped bare to its machinery. Nathanael's already questionable decision on a proper object-choice becomes even more suspicious in light of his dependence upon male confidants. Nathanael is a brother to Schreber and Freud's obsessive neurotics as well as to Lothar.

Even avoiding, for the moment, the centrality of father figures and surrogates to the story, Nathanael is an exemplary neurotic in more ways than one, a native son to the Modern age. Nathanael's paradigmatic status continues even when he veers away from activities that can be measured on the coordinates of dualism, when instead of vacillating between normal and "hypnoid states" or choosing an active/passive female object, he begins to repeat his experiences (and they begin to repeat on him). The father figures and father killers who recur in the story and trigger Nathanael's losses of control always draw attention to the problem of vision. Nathanael's father dies as he attempts to save his son's eyes from Coppelius. The uncannily similar Coppola is a peddlar of eyeglasses. As Samuel Weber has so ably demonstrated, the theme of vision does not play a subservient role to the castration complex, as Freud interprets the story; rather, this priority is reversed.[40] Nathanael's multiple fathers/castrators are masters of speculation. His moments of craziness do not occur in opposition to speculative activity but are instigated by it.

When Nathanael hurls himself to death from a tower of clear vision, having revolved out of control in the circles described in the epigraph to this section, he performs no activity that is not predicated by the philosophical bylaws of his age. Nathanael's revolution may in some sense repeat the clockwork movement of a doll vacant of subjectivity; it may also reenact the phantasmagoria and blindness that in the story have come to be associated with fatherhood and death. But for all the extremity of these circumstances, Nathanael has simply shifted over to the circular action at the end of logical suspense. Nathanael has entered the rotatory course that the conventions of speculation *provide* as their last will and testament.

Neurotic himself, Nathanael has fallen in love with a woman who figures subjectivity stripped bare. It is this infatuation that signals the helplessness of his condition. A maimed subject, a neurotic defined by his difference from the norm, Nathanael elects as his object the bare machinery of speculation. We cannot help surmising that Nathanael captivated Freud and became an insignia for the uncanny and the repetition-compulsion because somewhere, close to "On Narcissism," Freud had made a similar turn. Father of frankness and moderation, Freud himself is blinded and deranged by the sight of the open viscera of the speculative system that make his surmises possible.

Although broken, perhaps, and subject to mechanical failures and mental lapses, the neurotic is the central character of the Romantic-Modern age. This is so because the neurotic embodies a translation of the working principles of thought itself into the subjective domain. Not only does the literature of this age abound with neurotic characters, from Nathanael to Dickens's eccentrics, to Kafka's K.'s, Proust's Marcel, and Joyce's Bloom, but even the technical innovations in literary prose during this era may be regarded as dramatizing the states of neurosis. Perspectivism draws attention to the fissures within the divided mind. The interior monologue demands and reenacts the intense self-absorption of "hypnoid states." The spatio-temporal experiments giving *Ulysses*, *The Castle*, Proust's *Recherche*, and even such a conventional work as *The Magic Mountain* their distinctive quality in many ways duplicate the distortions by which Freud characterizes the neuroses.[41]

In literature as in life, the neurotic evokes a mixture of sympathy, admiration, contempt, and humor. Yet for all of his or her captivation—what Walter Benjamin would call aura[42]—the neurotic is merely a further declension of the speculating philosopher. The language that Freud applies to neurotics (and psychotics as well) is implicitly philosophical, a terminology that defines the procedural norms that the neurotic violates. If masterworks and central characters conceived and executed yet during this century bear striking genetic resemblances to their common ancestor, the speculative philosopher, can modernism be so modern?

[IV]

THE MEETING OF THE WAYS

. . . the boundless odor of the eucalypti
            Borges, "Death and the Compass," *Ficciones*

There are moments throughout the fictions of Jorge Luis Borges when from within the banality of ordered knowledge and everyday life a vast dimension of possibility and certainty *opens up*. Borges's fictive vocation may well have been to survey this border between limit and the untold potentials of literature. If vastness and expansion are literary qualities, they appear in Borges's fictions in a variety of contexts. In "Tlön, Uqbar, Orbis Tertius," a fictive world whose only judgments are subjective, whose numbers are relative, and which knows no concept of originality is discovered in a misprinting in a single set of the *Encyclopaedia Britannica.*[43] Yet this world of unmitigated indeterminacy assumes other forms: a vast game of chance that disrupts any notions of predictability or continuity that surrounds one's life ("The Babylon Lottery"); the library of Babel, whose "shelves contain all the possible combinations of the twenty-odd orthographic symbols."[44]

Expansion, then, is one of the key gestures by which Borges dramatizes the disruption of closed systems by the combinatorial potential of language. Odors, which *fill space* and radically transform the environment despite the fact that they are invisible, are a characteristic Borgesian figure for this literary expansion. In "Death and the Compass," from which the eucalyptus aroma at the head of this section derives, the movement of expansion finds a numerical expression. Throughout the story, in which an astute detective named Lönnrot reads his way both to the solution of a bizarre series of crimes and to his own death, attention is drawn to the border where sequential numbers expand into their squares. Attention is drawn to God's "ninth attribute," eternity, and to the ninety-nine names that the Tradition assigns Him. "The Hebraists attribute this imperfect number to the fear of even numbers; the Hasidim reason that this hiatus indicates a hundredth name—the Absolute Name."[45]

Lönnrot's death occurs at the site where the prime three expands into the perfect four. He smells the eucalypti when he learns that the triple pattern of murders that his interpretative capacities have enabled him to discern and unravel requires one additional point. The extra coordinate is the locus of his death and belongs to the plot of another, of Scharlach the Jew, who by killing Lönnrot not only achieves revenge for his brother's death but also reverses the Christian ascendency throughout two millennia of theological and political history. In seeking a literary escape from limit, Borges expands the constraining limits, whether logical, numerical, or historical, to death.

If Freud ever attains autonomy from the speculative system that determines the neuroses, it is similarly by expansion. We have already suggested the extreme unlikelihood, after a career spent in adapting speculative procedures, of Freud's ever being able to withdraw his work definitively from a dialectical superstructure. "Our views have from the very first been *dualistic,* and to-day they are even more definitively dualistic than before," writes Freud in *Beyond the Pleasure*

Principle (1920).[46] Yet for all this stubbornness, in Freud's writings on repetition, death, and the future surfaces a calm that metamorphoses the relation between the grammatical and speculative facets of his work from one of conflict to one of détente.

While colored by its explorations into the last things, *Beyond the Pleasure Principle* is also filled with the emergence of possibilities: for revision and renunciation but also for expansion. The immediate context for Freud's inquiry into systematic expansion in this work may be a stand-off between the organism's reception and deflection of stimuli. Yet the fluidity that Freud ascribes to the organism applies to the body of his work as well:

> We infer that a system which is itself highly cathected is capable of taking up an additional stream of fresh inflowing energy and of converting it into quiescent cathexis, that is of binding it psychically. The higher the system's own quiescent cathexis, the greater seems to be its binding force; conversely, therefore, the lower its cathexis, the less capacity it will have for taking up inflowing energy and the more violent must be the consequences of such a breach in the protective shield against stimuli. (*S.E.*, XVIII, 30)

Trauma rushes in where the psychic forces are unbound. The optimal conditions for mental health are expansiveness and a free flow of energy in and out of the subject. When this does not prevail, when cathexis is low, the stage is set for the eruption of unbound energy that constitutes trauma. A suspicious calm, a low-energy field, precedes the psychological storm.

In a very abstract manner, Freud characterizes here, among other things, the dimensions of expansion and contraction as they pertain to mental health. In light of the other innovations of *Beyond the Pleasure Principle*, this topic, however rarefied, could not be more germane. In this text, the death instinct breaks the dualistic equilibrium between the pleasure and reality principles, a structure that by Freud's own admission has been pivotal to his work. In *Beyond the Pleasure Principle*, Freud submits some of his most trusted judgments to revision.[47] In a dialectical fashion, he mediates certain of the oppositions providing his system with its fundamental equalizing torque. But precisely in the site of this ideological renunciation, even sacrifice, occurs the expansion, the suspension of limits, suggesting that Freud's grammatical project, while often obscured, was never abandoned.

In this text Freud grants, as we have seen, as much credence to the psychic functions that *protect against* stimuli as to those that *receive* them. He posits a regressive "backward path" of the instincts, toward "an old state of things, an initial state from which the living entity has . . . departed and to which it is striving to return" (*S.E.*, XVII, 42), as powerful as the relentless stream that dominated his early works. The structure of this backward impulse is repetition; its terminus is death. So compelling is this entropic force that under its influence Freud abandons one of the key articles of his faith.

> This would seem to be the place, then, at which to admit for the first time an exception to the proposition that dreams are fulfilments of wishes. Anxiety dreams, as I have shown repeatedly and in detail, offer no such exception. Nor do 'punishment dreams', for they merely replace the forbidden wish-fulfilment by the appropriate punishment for it. . . . But it is impossible to classify as wish-fulfilments the dreams we have been discussing which occur in the traumatic neurosis, or the dreams during psychoanalyses which bring to memory the psychical traumas of childhood. They arise, rather, in obedience to the compulsion to repeat . . . [*Sie gehorchen vielmehr dem Wiederholungszwang*]. (*S.E.*, XVIII, 32)

More than merely one more figure of intrapsychic activity, the repetition-compulsion represents an entire countereconomy to the imperatives of conflict and progress in the Freudian system. In the above passage, Freud detaches a certain segment of the dream-work from the service of volition. Yet far more is at stake in this emendation than merely the possibility of a dream that is not wish-driven. Severing the dream from the wish implies a renunciation of the entire scenario in which consciousness is folded upon itself in a conflictive involution. The repetitive activity that occurs for the sake of repetition itself is indifferent to the moral crises, the bad conscience, the sexual titillations that define the longest and predominant epoch of Freudian subjectivity. Just as Freud adjusts the centrality of volition in the dream-work, he recapitulates the history of his libido theory, revising his earlier distinction between the ego instincts and the sexual instincts. "Thus the original opposition . . . proved to be inadequate . . . the distinction . . . which was originally regarded as in some sort of way *qualitative*, must now be characterized differently—namely as being *topographical*" (*S.E.*, XVIII, 52).

It is within this overall context of hyperexpansion and revision that the repetition-compulsion and its complex arises as a renewed bond between the Freudian dialectics and grammar. Yet even in postulating a construct with such revolutionary repercussions on his work, Freud initially regresses to his most shopworn formulas in characterizing the repetition-compulsion. In the child's play, repetition serves as a shifter across the standard Freudian polarities: "At the outset he was in a *passive* situation—he was overpowered by the experience; but by repeating it, unpleasurable though it was, as a game, he took on an active part" (*S.E.*, XVIII, 16). "As the child passes over from the passivity of the experience to the activity of the game, he . . . revenges himself on a substitute" (*S.E.*, XVIII, 17). Just as Freud cannot broach the possibility of play without first registering it on the coordinates of activity/passivity and victimization/revenge, he must ascribe death, the orientation and terminus of repetition, to a vast evolutionary scheme. "If there is a 'beyond the pleasure principle', it is only consistent to grant that there was also a time before the purpose of dreams was the fulfilment of wishes" (*S.E.*, XVIII, 33). Always the patriarch, Freud situates the original inanimate state within a cosmological and physiological prehistory (*S.E.*, XVIII, 36, 50).

Repetition and death, however, point not only beyond the dominance of pleasure but also beyond the metaphysical superstructures that Freud compulsively applies to them. The adult variety of repetition offers no compensations in the form of revenge or sublime renunciation. The adult psychoanalytical patient who suffers from traumatic neurosis "is obliged *to repeat* the repressed material as a contemporary experience instead of, as the physician would prefer to see, *remembering* it as something belonging to the past" (*S.E.*, XVIII, 18). Only the physician is in a position to redeem this experience. In itself, this neurotic repetition leads nowhere, or if somewhere, only toward more signs of suffering that refuse to be assimilated within the mitigating clockworks of rationalization or time. Neurotic repetition is a self-enclosed but endless panorama of disquieting signs. The traveler on this expansive yet also circular way remains only partially a subject. To the extent that the neurotic repeats, he or she is severed from the subjective integrity and control that the course of therapy would restore.

True to his own prejudices, Freud assigns this mature repetition an origin and a terminus, which he calls death. But just as there is a repetition that does not salvage youthful self-esteem, there is a death that is not located either in a hypothetical prehistory or among the germ cells. The death of repetition is the dissolution of the subject upon a plane of signification. This death is anything but inanimate. It is the convulsive movement to which Nathanael is prone from the inception of adulthood, the death for which he yearns in his infatuation for a doll as well as in his fall from a high tower.

The deadly afterlife of repetition is filled with the hybrids of condensation, and it is at this point that Freud's grammatical aspirations merge into his final major revisions, after pursuing a largely digressive course. The death of repetition is merely the somber tone into which the joke-laughter subsides. Both condensation and the repetition-compulsion demand an intercourse of signification which is devoid of metaphysical aims. Both demarcate a domain in which signs vanish into signs, with no further reflection.

It is ironic, then, that in the late texts where Freud consolidates and confirms the dialectical underpinnings of his system, he also renews his commitment to cognitive grammar and rhetoric. The Freudian gravitation toward the widest horizon of speculation expands his dialectical machinery to such an extent that the free play of language again breaks out within its perimeters.

Freud accomplishes for modernism a decisive shift of the operations of speculation to the subjective sphere. Yet throughout this trajectory, in Freud as well as Hegel and Kierkegaard, the claims of dialectical precision and efficacy are subverted by an irreducible linguistic indeterminacy. It will come as no surprise, then, that the exemplary works of modernism remain in this impasse, hovering between the imperatives of speculative procedure and a textual network that will simply not give in.

FIVE

The Contours of Modernism

[I]

INTRODUCTION

The dawn of any century encourages claims of innovation, revolution, and decisive schism with the past. Our own century, the rumblings (or digital clicks) of whose decline may already be heard, began with an even exaggerated sense of newness. Not only did the final century of a millennium require a turn to the customary blank ledger but substantial changes in technology, social organization, and the conception and capacities of the political state added the aura of apocalypse to an already heady atmosphere of possibility.

The artifacts and developments grouped under the rubric "modernism" are too variegated, even contradictory, to evoke any uniform set of responses. Yet if any single sense accompanies the vast panorama of fictive, poetic, musical, architectural, and plastic innovations which comprise the modernist movement, it is one of rupture with the past, or indifference to it. Hence,

> modern architecture, modern music, modern philosophy, modern science—all these define themselves not *out* of the past, scarcely *against* the past, but in independence of the past. . . . Vienna in the *fin de siècle*, with its acutely felt tremors of social and political disintegration, proved one of the most fertile breeding grounds of our century's a-historical culture. Its great intellectual innovators—in music and philosophy, in economics and architecture, and, of course, in psychoanalysis—all broke, more or less deliberately, their ties to the historical outlook central to the nineteenth-century liberal culture in which they had been reared.[1]

Hence, "new readers can be electrified by exposure to [Wyndham Lewis's] *Tarr*, a book in which, as in few others, the sentence is reinvested with all the force of origins, as sculptural gesture and fiat in the void."[2] "Newton's universe—a mental, not a physical entity—was

gone: gone too the objects strewn through it in a state of 'rest,' await-
ing the impingement of causality: the metals waiting to be oxidized,
the water to be pumped, the poets to be 'influenced.'"[3]

Even in the access to the past that it could provide, modernism was
never less than groundbreaking. If not historical in any oppressive
sense, the turn of the century nonetheless closed a temporal bow,
facilitating a free intercourse with the long-forgotten and barely
known. "'Troy,' after Schliemann was no longer a dream, but a place
on the map."[4] Archaeological breakthroughs and the vast philological
collaborations of the era meant that "Joyce belonged to the first generation of young writers who could study their own language as his-
toric process by browsing in such a work [as Skeat's *Etymological
Dictionary*]."[5]

For all this intense atmosphere of freshness, one extending to material, formal, and tonal dimensions, the dawn of the century, like
Freud's work, occupies a place within the Hegelian aftermath. "For
the vortex is not the water but a patterned energy made visible by the
water."[6] Even if, following vorticism, all of modernism were to effect
a decisive shift from substance to movement, from stasis to dynamic
flow, like Ernest Fenollosa's ideograms,[7] the lines of force revealed in
the modernist current derive from the Hegelian physics. Despite its
pervasive aura of newness, which prompted Gertrude Stein to remark
America's uniquely intimate terms with the twentieth century, modernism does not revolutionize. At most, it displaces and transposes the
energy lines that prevailed in nineteenth-century speculation to the
surface of poetry, prose, and plastic material.

The break with the past, or indifferent turning away from it at the
head of the century, is not nearly as sharp or decisive as it would be
comfortable for critics and historians to surmise. To be sure, even a
shift from the procedures of philosophical discourse to the materials
and execution of esthetics is itself a major consequence, accounting
for many of the tonal innovations that took place around the beginning of the century. In the literary sphere, this moment is distinguished by the uniquely tactile relation that its major writers, of
prose as well as poetry, maintained with their language. Heidegger's
rhetoric of delving applies here.[8] Whether in the *bricolage* of Ezra
Pound, the suspended arcs of utterance in Proust and James, or the
truncated sentences that Kafka fashioned for German prose, writers
felt free to delve into the material qualities of language. But even if we
regard Joyce's technical innovations as unthinkable before the advent
of the twentieth century, the assertion of a general cultural revolution
or clear schism at this time is primarily in the interests of neatness and
a certain historical economy. A hypothetical nineteenth- / twentieth-

century break not only greatly simplifies the wide task of historical periodization but also supplies tangible distinctions that may be used to categorize the individual disciplines and genres.

The marked persistence of the Hegelian tropes within the seminal works of twentieth-century literature confronts any historical schema accounting for the rise of modernism with a notable exception. There can be little doubt that the possibilities afforded by internalization and externalization, reciprocal interplay, and inversion are of vital consequence to Yeat's *A Vision*, Joyce's *Ulysses*, Kafka's *The Castle*, Proust's *A la recherche du temps perdu*, and Henry James's major texts. These processes, which attain prominence in Hegel's discourse, shape the groundbreaking works of modern literature both as structures and as themes.

The striking works of this period are distinguished by their experimental quality. Not only of Proust's massive novel may it be said "that all great works of literature found a genre or dissolve one—that they are, in other words, special cases."[9] Because of their unrelenting experimentation with perspective, narrative voice, fictive time, characterization, and stylistic imitation and distortion, the most distinctively modern works are virtually all "special cases." Almost inherently, modernist fiction is experimental. One way of describing the modernist experiments is as plays upon operations that in the Hegelian discourse function as rules. In the pantheon of "classical" modern works, the Hegelian tropes no longer function within a speculative machine whose purpose is the approximation, if not the revelation, of some ultimate truth. In twentieth-century literature, the standard speculative gestures of philosophy stand apart, on their own, detached from the wider superstructure. These operations stand exposed. They have become, in their own right, esthetic "objects." At the turn of the century, structures and relations have become as esthetic and variable as the works in which they figure.

The persistence of the Hegelian operations over the watershed between the centuries and over the borders between and within the various genres presents any neat historical program with an embarrassment. Yet it would be an oversimplification to suggest that these operations, just because they endure, determine a static and unified epoch. The works of Henry James, Yeats, Proust, Joyce, and Kafka register neither a modernist repudiation of the past nor a capitulation to some overbearing epochal or formal continuity. Neither progressing nor regressing, the contributions of modernism register a transfiguration of movement, from truth to uncertainty, from speculative discourse to art. If modernism may be said to explore an esthetization of the procedures of philosophical speculation, this entire movement, a change of field, takes place under the purview of Kierkegaard's "Rotation Method." In the place of revolution, stasis, or simple repetition, modernism offers transvaluation and transfiguration, the dislocation of the figure. Modernism does not extend or preserve the organizing principles of philosophical discourse but rather shifts them to a different field and use.

Bizarre hybrids, not limited to Kafka's "Crossbreed" and Odradek, result from the modernist adaptation of Hegelian operations. Reflexive figures and acts can abound in such a text as *The Turn of the Screw* to such an extent that it reads almost as a catalogue of speculative gestures. Transposed to the sphere of James's tale, the operations, above all of bifurcation and reciprocity, gather full esthetic indeterminacy and resonance. *The Turn of the Screw* is an instance of a textually radical work inscribed fully within the perimeters of reflection. Such a work, which is not alone among the productions of modernism, questions the dependability of any divide that can be posited between reflexivity and nonreflexivity. The uncanny fusion of the speculatively familiar with the textually indeterminate effected by the story suggest that reflexivity and nonreflexivity are no more mutually exclusive than are the categories of modernism and "the nineteenth century."

In the enduring works of modernism, reflexivity and nonreflexivity interact through a doubly permeable membrane. The Hegelian tropes endure, but on the basis of their transposition to the esthetic domain, they become susceptible to losses of orientation, repeatability, and efficacy. If the disfiguration of the Hegelian tropes becomes an important item on the agenda of modernism, this enterprise is marked by the extreme idiosyncracy of its individual variations. In radically different ways, Kierkegaard, Kafka, Proust, Yeats, and Joyce react to a wide range of elements within the Hegelian arsenal. Not only do different speculative operations appeal to different authors as they go about the double task of appropriation and distortion; different tropes attain prominence within the various segments of the authors' literary production. Through these disfigurations, a broad cohesion of the Hegelian system nevertheless becomes discernible.

In the interest of exploring this persistence which is not permanent, this functional epoch which is not historical, this transposition which does not properly *move*, and a reflexivity whose limits and days are already numbered, the remainder of this chapter is devoted to two major modernist works, James's *The Turn of the Screw* and Proust's *Recherche*. These texts no more abolish the Hegelian tropes than they elevate them; they belong no more to a distinct outside of metaphysics than to an inside. Transitory works themselves, they illustrate the provisional status of all figures and philosophical operations.

[II]

PROUST: THE SEASCAPE OF GIRLS

We begin with Marcel Proust, an adept at fictionalizing speculative operations. For all the diversity of the fields that it touches and the breadth of its scope, the moving force behind Proust's epic *A la recherche du temps perdu* is love,[10] occupying the position held by *cathexis* in the Freudian system. Not only is the *Recherche* a love story: it is a serial romance as well. It derives its temporal structure, as well as the unforgettable figure of the maid tormented by the housekeeper Françoise in Combray, from Giotto's frescoes in the Cappella degli Scrovegni in Padua. Not only do Giotto's murals narrate the events of Christ's life: they encompass the narratives anticipating and succeeding this episode. The panels depicting the lives of Mary and Joseph before the nativity and the Last Judgment after the crucifixion are faithful to the sequence of the events in Christ's life. In Giotto's narrative the story focusing on Christ expands into a tripartite serial, the elements of which are in tandem. The succession of analogously structured episodes transforms a linear story into a stately cycle of repetition. Similarly, in the *Recherche*'s love epic the central episode, concerning the narrator Marcel's affair with Albertine, is announced by Swann's unhappy love for Odette and is succeeded by the homosexual romance whose crux is Charlus's passion for Charlie Morel.[11] As is described quite explicitly in the opening passage of *Cities of the Plain,* the heterosexual and homosexual romances of the *Recherche* are intertwined, literally impregnated with one another.

Within this sizeable framework, however, love, whatever its nature, is the driving force, that is, the energy moving characters toward and away from each other, the motivation behind desire, possession, and separation. Love is for Proust what force is for Hegel. In addition to his other metaphors for love, such as music or a disease, Proust couches romance in terms linking it unmistakably to the Hegelian enterprise. Whether as rehearsed by Charles Swann or as suffered by Marcel, love is the selection of the particular from the general and the torments of possessiveness occasioned by this choice. The agonies endured by Swann, Marcel, and Charlus are the logical as well as the emotional consequences of a bonding that begins in a random manifold, exemplified by the frieze or seascape of girls at Balbec, and that terminates in an intense obsession with, dependency on, and subjugation to the beloved. The grand passions of the *Recherche* thus retrace, in a fictive setting, the stages followed by the dialectic of particularity and generality in the Hegelian system.

Proust pursues the stations of the love attachment involving the central characters of the *Recherche* through a dual field. Throughout the *Recherche*, music is the artistic medium governing an interior, intrapsychic space of love. Music, in other words, is the internal symptom or accompaniment of love. This is particularly telling with regard to Swann's wooing of Odette. Vinteuil's "little phrase" is the "national anthem" of this passion. It is fitting that Charlie Morel, Charlus's great love, is a violinist. In the *Recherche*, music is the privileged grammar in the linguistics of love. Love transpires and grows within a language of tokens and gestures including gifts, euphemisms, and silences and absences. "Doing the catelyas," a euphemism which becomes Swann and Odette's private term for making love, is merely one pronounced element within an interior love language whose primary model is music.[12]

Yet the affinities and separations motivated by passion are by no means confined to a self-enclosed interior domain. If music exemplifies the language of the psyche for Proust, painting is the esthetic medium that prevails outside, in experiential or empirical space. If music is a shorthand for psychology, painting, specifically as practiced by Elstir, characterizes the realm of phenomenology, the set of spatial and temporal relations determining experience. By his elaboration of esthetic genres and his synthesis of exemplary works of art, Proust superimposes the exterior realm of the visual plane upon the interiority of the psyche, effecting an almost invisible seam between them. Elstir's paintings are esthetic miniatures of the grand map on which Proust situates the names of places, characters, and the history where places and names interact. When Marcel discovers his room at the Grand Hotel in Balbec-Plage at the beginning of "Place-Names: The Name," a visual field opens up for him and the reader. The seascape reflected on the glass panels of the bookcases in the room, an optical intersection of nature and language, becomes the occasion for a general, unspecified love, a love for a collective group of girls, a love with its own *force, laws*, and *field*. If painting joins music as a medium for love, the painter Elstir becomes Marcel's painting master and his guide to this newly opened visual and erotic field. Elstir's seascapes are emblems for this vague, collective, undifferentiated love, which enables Marcel, when he falls in love with Albertine, to fall in love with the entire "little band" as well. The seascape in which Marcel falls in love by taking the psychologically fatal step from the general to the particular, from the band, with such other enticements as Andrée, to Albertine, is thus a locus for a fictive working out of the struggle to distinguish the particular from the general, a procedure inherently necessary to each stage of systematic progress in Hegelian terms.

Marcel's first passion, the fatal step from general to particular love, takes place by the sea, in a setting characterized by endless expanse and by a dissolution of the boundaries separating land, water, and sky. And this stage is set within the frame of a painted surface no less general, disclosing the laws of space and perspective.

> Now the effort made by Elstir to reproduce things not as he knew them to be but according to the optical illusions of which our first sight of them is composed, had led him exactly to this point; he gave special emphasis to certain of these laws of perspective, which were thus all the more striking, since his art had been their first interpreter. . . . The continuity of the ocean was suggested only by the gulls which, wheeling over what, when one looked at the picture, seemed to be solid rock, were as a matter of fact inhaling the moist vapour of the shifting tide. Other laws were discernible in the same canvas. . . . This play of light and shade, which also photography has rendered commonplace, had interested Elstir so much that at one time he had painted what were almost mirages. . . . (I, 631)

What is perhaps most striking about this passage is the juxtaposition of its indefinite language of illusion and mirage and its rhetoric of abstraction. In this passage as in Hegel's scenario for "Understanding," a thoroughly ungovernable play of forces gives rise to the detached generalization of laws. Abstraction coexists with rather than negates what would seem least congenial to it, namely, a random flux so indifferent as to dissolve even the distinction between the rocks and the tide. Here as in Hegel's "Force and the Understanding," *illusion* is the double term both reflecting the indifference of the sea and giving rise to the laws of abstraction. Congruent with the frame of this painting is a physical field in which structures emerge only to dissolve. "The sea itself came cranking in among the land," "the roofs were overtopped . . . by masts which had the effect of making the vessels to which they belonged appear town-bred," "this fishing fleet seemed less to belong to the water than, for instance, the churches of Criquebec" (I, 629). The sea, Elstir's canvas, and this moment in Marcel's experience are all media that allow, by virtue of their seemingly endless breadth, a relaxation of the obsessive work of logic. Yet this ebb and flow that is so akin to the configuration, variation, and dissolution of structures in Proust's work and in texts in general posits its own laws, the laws of the written, painted, and musical media. And even though they pertain to the intangible, the indefinite, and the incongruous, these esthetic principles carry the force of law.

Even before Marcel first settles into his room at Balbec, he is at "one of those periods of our youth, unprovided with any one definite love, vacant, in which at all times and in all places . . . we desire, we seek, we see Beauty" (I, 595). Since he is engaged in a quest for abstract beauty, with a capital *B*, it is not an accident that before falling in love with Albertine, before relenting to a specific fixation on the basis of laws both accidental and arbitrary, Marcel should fall in love with a collective entity, like the Hegelian thing, a manifold of properties. Of the little band of *jeunes filles en fleur* he confesses, "I was in love with all of them, loving them all, yet the possibility of meeting them was in my daily life the sole element of delight" (I, 627). All of these girls "partook of the same special essence" (I, 627). The moment of first full flowering at which they all exist places them in a position, as a living mural or tableau, to function as collectively as their audience, Marcel, is predisposed to perceive in a general way. It is in a collective organism, compared to a coral reef, that Marcel first perceives discrete feminine entities and from which he will make a definite choice, pursuing love's trajectory from the general to the particular.

> Like those primitive organisms in which the individual barely exists by itself, consists in the reef rather than in the coral insects that compose it, they were still pressed one against another. Sometimes one pushed her neighbour over, and then a wild laugh, which seemed the sole manifestation of their personal life, convulsed them all at once, obliterating, confounding those indefinite, grinning faces in the congealment of a single cluster, scintillating and tremulous. In an old photograph . . . one cannot recognize them individually . . . save by a process of reasoning. (I, 620)

The organic fluidity that composes this group study partakes of the sea. The "little band" *is* the sea, is a translation into human terms of the philosophical conditions that Proust ascribes to the ocean and the seascape. As a group, the girls efface boundaries and distinctions, as Elstir's paintings of the region do.

The trajectory of love proceeds from this group portrait first to a stage of nascent individuation, at which the girls are easily replaced and substituted. It is at this stage that Marcel takes a number of liberties not without linguistic significance. In playfully directing attentions aroused by Albertine toward Andrée, in devising stratagems of deceit to manipulate a feminine frieze standing out in only partial relief, Marcel appropriates the linguistic capabilities defined by synecdoche and metonymy. Synecdochically, Albertine may disappear into the wholeness of the group. She may just as easily be summoned back into particularity. "As soon as she joined us I became conscious of the obstinate tip of her nose, which I had omitted from my mental pictures of her during the last few days . . . Albertine was built up afresh before my eyes" (I, 696). Albertine and Andrée, as Marcel plays them off against each other, stand in a metonymic relation.

Love, the fixation of an attachment or cathexis to one element of a composite entity, places a severe and ultimately fatal stress on the organic coherence of the little band. Like the Hegelian Thing, the "little band" undergoes an irreversible constitutional crisis when the demands of exclusive possession bring its constituent members to too stark a level of individuality. As Oscar Wilde was aware, love harbors killing powers. In loving, Marcel upsets the delicate ecological balance necessary for the survival of the group. When the "harmonious cohesion" of the group is "broken in Albertine's favor" (I, 688), a moment of exquisite variation in harmony ends.

[III]

THE SLEEPING ALBERTINE

It is often the case in Proust that no condition is more conducive to disease than the attainment of desire. Marcel may wish to possess Albertine exclusively; in his compulsion he may manage to break her off of the reef or detach her from the composite photograph. Yet the success of his schemes, the evolution of love from its softer to its harder and more particular stages, brings on the symptoms of an even crueler and more maddening condition. For after love has been detached from the feminine manifold and hoarded, what is one to do with it? This is precisely the problem that faces Marcel as he watches over and presumably entertains Albertine in his Paris apartment, having severed her from her context. Yet the torments of jealousy and uncertainty attached to the individuated Albertine define themselves in a manner not thoroughly inconsistent with the conditions of Marcel's nascent love. If that love hovers at the border of particularity and generality and settles, as Samuel Weber has demonstrated, in the figure of an indeterminate aquatic metaphor belonging completely to neither economy, then the torments of ripened love reside at the interstice of presence and absence.[13] The captive Albertine is that which is absent from itself and therefore not self-identical. She is never more enigmatic and exasperating than when, asleep, she is both absent and at the height of her affective powers. The sleeping Albertine illustrates the workings of the Hegelian dialectics at both their fullest efficiency and their failure.

Already by the ocean, both the setting and moment of blooming generality, Albertine reveals herself as a character with a generous but unsettling array of differences.

> On certain days, slim, with grey cheeks, a sullen air, a violet transparency falling obliquely from her. . . . On other days her face, more sleek, caught and glued my desires to its varnished surface. . . . At other times happiness bathed her cheeks with a clarity so mobile that the skin, grown fluid and vague, gave passage to a sort of stealthy and subcutaneous gaze, which made it appear to be of another colour but not of another substance than her eyes. . . . But most often of all she shewed more colour, and was then more animated; sometimes the only pink thing in her white face was the tip of her nose, as finely pointed as that of a mischievous kitten with which one would have liked to stop and play. . . . and each of these Albertines was different, as in every fresh appearance of the dancer whose colours, form, character are transmuted according to the innumerably varied play of a projected limelight. It was perhaps because they were so different, the persons whom I used to contemplate in her at this period, that later on I became myself a different person, corresponding to the particular Albertine to whom my thoughts had turned; a jealous, an indifferent, a voluptuous, a melancholy, a frenzied person. . . . For this is the point to which we must always return, to these beliefs with which most of the time we are quite unconsciously filled, but which for all that are of more importance to our happiness than is the average person whom we see. (I, 708)

The sea changes that so inform the person of Albertine are here transferred, first to the variety of Marcel's perceptions and then to Marcel's personality, which rapidly loses the joy and stimulation initially evoked by his beloved. The initial configuration of Marcel's association with Albertine, in which she is a panoply of sensations and he is a receptive audience and pursuer, itself changes. Albertine's seemingly endless variety awakens the desire to contain, control, and possess. From a rather clear-cut subject-object relation, Albertine and Marcel enter one of reciprocal influence, in which they both instigate and experience change. Yet if Albertine spawns a sequence of variants distributed over the expanse of the sea horizon, Marcel's frenzy assumes the form of troubled cycles whose stages include suspicion, manipulation, rage, and reconciliation. If Albertine's changes, like her sleeping body, are expansive in a horizontal way, Marcel is imprisoned in the rotatory movement rehearsed by Hegel's cycles, practiced by the Nathanael of Hoffmann's "Sandman," and marked as a fundament of human psychology by Freud's repetition-compulsion.

The love of Marcel and Albertine, like Hegel's initially playful exchange of forces, terminates in a bewildering cul-de-sac at which the partners reverse positions of superiority with bewildering acceleration.

Never is Albertine more beautiful and moving than during her sleep, in the intermediate state between death and active volition.

> I have spent charming evenings talking, playing games with Albertine, but never any so pleasant as when I was watching her sleep. . . . I seemed to possess not one, but innumerable girls. Her breathing, as it became gradually deeper, was now regularly stirring her bosom and, through it, her folded hands, her pearls, displaced in a different way by the same movement, like the boats, the anchor chains, that are set swaying by the movement of the tide. Then, feeling that the tide of her sleep was full . . . I crept without a sound upon the bed. . . . I myself was gently rocked by its regular motion: I had embarked upon the tide of Albertine's sleep. (II, 426–27)

The state of sleep is the paradoxical absence that makes Albertine more present than when she is actually "present" in mind. Asleep, Albertine becomes an image onto which Marcel can project his desires and with which he can exchange roles. Sleep is yet another sea overrunning the *Recherche,* and it maintains rather than diminishes Albertine's multiplicity.

The image of the sleeping Albertine becomes a talisman for the quality of her cohabitation with Marcel. Captive, enigmatic, exasperating, Albertine falls as much victim to Marcel's compulsions as she is a source of torment. In her waking life, Albertine assumes a variety of roles in relation to Marcel. She is a poetess of the everyday, composing epithets for the sweets that embellish their shared life (II, 468–69). Her accounts of her actions and whereabouts during her absences from Marcel make her a storyteller of the first order (II, 510). Her musical activities as a connoisseur of the chants of the street vendors (II, 486–88) and as a piano player (II, 640–41) associate her with this medium and link her to a motif beginning at the primal homosexual scene at Montjouvain and encompassing every significant personal interaction in the work. By the law of reciprocal interchange established when Marcel takes on her variance, Albertine becomes an artist in her own right. Her greatest esthetic achievement consists in composing the text over which Marcel is forever deliberating with endless worry and compulsiveness. Far more than merely the repository for Marcel's desire and affection, Albertine is his consummate work of art, the text that *he* composes and serves with a combination of subjection, fidelity, and hate.

It is as the sea, not the natural sea but the ocean of textual pos-sibilities, that Albertine delivers the "script" from which Marcel is left to divine her falsehoods (II, 441). The captive but fleeting Albertine is described in a manner situating her well within the tradition of the *Recherche*'s exemplary artworks and moments of esthetic apprehen-sion. She is both the artwork to which Marcel pays his obeisance and the text that he composes, a labor of servility whose only rewards consist of moments of textual apprehension.

> But did not my room contain a work of art more precious than all these—Albertine herself? . . . Her fingers, at one time trained to the handle-bars, now rested upon the keys like those of a Saint Cecilia. . . . I prolonged each of its [her face's] surfaces beyond what I was able to see and beneath what concealed it from me and made me feel all the more strongly—eyelids which half hid her eyes, hair that covered the upper part of her cheeks—the relief of those superimposed planes. Her eyes shown like, in a matrix in which the opal is still embedded, the two facets which alone have as yet been polished. . . . Her dark, curling hair, presenting a different appearance whenever she turned to ask me what she was to play next, now a splendid wing, sharp at the tip, broad at the base, feathered and triangular, now weaving the relief of its curls in a strong and varied chain, a mass of crests, of watersheds, of pre-cipices, with its incisions so rich and so multiple, seemed to exceed the variety that nature normally realises and to correspond rather to the desire of a sculptor who accumulates difficulties in order to bring into greater prominence the suppleness, the fire, the moulding, the life of his execution. . . . But no, Albertine was in no way to me a work of art.
> (II, 647–48)

The final disclaimer notwithstanding, Albertine *is* a work of art, but only among other things. In this passage Marcel weaves the figure of Albertine into a wide array of the narrative strands that have pre-viously touched upon the nature of the text, both as an object and an experience. As Saint Cecilia, Albertine joins the other characters in the *Recherche* who, by resemblance, enter privileged relationships with literary figures and works of art. Albertine *becomes* Saint Cecilia in the same sense that Françoise's unfortunate underling becomes indelibly marked by the *Charity* from Giotto's frescoes and Swann's Odette becomes a living personification of Botticelli's Jethro's daughter (I, 172). In all of these relationships, the characters comprising Marcel's domain and narrative become modified and redefined by the esthetic figures deriving from older (and often pictorial) works who are in effect grafted upon them. This process of personification by appro-priation of venerable esthetic figures is a highly estheticized version of metaphoric transposition. By means of this operation, works of art or their components become metaphors for fictive personalities. The paintings of Giotto, Botticelli, and Vermeer become the vehicles transporting tenors who are themselves constructs of narrative. This cultivated form of metaphor creates a fictive involution, a layering of synthetic construct upon construct, well-sustained by the other rhetorics of stratification in the above passage.

If Albertine is a work of art, she is so by more than allusion. As Marcel's eye caresses her, like a sculptor's overseeing his own work of art, she joins two realms of activity associated with esthetic complexity throughout the *Recherche*. As described in the above passage, Albertine resides at the junction between the activities of concealment and embroidery. She shuttles between two rhetorics, one of layering and superimposed strata or inscriptions and one of chain linkages, the spinning out of involuted skeins of association or movement. In its descriptions of the contours of Albertine's face as "superimposed planes," of her eyes as "a matrix in which the opal is still embedded," and of the "precipices" and "incisions" in her hair, the passage inscribes a set of multiple planes or backdrops upon her character. As a palimpsest, Albertine joins a sequence of artworks beginning with the Magic Lantern in little Marcel's bedroom that operate by concealment.[14] The effects of layering include the opening of an infinite regress and a disclosure of previously hidden complications where they had not been suspected. Marcel's Magic Lantern "substituted for the opaqueness" of the most intimate walls of his bedroom "an impalpable iridescence" (I, 7), a glow of submerged contours recurring, for example, whenever the metaphors of submarine landscapes and paintings enter the narrative.

Yet "the strong and varied chain" of her curls, the web lattice that they form, inscribes Albertine within yet another textual economy. Enigmatic in her strata, Albertine also initiates an endless chain of involution. Herself a textual strand with no inherent reason to terminate, Albertine figures the self-sustaining capacity of the work, the narrative links drawing vastly separated episodes and scenes together. Like one of the Paris *gares*, Albertine is a matrix where the novel's wandering threads, whether described as the Combray paths, the "little train," or the Balbec ditch, take off. As a figure of chain linkings of events and associations, Albertine is a descendant of the tea leaves that remain as the instigation and proof of time's capacity to open, of the control that the primary economy of the involuntary seizes over the most self-evident assumptions. Like Albertine's tresses, the remains of the tea that enable Marcel to yield to his suppressed apprehensions reside at the junction between a metaphor of layering and one of involution.

The drying of the stems had twisted them into a fantastic trellis, in whose intervals the pale flowers opened, as though a painter had arranged them there, grouping them in the most decorative poses. The leaves, which had lost or altered their own appearance, assumed those instead of the most incongruous things imaginable, as though the transparent wings of flies or the blank sides of labels or the petals of roses had been collected and pounded, or interwoven as birds weave the material for their nests. A thousand trifling little details . . . gave me, like a book in which one is astonished to read the name of a person whom one knows, the pleasure of finding that these were indeed real lime-blossoms. . . . (I, 39)

Descended, then, from the processes that comprise the very experiential basis for writing, the figure of Albertine encompasses the conditions and activities that make composition possible.[15] The uncertainties she awakens, the knowledge gaps she underscores, go hand in hand with the visual metaphors she epitomizes, both the panorama of disappearing surfaces and the labyrinth of untraceable turns. As a radical notation of textual activities, Albertine emanates from the inevitable moment of breakdown inscribed within the Hegelian dialectics. Marcel's original sin is that he separates Albertine, detaches her from the ebb and flow of particularity and generality. Once amputated from this organic movement, Albertine, for all her beauty, becomes a monster. She becomes the site and figure for that which refuses to be consistent with itself, for an identity forever receptive to difference and different from itself. The economies of layering and involution that she joins merely elaborate her radicality, as Marcel's caressing tributes fill in her beauty.

[IV]

THE PREGNANT INVERT

Only the narrowest of margins separates the moments of revelation in Proust from mere random occurrences. It is just such a scene, one both sought by its observer and taking him by surprise, that begins the volume of the *Recherche* known as *Cities of the Plain* (*Sodome et Gomorrhe*) and that permanently adjusts the work's economy. The naive Marcel happens to come upon, but does not interrupt, a homosexual act involving Baron Charles and Jupien, the "ex-tailor" whose shop adjoins the *hôtel* shared by the Duke and Duchess of Guermantes and Marcel. Not only does this scene trigger a lengthy meditation on the biological, philosophical, and esthetic nature of homosexuality on the

part of the narrator; it discloses the existence and uninterrupted operation in the novel of a countereconomy to the model of heterosexual love and desire. The romance whose main episode is Charlus's
love for Morel *takes up* the thematic strands woven into *Un Amour de
Swann* but utilizes them in its own contrary way. Yet the *Recherche* not
only intertwines narratives whose cores happen to be homosexual and
heterosexual romances. Far from being mere modes of sexual gratification, homosexuality and heterosexuality comprise entire counter-
systems of thought and structuration operational throughout the text.
What may well be most crucial about the scene initiating *Cities of the
Plain* is that the homosexual economy it announces relates to heterosexuality and reproduction *both* in a dialectical way *and* as a parable of
writing. The subeconomy of homosexual relations may be the logical
other of heterosexuality and the teleological aspirations implicit in
reproduction, but as described by Marcel in this passage, it is also a
model for the displacement, substitution, and supplementarity of
writing.

The scene of Charlus's encounter with Jupien is set in an elaborate
stage machinery, itself with ample precedents in the novel and going
back to the deepest strata of Marcel's experience. When Charlus enters the range of Marcel's observation, the latter is actually recon-
noitering the movements of the Duke and Duchess of Guermantes
from a hidden vantage point, a staircase in the house that Marcel
terms a "watch-tower" (II, 3).[16] This is a type of architectural setting
for observation similar to the one that Henry James constructs for the
governess in *The Turn of the Screw*. This framework, which both sets in
relief and impedes the viewing of the scene to take place, recalls the
novel's *primal* homosexual scene, at Montjouvain, and the towers that
form so characteristic and strategic a part of the landscape at
Combray.

Just as Marcel becomes the unwitting accessory to Charlus's coupling with Jupien, in "Combray" he views through the manifestly
theatrical setting of an open window the intimacy and conspiracy
joining Mlle. Vinteuil and her friend (I, 122–27). Not only does Marcel witness the physical side of their relation; he watches as they dese-
crate, by spitting on it, a photograph of Mlle. Vinteuil's recently de-
ceased father, the composer. Of particular consequence is the
structural analogy between the two homosexual scenes. In both cases,
the moment of observation, of absorption in the events at hand, is
succeeded by an interpretative statement. The Montjouvain scene
inspires a brief homiletic on sadism. In keeping with the Proustian
dictum that falsifies all appearances, this first impression of the bru-
tality of Vinteuil's survivors will be reversed by the later revelation of

their boundless generosity, above all on the part of Mlle. Vinteuil's consort, in deciphering and transcribing the composer's musical remains (II, 562–63). Similarly, the intercourse between Charlus and Jupien is the occasion for the novel's global commentary on homosexuality.

The initial moment of both scenes, then, consists in an encounter between (homosexual) actors and an audience (Marcel), himself in the position of the classical speculative subject or observer. The theatrical act, however, whose framework imposes a barrier between the audience and the stage, soon gives way to a commentary behind which Marcel is the moving force. In this fashion, the homosexual act *engenders* Marcel's existence as a writer. Although divorced from the system of human reproduction, homosexuality nevertheless plays a formative role in the production of writing.

The *dramatic* encounter between Charlus and Jupien serves as the allegorical kernel of an extended discourse on homosexuality which has, given its rhetorics of nature and law, no less than scientific aspirations. This commentary will insist on homosexuality's equiprimordiality with heterosexuality, on the coexistence of both modes within the sphere of nature. It will describe homosexuals sociologically as a race of the dispossessed and deterritorialized. On the highest level of hypothesis, homosexuality becomes a matrix of esthetic activity, a site of principles and operations that throughout Proust undermine and complicate the surface level of reality. In this regard, homosexuality involves intricate camouflages, dissimulations, distortions of identity, and innovative syntheses in the relation between the subject and the other.

As the impetus behind, the *illustration* motivating, this allegorical sermon, the scene between Charlus and Jupien is geared toward confirming these observations. Particularly prominent in the description of the scene are rhetorics of *law* and *nature*. The homosexual setting discovered by Marcel will be no less scientific, no less determined by laws of generality, than the phenomenological space depicted in Elstir's landscapes of Normandy. In anticipating Marcel's insistence on the equality and complete parity of homosexuality with any other order in terms of naturalness and cultural venerability, the scene paints Charlus's intercourse with Jupien in pointedly natural terms. Their coupling is described as closely analogous to the fertilization of an orchid by an insect.

> Then, realising that no one could see me, I decided not to let myself be disturbed again, for fear of missing . . . the arrival . . . of the insect sent from so far as ambassador to the virgin who had been so long waiting for him to appear. I knew that this expectancy was no more

passive than in the male flower, whose stamens had spontaneously curved so that the insect might more easily receive their offering; similarly, the female flower that stood here, if the insect came, would coquettishly arch her styles [*styles*], and, to be more effectively penetrated by him, would imperceptibly advance, like a hypocritical but ardent damsel, to meet him half-way. The laws of the vegetable kingdom are themselves governed by other laws. . . . My reflexions had followed a tendency which I shall describe in due course, and I had already drawn from the visible stratagems of flowers a conclusion that bore upon a whole unconscious element of literary work, when I saw M. de Charlus coming away from the Marquise. (II, 4–5)

This passage is an allegory within an allegory, an ostensibly natural description setting the stage for the concrete act that will transpire between Charlus and Jupien. By its end, the passage discloses both an "unconscious element" of the literary work, one running through the entire *Recherche,* and the "other laws" of the vegetable kingdom. What the unconscious literary element and the other, vegetable laws have in common is that they do not exclude homosexual activity. The mating ritual between the insect and the flower described earlier in the passage tolerates a variation and transposition of masculine and feminine roles. In the domain of nature, the coquettish female flower is more pronounced in her activity than the male flower, whose stamens stand erect in the expectation of the insect's dominance. In nature, the logic of this description runs, the status of the male is complex rather than monolithic. The masculine does not simply project spatially or assert itself. In nature the masculine is already sundered between erection and passive expectation. The natural domain of this fertilization is both primordial and advanced, exists both at the same prescientific origin from which heterosexuality is descended and as an experimental medium, subject to botanical and zoological laws. The passage determines homosexuality both as nature and law.

The "other" law of autofecundation, the law receptive to variation and synthesis between active and passive postures, is also akin to the "unconscious" element within the *Recherche,* that is, to the network of homosexual relations that have flourished since Montjouvain and Odette's adventures but enter full bloom only around the figure of Charlus. The dialectical possibilities entertained by homosexuality, the hybrids produced through the crossings of masculine and feminine roles, thus extend into literary ramifications. The literary dimension of the above scenario becomes quite explicit in the description of the female element of the flower as *styles*, both stylistic unities and styluses. The interchangeability of the masculine and the feminine in the world of "natural" laws and the complex crossings that they produce thus engender an entire esthetics, one which is always already present in the *Recherche* but which the figure of Charlus allows to be explicit. The "coming out" of these autoerotic laws and esthetic principles is akin to the unmasking of the unconscious in psychoanalysis.

It is in the context of the bizarre crossing between the necessity of natural behavior and the detachment of scientific law that *we*, sharing Marcel's vantage point, observe the behavior of Charlus and Jupien. Proust's scientific rhetoric allows the scene to take on a slapstick quality, as if under the special effects of stage lighting, two people are suddenly metamorphosed into creatures of a lower order. Jupien "takes root" in the "ground before M. Charlus . . . like a plant" (II, 5). Having "thrown up his head, given a becoming tilt to his body, placed his hand with a grotesque impertinence on his hip, stuck out his behind," Jupien poses himself "with the coquetry that the orchid might have adopted on the providential arrival of the bee" (II, 5–6). The "inarticulate sounds" (II, 9) that these men, functioning as caricatures of lower organisms, produce is a parodic natural language. Yet the comic "as if" that makes Jupien an orchid and Charlus a bee does not account for the totality of the scene, as Marcel specifies. "The scene was not, however, positively comic, it was stamped with a strangeness, or if you like a naturalness, the beauty of which steadily increased" (II, 6). By this equation, an uncanniness or alienation accompanies the comic nature of the homosexual realm.

This tragicomic sense of chance conjunction gives rise to an extended meditation on the subject of homosexuality, one notable for its emotional intensity as well as its thematic scope. This long apostrophe is divided between a sociological survey of the homosexual predicament, experienced individually and collectively, and an excursis on the wider epistemological, ontological, and interpretative problems that sexual inversion raises. On a sociological level, Marcel characterizes the collectivity of inverts as a disenfranchised and universally suspect group of outcasts akin to the Jews:

> Their honour precarious, their liberty provisional . . . their position unstable, like that of the poet who one day was feasted at every table, applauded in every theater in London, and on the next was driven from every lodging, unable to find a pillow on which to lay his head, turning the mill like Samson and saying like him: "The two sexes shall die, each in a place apart!"; excluded even, save on the days of general disaster when the majority rally round the victim as the Jews rallied round Dreyfus . . . like the Jews again . . . shunning one another, seeking out those who are most directly their opposite, who do not desire their company . . . but also brought into the company of their own kind by the ostracism that strikes them . . . and going in search . . . of cases of

inversion in history, taking pleasure in recalling that Socrates was one
of themselves, as the Israelites claim that Jesus was one of them, without
reflecting that there were no abnormals when homosexuality was the
norm, no anti-Christians before Christ . . . a reprobate part of the
human whole, but an important part, suspected where it does not exist,
flaunting itself, insolent and unpunished, where its existence is never
guessed; numbering its adherents everywhere. . . . (II, 13–15)

Astonishing as it may seem, this extract derives from a single attenuated sentence, the longest in the *Recherche*, a verbal ejaculation trig-
gered by the explicitness of the Baron's activities. The sentence is a
rising refrain of the injustices committed against homosexuals, by
themselves and by others, in thought and act. In its argumentative
thrust, the passage again stresses the equiprimordiality of inversion.
Just as nature provides for autofecundation and male passivity, so
there is no original order that homoeroticism violates. Inverts and
Christians become deviant only after there are sexual mores and anti-
Christians to persecute them. Homosexuality thus resides in the position of the Derridean supplement. Like Derrida's trace, homosexuality is effaced by the social organization in which it plays an integral
role.[17]

It is in the context of such categorical yet irrational exclusion that
the more theoretically interesting implications of homosexuality
arise—the dissimulations, the confused identifications, the un-
answered quests, and the betrayals. The logical complexity attached
to the situation of a Charlus is considerable: his temperament belies
his appearance; he seeks what he physically resembles; he resembles
temperamentally the antithesis of his physical gender. The difficulty
of Charlus's position accounts for the implicit exasperations of homoerotic yearning: "they fall in love with precisely that type of man who
has nothing feminine about him, who is not an invert and consequently cannot love them in return" (II, 13). Such logical and logisti-
cal difficulties arise from a system of generic categories that is inherently inefficient, that fails to engender. It is by virtue of the implicit
duplicities within the system of gender that sexual identity is always
mistaken identity, that innuendoes and aspersions are structurally
false.

Yet for all its encyclopaedic breadth, the greatest achievement of
the homoerotic manifesto that erupts from Marcel may well take
place on the metaphoric and stylistic levels. On no less than three
occasions, Marcel qualifies the conditions and activities of homosexuality in terms of pregnancy and birth. Pregnancy, a state seemingly
reserved for the economy and metaphysics of reproduction, is the

metaphoric correlative for the *style* in which this definitive statement is couched. Marcel's declaration and plaint is filled with tangents, involuted with parenthetical introjections, no more so than in the runaway sentence alluded to and cited in part above. Ironically, the style that Proust fashioned for a homosexual discourse is *pregnant*, just as on the metaphoric level Marcel repeatedly describes homoeroticism in terms of birth. This structure reproduces itself on the widest level. Within the narrative structure of the novel, the romances of Marcel with Albertine and Charlus with Charlie, both predicated on the Swann overture, are impregnated with each other. The love stories of Marcel and Charlus are counter homosexual and heterosexual narrative strands coiled around a foetal center of textual apprehensions common to both.

The metaphor of impregnation invades the multiple dimensions of the homosexual matrix. On the most concrete level, Marcel compares the inarticulate noises emitted by Charlus and Jupien to a mother's birth cries: "I concluded from this later on that there is another thing as vociferous as pain, namely pleasure, especially when there is added to it—failing the fear of an eventual parturition, which could not be present in this case . . . an immediate afterthought of cleanliness" (II, 9). Even while formulating the remoteness of homosexuality to human reproduction, this passage metaphorically bonds the two subsystems. The wider interpretative problems posed by homoeroticism also open themselves to the image of pregnancy. Marcel repeatedly describes the homosexual mode as an effaced script or cipher in an individual that, once rendered legible, illuminates the person in a new light and discovers a new coherence for his traits. In this regard, homosexuality becomes a new legibility that decodes a hitherto incongruous character. Marcel figures this recognition as a sentence "broken up in letters scattered at random upon a table" that becomes, arranged properly, "a thought which one can never afterwards forget" (II, 13). And specifically with regard to Charlus, Marcel compares the new intelligibility of his actions and tastes to the discovery of pregnancy in a woman: "Until that moment I had been, in the presence of M. de Charlus, in the position of an absent-minded man who, standing before a pregnant woman whose distended outline he has failed to remark, persists, while she smilingly reiterates: 'Yes, I am a little tired just now,' in asking her indiscreetly: 'Why, what is the matter with you?' But let some one say to him: 'She is expecting a child,' suddenly he catches sight of her abdomen and ceases to see anything else. It is the explanation that opens our eyes; the dispelling of an error gives us an additional sense" (II, 12). It is a distended but previously unnoticed line that revolutionizes the image of Charlus for Marcel, a line emanating from a pregnant woman that becomes the trait of Charlus's current activities.

The metaphor of pregnancy extends into Marcel's sociological profile of homosexuality as well. Momentarily eschewing the activities of sadists and transvestites, Marcel characterizes the predicament of what he terms the "solitary invert" (II, 19). The hypothetical case that he formulates is endowed with the indefinite and timeless setting of a Kierkegaardian or Kafkan parable. The shame, ostracism, and isolation endured by the nameless "solitary" graphically illustrates the conditions set down in Marcel's attenuated (juridical as well as discursive) sentence. Among the punishments to which the invert is condemned is an ongoing insecurity in his relationships, a continuous threat of betrayal. He is taken up and abandoned at will, according to the dictates of social propriety and circumstance. In the jarringly uneven relationship between the hypothetical "solitary" (whose impersonality only underscores his closeness to "Marcel") and a "boyhood's friend," this is precisely what happens. The image of pregnancy intervenes in this association as well, both as a figure for the forces that interrupt the homoerotic liaison and as the circumstances that bring it about.

> Meanwhile the married neighbor of our recluse has returned; before the beauty of the young bride and the demonstrative affection of her husband, on the day when their friend is obliged to invite them to dinner, he feels ashamed of the past. Already in an interesting condition, she must return home early, leaving her husband behind; he, when the time has come for him to go home also, asks his host to accompany him for part of the way; at first no suspicion enters his mind, but at the crossroads he finds himself thrown down in the grass. . . . And their meetings begin again, and continue until the day when there comes to live not far off a cousin of the young woman, with whom her husband is now constantly to be seen. And he, if the twice-abandoned friend calls . . . is furious, and repulses him with indignation that the other has not had the tact to foresee the disgust which he must henceforth inspire. (II, 21)

Pregnancy inserts itself at the "crossroads" which is the site of the invert's ongoing quandary. The invert is vulnerable to betrayal occasioned both by other men and women. He stands at a crossroads in time as well as between the sexes. The friendships of the past may recur, but there is no telling when they will be severed by the revelations and hypocrisies of the future. In this fragile position, akin to the passive extension of the male flower, the homosexual is in a secondary role, subject to the whims and fashions of his *other*. He occupies the marginal station of the dispensable but structurally implicit supplement.

By its persistence, however, the metaphor of pregnancy invoked in these passages suggests that the homoerotic matrix, for all its dissimulation, sterility, and marginality, never thoroughly detaches itself from the heterosexual economy of reproduction. The relation between the two countermodels is one of intertwining, of mutual impregnation, rather than of simple contradiction. On a metaphoric level at least, the self-fertilizing order of homosexual relations never definitively cuts the cord leading to its reproductive counterpart, just as Marcel, on that fateful childhood night informed by Swann, cannot relinquish his mother. From the pregnant woman may descend an invert, an entire order of inversion, rife with logical and epistemological complexities. But this turn of events does not sever the "exquisite thread" (I, 23) to the mother or between the countermodels.

If both strands of the *Recherche*'s double romance are twined around a common foetus, the scientific laws of inversion may illuminate the contents of that evident but dark womb. Primarily in its logic and logical permutations, the homosexual matrix is descended from the father. Charlus's situation and the difficult position of all inverts spawns a calculus of identifications and analogies. In a passage we have already touched upon, Charlus is *like* a woman in temperament, *like* a man in physique. Even where they discover hybrids and deviations, such logical qualifications stem from a hierarchical and paternal system of identities and determinations (the latter being the philosophical correlative to biological reproduction). The father is not a very prominent or, for that matter, even consistent figure in *Swann's Way*. He merely sires a few interdicts. A far more persistent fossil of his presence is the logic by which homoeroticism is measured and categorized.

Yet as we have seen, homosexuality is also a revolutionary code within a code, a partially effaced legend that transforms the nature and signification of its referents. The umbilical cord that the homoerotic matrix never finally severs from the economy of reproduction spins itself into narrative and the operating principles of texts. A work of remembrance, the *Recherche* never forgets its prehistoric debt to the womb as a generatrix of textual activity and awareness. Acknowledging this attachment, Proust fashions both a pregnant discourse and a pregnant narrative structure. The *Recherche*'s widest units, its romances and the episodes that encompass entire social coteries, may supplant each other, but they intertwine in such a way that they may all be continued in *The Past Recaptured*. And this weave mimics the complications—the introjections, the parenthetical remarks, the organic bubbles—that Proust encompassed within the microscopic medium of his style.

The figure of the pregnant invert, the undermining of formal injunctions that is nonetheless filled with a certain expansive plenitude—this metaphor encompasses the *Recherche* but locates the other major experiments of modernism. When the image of pregnancy is first encountered in the *Recherche,* in conjunction with the unfortunate maid who resembles the *Charity* of Giotto (I, 61–62, 92–95), the text is exuberant in the expanse of its yet-unlimited suggestiveness. The persecuted maid joins the novel's other characters, such as Odette, who by resemblance inhabit and test the threshold between art and life. The maid is also well cast in the comedy surrounding Françoise's domestic sadism. The occasion discloses both an unsuspected cruelty and compassion on the part of Françoise, and provides another illustration of the great law of *Swann's Way:* that appearances invariably deceive.

The pregnant invert may be a degenerate descendant of Giotto's *Charity,* whose plenitude has been tempered by a familiarity with the numerous culs-de-sac that inhabit and structure the *Recherche.* Yet for all the limits disclosed in the course of the novel, for all its evidences of structural, logical, and moral decadence, the pregnant invert continues to partake of metaphoric wealth, an Ali Baba's cave of association.

Suspended between dialectical qualification and textual production, the figure of the pregnant invert illustrates the global scene at the rise of modernism and the options available to the Hegelian aftermath. The international scope of this setting can be documented by turning to Henry James, whose *The Turn of the Screw* shares with the Proustian synthesis a common stage.

[V]

JAMES: TWISTS OF THE GOVERNESS

The central actor in Henry James's *The Turn of the Screw* and his other ghost stories may well be the human nervous system.[18] As the narrative moves through a sequence of sudden reversals of readerly expectations and toward the vertiginous plateau where none of its frames of reference hold fast or provide perspectival consistency, it is the nerves, our own as well as the governess's, which pay for the groundless footing. Our suspicions may dart from Flora and Miles to

Mrs. Grose and may even alight upon the governess and Douglas, the final authorities to which the story grants us appeal, yet the narrative's demonic shifts are finally inscribed upon the organic system of the affections itself.

The story was composed at a time when Freud was supplementing his neurological account of consciousness with metaphysical and psychological constructs.[19] While the sources of stimulation, narrative as well as physiological, may be infinite, considerable coordination is required to marshal a set of facts and possibilities to the point where they effect a discharge of the nerves in anxiety. Yet it is precisely toward this effect that *The Turn of the Screw* is directed. The story is a meticulously constructed generator of a shock closely akin to the one that Walter Benjamin underscored as the insignia of the Modern age. Just as the Freudian trauma penetrates the psyche's own shield of defenses, the shocks almost tangentially disclosed in the course of the story undermine the reassurances that the text itself has volunteered.

The Turn of the Screw hovers in the uncertainties entertained by the too fertile imagination of a governess. The story, to whatever extent a jarringly abrupt narrative allows for one, concerns the degree to which the governess's suspicions as to the apparitions that she witnesses at Bly infect her relations with her charges, two children, her colleague, and herself. The basic unit of the story's momentum and force is the intellectual gesture in which an idle speculation becomes a conclusion, in which a precipitous determination predicates subsequent beliefs and actions. Through the repetition of this reflexive gesture on the part of the governess, the story becomes a vertiginous fabulation of hastily (if not falsely) drawn conclusions.[20]

Although the governess, as the story eventually and cruelly reveals, *governs,* she is initially cast in the role of an exemplary reader. Like Hegel's Antigone and Kierkegaard's women, at first she occupies the passive position of the observer and receptor. If the governess's hallucinations evolve from privately witnessed aberrations to actual personages in collusion with the children, if her anxieties progress beyond her psyche to the point where one of her charges dies of fright, this may be easily dismissed as a distinctly feminine hysteria. The core of the story, consisting of the governess's own written account of her stay at Bly and interactions with the children, Mrs. Grose, and the apparitions, is surrounded in a double narrative frame. Apart from serving as a setting for the governess's text, this framework provides the background and conditions of what might be considered a fictive case history of hysteria.

One element of the narrative framework concerns the rather practical question of how the governess's tale is to reach the hands of

Douglas, host of a Christmas Eve gathering at which the story's narrator is a guest, so that he may read it aloud. Nothing could be more intimate than a story, even a ghost story, told around a fire at the most familial moment of the year, radiating a trust and warmth that would seemingly extend to the rapport between a governess and her charges. Yet at every turn the governess's narrative undermines the Kierkegaardian intimacy of this initial setting.

The story's first suspense is the waiting the guests must tolerate until the governess's manuscript arrives in the London post. Douglas informs his audience that the woman in question was his sister's governess, a tangential fact of some consequence, since it places him in the position of little Miles. It is Douglas who forges the central tale's setting in a second sense. By virtue of his "personal connection" to the governess, he can fill in other incidental but decisive details, specifically those relating to the circumstances and motives surrounding the governess's original acceptance of her position. It is from Douglas that we learn how "handsome and bold and pleasant, offhand and gay and kind" Bly's absent master was (p. 4); the condition "that she should never trouble him—but never, never: neither appeal nor complain nor write about anything; only meet all questions herself" (p. 6); and that having seen the master "only twice" and receiving only one handshake in thanks "for the sacrifice, she already felt rewarded" (p. 6). Apart from performing narrative groundwork, the story's frame thus qualifies all that follows by a specific symptomology, the pathology of hysteria. Hopelessly in love with an absent master, deprived not only of sexual gratification with him but even of words, the governess seems a textbook case of hysteria. The textbook, by Freud and Breuer, appeared in 1895, three years before James's story. The governess's visions, her hypnotic moments when time seems to stop, her machinations in winning Mrs. Grose to her point of view, and the ultimate transference of her anxiety to the children she ostensibly protects all seem to be hysterical manifestations that arise in the place of the master. In this regard, it would seem possible to dismiss both the governess and her narrative as mere onsets of "female trouble," a generically marked exaggeration to be deflated through the application of some measure and restraint.

To be sure, the parallels between the governess's experiences at Bly and the symptoms of hysteria set out in Breuer and Freud's *Studies on Hysteria* are nothing less than uncanny. In their treatise, the first major code of psychoanalytical research, Breuer and Freud settle on a group of recurrent hysterical symptoms, including "surplus excitation," "hypnoid states," and "splitting of the mind" or "double conscience," which they ascribe to sexual repression. In a striking number of instances, the governess's conditions at Bly correspond to ones characterizing the cases of the seminal patients of psychoanalysis, such as Fraüleins Anna O. and Elisabeth von R. By her own account, the governess's visions are hypnotic and marked by division. The repressively unselfish role of guardian (or nurse) is regarded by both Breuer and Freud as one particularly conducive to anxiety. The child-care situation was, for the progenitors of psychoanalysis, the breeding ground for premature sexual activity in children, another of the standard preconditions for adult neurosis. In this regard, the governess is more the cause than the sufferer of hysteria, yet Freud observes that child molestation often repeats abuses suffered earlier by the perpetrator. Not a case history in the formal sense, James's story stops at introducing material from the governess's past in explanation of her behavior.

Yet if we wish to write off the governess as a repressed hysteric, James offers us literary aids for this task beyond the aims and institution of psychoanalysis.[21] The arbitrary manner in which the governess forces interpretations upon both the phenomena she observes and the words she hears comprises a kind of inferential hysteria. The rigidity of her conclusions often far exceeds the uncertainty that prompted them, suggesting a logical hyperexcitability installed within her character. In her only promiscuity, the governess entertains a wide array of possibilities while she is at Bly: that the place is haunted altogether, who the apparitions are, that the children are their victims or their allies. Yet her logical point of departure at any given moment, her temporary working assumption, is almost invariably reached through this process of reading in, which is analogous to *projection* in psychoanalytical theory. The formative role of this inferential leap in her psyche has even penetrated her *conscious:* "by the time the morrow's sun was high I had restlessly read into the facts before us almost all the meaning they were to receive from subsequent and more cruel occurrences" (pp. 27–28). "I only sat there on my tomb and read into what my little friend had said to me the fulness of its meaning" (p. 57). It is on the basis of this projective mode of reading that the governess *decides* that Mrs. Grose speaks of someone *beside* the master (p. 12), that the apparition known as "Quint" is after Miles (p. 25), and that the children are in collusion with the ghosts that only she sees (pp. 52–53).

On the basis of this literary instance of hypersuggestibility and the affinities between the governess's conditions and those outlined in the Freudian textbook, it would seem perfectly appropriate to dismiss both the governess and the story as illustrations or caricatures of the theory of hysteria. Yet such an application terminates with an abruptness belying the prolonged indeterminacy that the story sustains. Even deeper than the governess's tendencies to hysteria are the roots of its uncanny moments of "visitation" in the matrix of Hegelian operations also underlying Freudian neurosis. When we turn to those horrifying and still scenes that serve as the "episodes" in her disease and as strategic turning points in her conquest of Bly, we see that they are catalogues of long-established reflexive and speculative operations.

> It was plump, one afternoon, in the middle of my very hour: the children were tucked away and I had come out for my stroll. . . . Someone would appear there at the turn of a path and would stand before me and smile and approve. . . . What arrested me on the spot—and with a shock much greater than any vision had allowed for—was the sense that my imagination had, in a flash, turned real. He did stand there! but high up, beyond the lawn and at the very top of the tower. . . . This tower was one of a pair—square, incongruous, crenelated structures— that were distinguished, for some reason, though I could see little difference, as the old and the new. They flanked opposite ends of the house and were probably architectural absurdities. . . . I admired them, had fancies about them . . . yet it was not at such an elevation that the figure I had so often invoked seemed most in place.
>
> It produced in me, this figure, in the clear twilight, I remember, two distinct gasps of emotion. . . . My second [surprise] was a violent perception of the mistake of my first: the man who met my eyes was not the person I had precipitately supposed. . . . It was as if, while I took it in— what I did take in—all the rest of the scene had been stricken with death. I can hear it again, as I write. . . . The rooks stopped cawing in the golden sky and the friendly hour lost, for the unspeakable minute, all its voice. The gold was still in the sky . . . and the man who looked at me over the battlements was as definite as a picture in a frame. . . . He was in one of the angles. . . . He turned away; that was all I knew (pp. 15–17)

The governess's first horror, a specifically reflexive nightmare, takes place amid the benign plumpness of the afternoon, at her own special hour, when the children are "tucked away." The warmth of this golden "friendly hour" recalls the governess's first images of Bly: the "bumping, swinging coach" that brings her there, the "most pleasant impression" she has of "the broad, clear front, its open windows and fresh curtains . . . the lawn and the bright flowers" (p. 7). The harbinger of horror in the story is often an emotional release figured in intimacy and breadth, a relaxation of the defenses.

And yet, what exactly is the terror of this episode? On one level, the trauma is described as one that takes place on the border between the outside and the inside. And this particular shock allows for no exit. At first the governess is shaken by the uncanny *correspondence* between her sexual fantasy of the handsome "someone" and what she actually sees. Yet no sooner does this fright take place, of the imagination's "turning real," than it is compounded by an awareness of the discrepancy between the projection and the actuality: "he" stands not at the expected elevation. In both of its possible ramifications, then, the discrepancy between the outside and the inside upsets the governess. A reality that confirms fantasy is horrifying, and this shock is only aggravated when the correspondence begins to unravel. One dimension of the governess's terror, then, is the unmitigated unsettling caused by the compulsive displacement that transpires between the outside and the inside, among the most fundamental momentums of the Hegelian text.

Accompanying this compulsive and fatal comparison between the interior and the exterior are the fantastic symmetry and division that prevail within both the scene and the governess's reactions to it. The double towers flank the house symmetrically. The triggering of the hallucination provokes "two distinct gasps of emotion" in the governess. Yet this pronounced doubling or bifurcation dominates the scene not by virtue of its status as a formal category so much as in the relations of reciprocity that it initiates. In the sense that the male figure in this scene is a projection of the governess's, he exists as her double. More unsettling than this hypothesis are the implications, noted by the passage, that as a double of the governess, the apparition usurps her claims to "reality," becomes exactly as actual as she is. The ornamental doubling in the landscape underscores a much less palatable speculation: that the figment of the imagination has become as "real" as the "person," the thinking subject, the governing governess.

The schizoid mutuality of the relationship between the subject and the image is what gives the consummating horror to those moments in the visitations when the apparitions *stare back*. Shortly after the above citation ends, we read: "So I saw him as I see the letters I form on this page; then . . . as if to add to the spectacle, he . . . passed, looking at me hard all the while. . . . Yes, I had the sharpest sense that during this transit he never took his eyes from me" (p. 17). It is the imagistic autonomy attained by the governess's projections when they stare back that endows her visions with their fullest horror. And the reciprocity most succinctly abbreviated in the figure of the simultaneous and mutual regard of entities that may or may not share the same status, this sustained parity forms an economy governing the entire story. The story is calibrated according to a calculus of uncanny reciprocities, in love, communication, dissimulation, and protection. At several moments in the text, the governess assumes that Mrs. Grose and the children are concealing something from her. But the governess's suspicions that Mrs. Grose camouflages the apparitions at Bly (pp. 11–12, 27) and that the children conspire with the visitors (p. 52) do not preempt her own dissimulations (pp. 38–39). In a similar vein, the governess stifles any attempted contact between her companions and the absent master (p. 54), just as by contract she must repress her communicative urges. A final irony of the story is that little Miles, having been fatally influenced by the governess's projections, assumes the same protective stance toward her that comprises only one limited facet of her relation to the children (p. 66). And why should the reciprocal scrutiny that is a constitutive element of the governess's visitations not extend into every aspect of a story that *she* composes?

Doubling—in the above passage of towers, gasps, figures, and regards—is the basic unit of repetition, its primary instance. And the passage we read certainly harbors the seeds of the story's compulsive repetitions. The strange figure appears before the governess "at the turn of a path," and in recording the scene, in writing it, she can "hear" its sounds "again." The governess's horror accumulates in the persistence of scenic repetition. As in the case of Kierkegaardian repetition, the scenes vary as they transpose certain basic elements. As the first visitation, the scene we presently scan may contain the fullest vocabulary of elements: doubles, reciprocal regards, stillness, scaffolding and other frameworks, angles, and distortions. Subsequent scenes supplement this vocabulary; they also edit out certain of the elements. Quint's second visitation, for example, takes place indoors, enabling the implicit rhetoric of reflection in the first to become overt. Quint peers at the governess through a window (a "glass," also suggesting a mirror) situated near a staircase, an addition to the earlier external scaffolding (p. 20). In the third visitation, the apparition's participation is so intense that he becomes the scene's "spectator" (p. 29). It is in this episode that the story's imagistic *mise en scène* expands. Not only does the governess suffer the agonizing tension of her parity with an uninvited voyeur: she begins to measure the impact of the scene of a third party, in this case Flora. The governess awaits "what a cry from her, what some innocent sign either of interest or alarm, would tell me" (p. 30). Expanded to its full complexity, the visitation scene places the governess midway in a specular quandary. Simultaneously, she must mark both the unwanted visitor already gazing at her and the impact of the scene, whether "real" or invented on another audience, comprising Mrs. Grose and the children.

These scenes are divided off from the rest of the narrative by framing devices as effective as the scaffolding that often becomes part of the stage props. Specifically, it is the sudden hush that comes over these moments, their unbearable stillness, that separates them from the overall narrative flow. In fashioning a narrative that fluctuates between intimate storytelling and rigorously autonomous scenes, the governess experiments in that imagistic tradition synthesized in Kierkegaard's *The Concept of Irony*. The story's ample rhetoric of *fixing*, in the sense both of staring and of holding fast (pp. 3, 41), is indicative of the power of the stasis that prevails within the image. For James as for Kierkegaard, the self-enclosure of the image precludes the possibility of progress by bringing it to a halt.

Time stops during the scenes of visitation because they are so totally *absorbing*. For the governess, their fascination is itself a trespass, ending "the general high propriety" that rules at Bly when she first arrives (p. 15). The stoppage of time effected by the visitation scenes is in direct proportion to the degree to which the governess is captivated by her charges. In her attempts to definitively know and fix the children, the governess is in a position similar to Winterbourne's in relation to Daisy Miller. Daisy Miller so fascinates Winterbourne that he surveys her from every angle, but most of what he finds, by virtue of the standards he applies, is impropriety. Miles and Flora pose a similar riddle to the governess. In her attempts to resolve her interpretative problem, the governess treats the children as an imagistic surface to be *filled in* by projection: "They had nothing but me, and I—well, I had *them*. . . . This chance presented itself in an image richly material. I was a screen—I was to stand before them. The more I saw, the less they would. I began to watch them in a stifled suspense . . ." (p. 28). As in the case of Daisy Miller, the blank image under scrutiny is to be not only filled in by the observer but stifled and abused.[22] The children are eventually pushed out of the picture and blinded. Miles's beauty places the governess "under the spell" (p. 20), and for this reason, perhaps, he does not escape her. The girl-child is more vigorous. By virtue of either extreme innocence or depravity, Flora refuses to be shaken and thus denies the governess confirmation of her uncanny experiences. In the line of Daisy Miller, Flora "absolutely declined to be puzzled" (p. 43), to her warden's desperation. Not only, then, does the governess's experience break down with a sequence of imagistic moments, episodes informed by the Romantic tradition of the image. The governess's interactions take the form of imagistic activities: interpretation, projection, captivation, enclosure.

In James's vocabulary as in Hegel's, turning is the basic metaphor for repetition. James's screw may penetrate deeper (or tighten); its threads may move. But the activity of revolution characterizes the story's compulsive recurrences. And yet, not only do the story's apparitions turn their backs on the observer (pp. 17, 41); not only does a reciprocal, reflexive vocabulary of fright *re*turn. The turns of the screw are upheavals, unmaskings, and debunkings of the presuppositions that the text offers as givens. The turns of the screw effect a series of fictive negations that are all the more bewildering because the assumptions undermined are not abstract philosophical terms but items derived from a language of consciousness and life. It is in the sense of such turns that the governess passes from an intimate colleague and protectress to an author, the author of Mrs. Grose's unhinging and Miles's death as well as of the narrative. The governess *speaks* a language of nurturing and salvation (pp. 28, 65, 79, 81), but she composes one of bewilderment and wild suggestion. By the same token, Mrs. Grose and the children *turn* from dissimulations and conspirators to victims of a master, not an absentee one but an authoring one. In its vacillations between threat and protection, vulnerability and abuse, the story explores the potentials released by the Hegelian dialectic of the master and the slave.

As writer and author, the governess offers an alternate mastery to the one to which she initially subordinates herself. As the orchestrator of scenes of reciprocal indeterminacy and the impetus for the story's turns of the screw, she composes a world that supersedes the conventions from which it is derived. We have already cited some of the evidence that suggests the *story's* grounding in operations of internalization and externalization, bifurcation, reciprocity, and circularity. As we have seen, this matrix underlies not only the story but also the Freudian constructs according to which it may be read. Yet as an author, as a writer in the text, the governess composes a domain unified by no center or consistency. The story is a collage of mutually untenable logical conditions.

In the story's third and fourth sections, the narrative transcribes the voice of a governess who regards herself as the victim of strange visitations. In section 7 we witness a governess who assumes that the children know of the visitations. In sections 10 and 11 we read a narrative voice assuming the children to be in treacherous collusion with the visitors. In section 20, the governess sees figures that no one else sees; in the very next section we find Flora in absolute terror of her protectress. And in the final section, the governess embraces Miles with clutches as deadly as they are affectionate. These logically incongruous pictures come to us via the medium of a voice consistent in its intimacy. But this vocal steadiness betrays us, as the children are betrayed.

Rather than a narrative transcribing the presence of a *centered* self or personality, what we have in this text is a story without a center. This story shifts between assumptions so incongruous as to suggest either the absence of any central personality or authorship or, if some origin be required, the presence of a subject so fragmented and split as to be held together by no logic other than madness. The story becomes a recording of a decentered voice, hence one with no master, a narrative beyond control.

But the governess *is* the story's author. In fabulating a story beyond consistency and logic which nonetheless appropriates the Hegelian matrix of speculative operations, she removes the text from the space of mastery and inscribes it within the problematic of writing. To the extent that the governess does suffer from hysteria, it is not as a psychological category but as a condition of writing. It is the implicit hysteria of writing that imprisons the author in a self-enclosed domain and fabulates a miasma of repetitive yet shifting details.[23] The governess authors the story in the absence of the master's love, phallus, protection, and control. That the text replaces the dominant orders of reflection and hysteria with its own economics of writing in no way denies its debt to Hegelian operations. This, in a word, is the locus of the seminal works of modernism, moving toward a problematic of writing from within a framework of reflexive gestures.

The moments of textual violence that break out within Kafka's novels, as well as the intricate Proustian artifacts, are also situated in the transition charted by *The Turn of the Screw*. These and other distinctively modern experiments benefit from the dual possibilities afforded by the governess's story. The resources of fiction can move toward an explicit acknowledgement of the dynamics of writing without relegating the discursive activities here associated with "Hegel" to some closed and rigid otherness or past. Too much exuberance surrounds the groundbreaking explorations of modern literature to warrant a decisive threshold separating the outside and the inside of systematic thought. As both Hegel and Kierkegaard demonstrate, too much play and inefficiency are accommodated within philosophical speculation to definitively close it off from the textual activity of the artifacts that have recourse to it.

The impelling question facing modernism at the beginning of the twentieth century concerns the relation between the outside and the inside of the system of speculative thought. While within the field of critical theory this question has been specifically posed since 1967, with the appearance of three groundbreaking works by Jacques Derrida, the problem and its ramifications continue to undergo refinement.[24] If we follow the lead of such modernists as Proust and James, who examined the nature of language and the literary text from within the Hegelian aftermath, the border between the outside and inside can continue to be a threshold of *ouverture* and discovery.

NOTES

ONE

Introduction: From Philosophy to Poetics

1. Jacques Derrida is responsible for endowing this question with its full urgency and range of implications. See Jacques Derrida, *Of Grammatology*, trans. Gayatri C. Spivak (Baltimore: Johns Hopkins University Press, 1976), pp. 27–35, 44–52.

2. For a superb investigation into the possibilities of a tropological history, see Hayden White, *Tropics of Discourse* (Baltimore: Johns Hopkins University Press, 1978), pp. 1–25. For a discussion of the ironic perspective ingrained into Hegel's thought and inherited by his followers, see idem, *Metahistory* (Baltimore: Johns Hopkins University Press, 1973), pp. 43–85.

3. Friedrich Nietzsche, *The Gay Science*, trans. Walter Kaufmann (New York: Random House, 1974), pp. 163–64.

4. Walter Benjamin, *Illuminations*, ed. Hannah Arendt (New York: Schocken Books, 1969), pp. 116–17, 204–5.

5. Jean Baudrillard, *The Mirror of Production*, trans. Mark Poster (St. Louis: Telos Press, 1975), p. 39.

6. Ibid.: "Work and non-work: here is a 'revolutionary' theme. . . . The end of the end of the exploitation by work is this reverse fascination with non-work, this reverse mirage of free time (forced time-free time, full time-empty-time. . . ."

7. Ibid., pp. 114–15.

8. Ibid., p. 29. For Baudrillard's discussion of the subjective implications of utility, see his *For a Critique of the Political Economy of the Sign*, trans. Charles Levin (St. Louis: Telos Press, 1981), pp. 132–36.

9. Walter Benjamin, "On Some Motifs in Baudelaire," in *Illuminations*, pp. 155–63.

10. Hugh Kenner, *The Pound Era* (Berkeley and Los Angeles: University of California Press, 1971).

11. Philippe Lacoue-Labarthe and Jean-Luc Nancy, *L'Absolu littéraire: Théorie de la littérature du romantisme allemand* (Paris: Seuil, 1978).

12. This point is established, and its theoretical ramifications explored, by Rodolphe Gasché in "Deconstruction as Criticism," in *Glyph 6: Textual Studies* (Baltimore: Johns Hopkins University Press, 1979), pp. 177–215.

13. See Jacques Derrida, *Speech and Phenomena*, trans. David B. Allison (Evanston: Northwestern University Press, 1973), pp. 40–44, 56–60, 68–69, 75–80.

14. See Jacques Derrida, "Ousia et grammé," in *Marges de la philosophie* (Paris: Minuit, 1972), pp. 33–38, 50–51, 59, 75–78.

TWO

Five Hegelian Metaphors

1. George Wilhelm Friedrich Hegel, *Phenomenology of Spirit*, trans. A. V. Miller (Oxford: Oxford University Press, 1977), pp. 31–33, 37–38. Citations and page num-

bers refer to this translation. German phrases derive from Hegel, *Phänomenologie des Geistes* (Hamburg: Meiner, 1952).

2. Ibid., pp. 16–19.

3. Ibid., pp. 9–10.

4. Ibid., p. 11.

5. Ibid., pp. 36–38.

6. Ibid., pp. 35–36, 41.

7. See, for example, M. H. Abrams, *Natural Supernaturalism* (New York: Norton, 1971), pp. 229–37.

8. See, for example, Søren Kierkegaard, *The Concept of Dread*, trans. Walter Lowrie (Princeton: Princeton University Press, 1957), pp. 10–12; and idem, *Concluding Unscientific Postscript*, trans. David F. Swenson and Walter Lowrie (Princeton: Princeton University Press, 1968), pp. 100–107. Also see Arthur Schopenhauer, *The World as Will and Representation*, trans. E.F.J. Payne (New York: Dover, 1966), I, 429, and II, 40.

9. Immanuel Kant, *Prolegomena to Any Future Metaphysics* (Indianapolis: Bobbs-Merrill, 1950), pp. 29–31, 39–41, 51.

10. Ibid., pp. 34–36.

11. Ibid., pp. 38–39.

12. Ibid., pp. 35–36, 39.

13. Ibid., p. 45.

14. Ibid., p. 90.

15. The "character" "consciousness" is also the most fully elaborated metaphor in the work. The reader of this chapter will not be able to avoid noticing that I qualify the term "consciousness" and its various forms (e.g., "self-consciousness") by means of quotation marks. Through the admittedly superficial expedient of quotation marks I intend to emphasize the metaphoricity of "consciousness," which is at once the *Phenomenology*'s central and widest category. It is at this point that my reading diverges from those which, like Jean Hyppolite's, regard the work primarily as a development or genealogy of "consciousness" through experience. See Jean Hyppolite, *Genesis and Structure of Hegel's "Phenomenology of Spirit,"* trans. Samuel Cherniak and John Heckman (Evanston: Northwestern University Press, 1974), pp. 11–15, 39–41.

16. For an elucidation of the problems attending the notion of iterability, see Jacques Derrida, "Signature Event Context," in *Glyph 1: Johns Hopkins Textual Studies* (Baltimore: Johns Hopkins University Press, 1977), pp. 172–97.

17. Dorrit Cohn elaborates the nature and operation of this narrative voice within the framework of literary works in her essay "The Narrated Monologue: Definition of a Fictional Style," *Comparative Literature*, 18 (1966), 97–112.

18. For example, Hegel, *Phenomenology*, p. 52: "thus the standard as such (and Science likewise if it were the criterion) is accepted as the *essence* or as the *in-itself*. But here, where Science has just begun to come on the scene, neither Science nor anything else has yet justified itself as the essence or the in-itself; and without something of the sort it seems that no examination can take place."

19. Ibid., p. 138: "For the surrender of one's own will is only from one aspect negative; in principle, however, or in itself, it is at the same time positive, viz. the positing of will as the will of an 'other,' and specifically of will, not as a particular, but as a universal will."

20. Ibid., p. 10: "But this *in-itself* is abstract universality, in which the nature of the divine life *to be for itself*, and so too the self-movement of the form, are altogether left out of account."

21. Ibid., p. 52: "This conceit [*Eitelkeit*] which understands how to belittle every truth, in order to turn back into itself and gloat over its own understanding, which

knows how to dissolve every thought and always find the same barren Ego instead of any content—this is a satisfaction which we must leave to itself, for it flees from the universal, and seeks only to be for itself."

22. See Jacques Derrida, *Speech and Phenomena*, trans. David B. Allison (Evanston: Northwestern University Press, 1973), p. 104.

23. For the place of the synecdochical relationship between the seed or germ and the living being within the ideology of the organic, see Philip C. Ritterbush, *The Art of Organic Forms* (Washington, D.C.: Smithsonian Institution Press, 1968), pp. 16–27. Drawing largely on Goethe, Keats, and Coleridge, Ritterbush synthesizes a model of the organic whose attributes include, in addition to the continuity between the whole and its parts: life, internal integration, evolution, and symmetry. Particularly in the attention paid by eighteenth- and early nineteenth-century scientists to symmetry, whether axial or in terms of repeating patterns such as the spiral, there is a rich analogy between the biological notion of the organic and the techniques of resolution and coordination within the Hegelian text.

24. The rhetorical correlative to this logical and epistemological reversal is chiasmus. For a discussion of the reversals effected by this trope in Rilke's poetry, see Paul de Man's introduction to Rainer Maria Rilke, *Oeuvres*, ed. Paul de Man (Paris: Seuil, 1972), pp. 22–26, 32–33, 36–38. Jacques Derrida characterizes the term and the crossings it effects in *La Dissémination* (Paris: Seuil, 1972), pp. 41, 52, 403. For another important treatment of chiasmus, as well as an excellent reading of the text, see Barbara Johnson's essay, "Melville's Fist: The Execution of *Billy Budd*," in her *The Critical Difference: Essays in the Contemporary Rhetoric of Reading* (Baltimore: Johns Hopkins University Press, 1980), pp. 79–109.

25. Hegel's hypothetical characterization of the thing of perception by means of its attributes and his description of the thing's disintegration follow and to an extent parody parallel passages in Plato's *Sophist*. The relevant Hegelian passages are to be found on pp. 96–100. The Platonic models for these passages are *Sophist* 245, 253b–e, 258e, and 259. See *Sophist*, trans. F. M. Cornford, in *The Collected Dialogues of Plato*, ed. Edith Hamilton and Huntington Cairns (Princeton: Princeton University Press, 1973), pp. 989, 998–99, 1005–6. I owe this observation to Horace Fairlamb.

26. For a discussion of the fundamentally linguistic constitution of both the Hegelian subjectivity and objectivity, see Josef Simon, *Das Problem der Sprache bei Hegel* (Stuttgart: W. Kohlhammer, 1966), pp. 11–47, 55–62, 66–84. Simon pays particular attention to the relationship between the narrative voice and Hegelian experience.

27. Another telling ambivalence in Hegel's relation to the tropes that he deploys in his account of philosophical language is to be witnessed in his attitude toward circularity. Hegelian uses of the circle will characterize writers from Hoffmann and Nietzsche to Kafka and Freud, yet even in the *Phenomenology* circles appear both as emblems of organic completion and as mechanical indications of a loss of subjective control. Two passages from the "Preface" should illustrate this ambivalence. In the first the circle emblematizes an *integral* generation of the truth within the philosophizing subject: "Only this *self-restoring* sameness, or this reflection in otherness within itself . . . is the True. It is the process of its own becoming, the circle that presupposes its end as its goal, having its end also as its beginning; and only by being worked out to its end, is it actual" (p. 10). This circle of self-evolution (or self-determination) is to be sharply distinguished from the circle of formalism and death: "This formalism . . . imagines that it has comprehended and expressed the nature and life of a form when it has endowed it with some determination of the schema as a predicate. . . . In this sort of circle of reciprocity one never learns what the thing itself is, nor what the one or the other is" (p. 29). This latter passage directs suspicion not only toward the

figure of the circle but also toward the reciprocity (*Gegenseitigkeit*) that is the basic mechanism of the Hegelian physics. For equally problematical references to circles, also see pp. 18, 20.

28. To describe the resolution effected by the curtain, we may say either that the episode culminates in an interior/exterior shift (in this case, to the interior) or, more skeptically, that the curtain conceals or disguises an abrupt termination at a dead end, that the curtain indicates a continuity where there has in fact been a definitive break in the narrative. The episode thus illustrates some of the possibilities open to Hegelian resolution in general. The most prevalent modes by means of which conflicts are resolved and narrative continuity is assured in the Hegelian text include the following: interior/exterior shifts, transcendence (disqualifying a prior stage *for the purpose* of reaching a higher one, a continuous movement), simple suppression (*dis*continuous abandonment of a prior stage in the absence of a resolution), and a mutual relinquishing of self-interest on the part of the two sides in a conflict, the becoming transparent of an opposition. For interiorization, see pp. 102–3, 126–27; for exteriorization, pp. 83–84, 107–9, 370, 383–84; for transcendence, pp. 260–61, 373, 380–82; for simple supersession, pp. 118–20; and for the cancellation of opposition, pp. 94–95, 111–12, 386–87.

29. For a discussion of the retrospective self-confirmation performed by the Hegelian text, see Andrzej Warminski, "Pre-positional By-play," in *Glyph 3: Johns Hopkins Textual Studies* (Baltimore: Johns Hopkins University Press, 1978), pp. 98–117.

30. In recent work, J. Hillis Miller has performed the invaluable task of adapting the arena of intersubjective relations to the dynamics of textuality. He does this by exploring the metaphoric specificity and rhetorical implications of linear imagery in certain exemplary novels. See J. Hillis Miller, "Ariadne's Thread: Repetition and the Narrative Line," *Critical Inquiry*, 3 (1966), 57–78; and idem, "A 'Buchstäbliches' Reading of *The Elective Affinities*," *Glyph 6: Textual Studies* (Baltimore: Johns Hopkins University Press, 1979), pp. 1–23.

31. The fullest placement of Hegel within the context and particular crystallizations of Western thought is Jacques Derrida's *Glas* (Paris: Galilée, 1974). With a mastery that he would only question in the Hegelian text, Derrida assembles the diverse components that Hegel synthesizes into a self-confirming and self-perpetuating speculative system. Derrida isolates and painstakingly combines the theological, ontological, anthropological, economic, and psychosexual elements of the matrix of Hegelian speculation. Derrida's combinatorial feat consists not only in the range of the elements that he isolates but also in the degree to which he provides "coverage" of the Hegelian corpus, including the often forgotten or neglected parts. The present essay, on the other hand, limits itself to a section of the *Phenomenology* that has received only too much commentary. It confines itself to the transition between the physical and the metaphysical domains of the Hegelian discourse, a necessary condition for the advanced crystallizations of theology, political organization, and art. The main part of the Derridean commentary presupposes this transition and arises at a moment when the formal tropes I discuss have already been rehearsed, repeated, and domesticated.

32. Shock is a rubric under which Walter Benjamin places many of the societal and intellectual effects of the industrial revolution and advanced capitalism. The techniques of industrialism are themselves defined by a problematic of repetition ("mechanical reproduction"). See Walter Benjamin, *Illuminations*, ed. Hannah Arendt (New York: Schocken Books, 1969), pp. 217–51.

33. Here one could draw a direct line from the images of music and Don Giovanni in Kierkegaard's *Either/Or* to the centrality of adultery in such a modern text as James Joyce's *Ulysses*. Kierkegaard's esthetic domain is characterized by an uncontained sexual

expenditure and an uncontrollable repetition that implicitly, if not explicitly, oppose the resolutions reached in the Hegelian evolution of stages. Organized around a discussion of adultery, parricide, fratricide, and homosexuality both in Shakespeare's plays and life, the "Scylla and Charybdis" episode of *Ulysses* focuses and elaborates the types of displacement and breakdowns of intentionality and causality that govern the rest of the novel. See Søren Kierkegaard, "The Immediate Stages of the Erotic," in *Either/Or* (Princeton: Princeton University Press, 1971), I, trans. Walter Lowrie, with revisions and foreword by Howard A. Johnson, pp. 43–134. Also see James Joyce, *Ulysses* (New York: Random House, 1961), pp. 184–216.

34. John Keats, *The Poems of John Keats,* ed. H. W. Garrod (London: Oxford University Press, 1966), p. 207, l. 16.

35. William Wordsworth, "Preface to the Second Edition . . . of 'Lyrical Ballads,'" in *The Poetical Works of William Wordsworth,* ed. E. de Selincourt (Oxford: Clarendon Press, 1944), IV, 387–88, 390–91, 393, 396–98.

36. Johann Wolfgang von Goethe, *Hamburger Ausgabe: Goethes Faust* (Hamburg: Christian Wegner, 1963).

37. William Butler Yeats, *The Collected Poems of W. B. Yeats* (1933; reprint ed., New York: Macmillan, 1966), pp. 129–30, 191–92, 211–12, 243–44.

38. Ibid., pp. 251–65.

39. William Butler Yeats, *A Vision* (1937, reprint ed., New York: Macmillan, 1965), pp. 67–104.

40. Yeats, *Collected Poems,* p. 184.

41. Marcel Proust, *A la recherche du temps perdu,* ed. Pierre Clarac and André Ferré, 3 vols. (Paris: Pléiade, 1954), III, 256, 259–60.

42. Walter Benjamin, "Franz Kafka," in *Illuminations,* p. 117.

43. Hegel, *Phenomenology,* pp. 267–94.

44. Sigmund Freud, "Repression" (1915), in *The Standard Edition of the Complete Psychological Works of Sigmund Freud,* ed. James Strachey and Anna Freud (London: Hogarth, 1953–74), XIV (1957), 147.

45. Sigmund Freud, "On the Mechanism of Paranoia," in "Psycho-analytical Notes on an Autobiographical Account of a Case of Paranoia (Dementia Paranoides)," *Standard Edition,* XII (1958), 66.

46. Ibid., pp. 60–61.

47. Sigmund Freud, *The Ego and the Id,* in the *Standard Edition,* XIX (1961), 25.

48. Sigmund Freud, *Beyond the Pleasure Principle,* in the *Standard Edition,* XVIII (1955), 7–64.

49. Ibid., p. 36.

50. Ibid., p. 27.

THREE

Søren Kierkegaard and the Allure of Paralysis

1. Especially given the poetic qualities that Kierkegaard's writings appropriated for philosophy, Harold Bloom's notion of poetic influence is relevant to this essay. The entire transition from Hegelian tropes to modernism traced by this book is close to the anxieties, resistances, and adaptations that take place in influence—with the primary exception that the play of sexual roles and postures along this course is more varied than Bloom's oedipal scenario for influence explicitly dramatizes. See Harold Bloom,

The Anxiety of Influence (London and New York: Oxford University Press, 1973), pp. 6–45.

2. The following abbreviations have been employed in referring to the editions of Kierkegaard's works cited in the essay:

E: Either/Or (Princeton: Princeton University Press, 1971), I, trans. David F. Swenson and Lillian Marvin Swenson (cited in the text as "the *Either*").

O: Either/Or (Princeton: Princeton University Press, 1971), II, trans. Walter Lowrie, with revisions and foreword by Howard A. Johnson (cited in the text as "the *Or*").

F&T: Fear and Trembling and The Sickness unto Death, trans. Walter Lowrie (Princeton: Princeton University Press, 1968).

R: Repetition: An Essay in Experimental Psychology, trans. Walter Lowrie (New York: Harper & Row, 1964).

CI: The Concept of Irony: With Constant Reference to Socrates, trans. with notes by Lee M. Capel (Bloomington: Indiana University Press, 1965).

Concluding Unscientific Postscript, trans. David F. Swenson and Walter Lowrie (Princeton: Princeton University Press, 1968).

3. For a groundbreaking exploration into the fictionality of the Kierkegaardian discourse, see Bertel Pederson's article, "Fictionality and Authority: A Point of View for Kierkegaard's Work as an Author," *MLN*, 89 (1974), 938–56. In addition to accounting for Kierkegaard's pseudonymity and the role of Menippean satire in his work, Pederson provides a rare glimpse into the wordplay permeating his language.

4. In his full-length study of fictive surrogation in Kierkegaard's writings, Mark C. Taylor bonds the pseudonymous authorship to "a basic vision of the nature of the self and what it means to attain authentic selfhood." According to Taylor, Kierkegaard's pseudonymy does not so much fragment the structure of the self as confirm it, even as it evolves in time. See Mark C. Taylor, *Kierkegaard's Pseudonymous Authorship* (Princeton: Princeton University Press, 1975), pp. 19, 23, 81–91, 108–26.

5. See "The Ethical World" and "Ethical Action" in G.W.F. Hegel, *Phenomenology of Spirit*, trans. A. V. Miller (Oxford: Oxford University Press, 1977), pp. 267–89. We will return to these passages in discussing Kierkegaard's appropriation of the figure of Antigone in the *Either*.

6. It is in this regard that Kierkegaard attains importance to contemporary critical theory, as a writer who inherited the speculative conventions of Romanticism but continually attempted to articulate their limits. In elaborating the countercurrents to the mainstream of Western thought, whether in the figure of Socratic irony or of Don Juan's music, Kierkegaard is quite close to Jacques Derrida's critiques of the logocentric imperatives dominant in the same tradition. Kierkegaard's emphasis on the linguistic figure as the basis and form of any substantive philosophical category, including reality, anticipates a parallel insistence in the work of Paul de Man. Derrida has pursued the tension between the ideational and deterministic mainstream of Western thought and what it excludes, to which he applies a number of terms, including "writing" (*écriture*) and "difference" (*différance*), in a wide variety of contexts from Plato to Heidegger. Yet the strategic affinity between the questions that he poses and Kierkegaard's undertaking may still be most evident in *Of Grammatology*, trans. Gayatri C. Spivak (Baltimore: Johns Hopkins University Press, 1976), pp. 17, 29, 34, 43, 56, 156–57, 226. For de Man's elaboration both of the decisiveness and of the inevitable distortion of figuration, see his "Shelley Disfigured," in *Deconstruction and Criticism* (New York: Seabury, 1979), pp. 61–69.

7. The theological mainstream of Kierkegaard criticism, exemplified by Walter Lowrie, insists on treating Kierkegaardian anxiety, dread, and even eroticism as almost

tangible spiritual states. Yet Kierkegaard qualifies these conditions, even in texts where he dramatizes the conflicts of faith, in terms of their implicit linguistic postures and activities. Thus, the presumably religious quandary in which Sarah, daughter of Raguel and Edna, and her suitors find themselves because Sarah's first seven husbands died in the bridal chamber is primarily an exploration into repetition and differentiation (*F&T*, pp. 111–15). Virtually all examples of the leap of faith cited in this section of *Fear and Trembling* ("Problem III") implicate problems of reading and interpretation. The story of Agnes and the merman suggests that if anything, the leap of faith and crisis of decision are subcategories of the narrative dynamics of seduction, not vice versa (*F&T*, pp. 103–9). For a characteristic assessment of Kierkegaard's importance in theological terms, see Walter Lowrie, *Kierkegaard* (New York: Harper & Brothers, 1962), I, 14–15, 232.

8. For a far more direct assessment of Hegel's influence on Kierkegaard than would be entertained by Harold Bloom's scenarios of anxiety and misreading, for a reading in which Kierkegaard *extends* rather than disfigures Hegelian thought, see Niels Thulstrup, *Kierkegaards Verhältnis zu Hegel* (Stuttgart: W. Kohlhammer, 1969).

9. For an excellent introduction to Kierkegaard, one itself shaped by the discursive qualities here attributed to the "Diapsalmata," see Sylviane Agacinski, *Aparté: Conception et morts de Sören Kierkegaard* (Paris: Aubier-Flammarion, 1977). In addition to her own Kierkegaardian asides, Agacinski contributes a fine discussion of Kierkegaardian irony suggestive of its varied identities and functions.

10. For a discussion of the solitude that Kierkegaard attributes to the esthetic mode, and regarding Kierkegaard's placement in a tradition of writers concerned with esthetic isolation, see Ralph Harper, *The Seventh Solitude* (Baltimore: Johns Hopkins University Press, 1967), pp. 19–30.

11. See Stéphane Mallarmé, "Un Coup de dés," *Oeuvres complètes* (Paris: Pléiade, 1961), pp. 457–77.

12. Marc Shell provides the most exhaustive current exploration into the economic correlatives to literary activities, including substitution and displacement. See Marc Shell, *The Economy of Literature* (Baltimore: Johns Hopkins University Press, 1978), pp. 5–10, 89–95. Kierkegaard's economic imagery is not limited to *Either/Or*. See *F&T*, pp. 22, 49, 51, 53, 95, 117.

13. A counterinstance of this ascription of eroticism to an inert deity would be the shocking discovery that one's beloved is of a different sexual identity than has been presupposed. This is the turning point in Balzac's story "Sarrasine," a text presented and meticulously explicated in Roland Barthes' *S/Z: An Essay*, trans. Richard Miller (New York: Hill and Wang, 1974).

14. Marcel Carné, dir., *Les Enfants du paradis* (1944–45), script by Jacques Prévert, with Pierre Brasseur, Jean-Louis Barrault, Marcel Herrand, and Arletty.

15. For Hermann Diem, the dialectical framework in Kierkegaard's works is a source of movement rather than stasis. Diem's application of the dialectical structures in Kierkegaard's work to a theological master plan retracts any development that might have taken place since Hegel. In Hegel, the machinery of dialectics, although ultimately in the service of a teleological scheme, is couched in terms of a neutral, formal rhetoric. Diem transforms Kierkegaard's play on dialectics into a direct religious allegory. See Hermann Diem, *Kierkegaard's Dialectic of Experience* (Edinburgh and London: Oliver and Boyd, 1959).

16. This parody of the Hegelian rhetoric and operations may well reach the height of its overtness in *Fear and Trembling*, where the narrator professes that he "has not understood the System" and that his discourse "is not the System." Both in this work

and in *The Sickness unto Death* at times the material is rigidly and hilariously molded to fit tripartite schemes of argumentation strongly reminiscent of the Hegelian discourse. See *F&T*, pp. 23–24, 100, 120, 146.

17. As we shall see, certain elements in this complex, specifically those related to reflection, hovering, the image, and infinity, emerge from speculative models whose operation within the history of philosophy is venerable if not archaic. Recent critics such as Philippe Lacoue-Labarthe, Jean-Luc Nancy, and Rodolphe Gasché have rendered the inestimable service of placing the economies of reflection and imaging within the general context of Romantic thought. If, in isolating the elements of irony, I temporarily reserve judgment as to their relative centrality or marginality to the Western metaphysical tradition, it is out of my own fascination with their interaction within an idiosyncratic and uneven machine. For discussions placing the types of subjective freedom, reflection, imaging, and hovering infinity in Kierkegaardian irony within their widest philosophical contexts, see Philippe Lacoue-Labarthe and Jean-Luc Nancy, *L'Absolu littéraire: Théorie de la littérature du romantisme allemand* (Paris: Seuil, 1978), and Rodolphe Gasché, "Deconstruction as Criticism," in *Glyph 6: Textual Studies* (Baltimore: Johns Hopkins University Press, 1979), pp. 177–215.

18. The point of departure for Theodor Adorno's reading of Kierkegaard is precisely the conjunction between a subjective interiority and the space of esthetics, and this despite Kierkegaard's insistence on an external setting for art. Adorno's discussion emphasizes the manner in which Kierkegaard continued time-honored philosophical distinctions between form and content, outside and inside, and subject and object. His discussion concerns itself more with establishing a philosophical context for Kierkegaard's writings than with demonstrating the philosopher's thrust in the direction of discursive limits. See Theodor W. Adorno, *Kierkegaard* (Frankfort: Suhrkamp, 1966), pp. 29–39, 51–57, 75–86.

19. See Hegel, *Phenomenology*, pp. 94, 99, 106–8.

20. I refer to the extreme importance attached to "spots of time" in Wordsworth's *Prelude*, book 13, ll. 208–25, as moments or scenes endowed with incalculable affective power. Hawthorne's novel comes at the end of this tradition. Published in 1860, it demonstrates the time that was required for European Romantic conventions to become registered in American fiction. No less than Wordsworth's "spots of time" is this novel concerned with the power of images of all sorts: paintings, statues, gardens, and even the city of Rome are subjected to the minute and reverential scrutiny reserved for images.

21. In this regard, I concur with Louis Mackey, who observes a pronounced predominance of the esthetic over the ethical throughout Kierkegaard's works, including the so-called "religious" writings. The esthetic and the ethical *agree* because they are both ironic. Mackey reads the *Concluding Unscientific Postscript* as an extension, rather than a repudiation, of esthetic excess. On this major point, Mackey thus takes issue with such interpreters as Walter Lowrie, who postulate a retreat into religiosity and moralism in the aftermath of Kierkegaard's abortive engagement. See Louis Mackey, *Kierkegaard: A Kind of Poet* (Philadelphia: University of Pennsylvania Press, 1971), pp. 137–38, 142–43, 149, 157.

22. Allan Stoekl provides an excellent discussion of the notion of heterogeneity in relation to Georges Bataille's works in "The Commander in the Text: The Theory and Novels of Georges Bataille" (Ph.D. diss., State University of New York at Buffalo, 1980).

23. Marcel Proust, *A la recherche du temps perdu,* ed. Pierre Clarac and André Ferré, 3 vols. (Paris: Pléiade, 1954), I, 43–48.

24. See Johann Wolfgang von Goethe, *Faust,* pt. 1, ll. 1649–1706.

25. Proust, *A la recherche du temps perdu*, I, 788–98, 894–95.

26. See Ferdinand de Saussure, *Course in General Linguistics,* trans. Wade Baskin (New York: McGraw Hill, 1966), pp. 12–20.

27. Cf. Dorrit Cohn, "The Narrated Monologue: Definition of a Fictional Style," *Comparative Literature,* 18 (1966), 97–112.

28. Within the field of modern physics, "complementarity" is the term for the reciprocal interaction between the scientific experiment and the observer that is reminiscent of the interplay between Kierkegaard's lovers. For a discussion of Kierkegaard's possible influence on Niels Bohr and modern physics, see Gerald Holton, *Thematic Origins of Scientific Thought* (Cambridge, Mass.: Harvard University Press, 1973), pp. 118–24, 144–47. I am indebted to James Bunn for this reference.

29. I think specifically of Joyce's *Ulysses,* Faulkner's *As I Lay Dying* and *The Sound and the Fury,* Woolf's *The Waves,* and Kafka's "Description of a Struggle."

30. The judge's vision of domesticity is reminiscent of Freud's selection of soap as "the yardstick of civilization." See Sigmund Freud, "Civilization and Its Discontents," in *The Standard Edition of the Complete Psychological Works of Sigmund Freud,* ed. James Strachey and Anna Freud (London: Hogarth, 1953–74), XXI (1961), 93–95.

31. It is precisely at this point that existential readings of Kierkegaard have tended to intervene. Walter Kaufmann defines the "heart of existentialism" as "the refusal to belong to any school of thought, the repudiation of the adequacy of any body of beliefs, and a moral dissatisfaction with traditional philosophy." William Barrett concurs with this implicit vision of Kierkegaard as a promulgator of iconoclastic and personal choice. For him, Kierkegaard belongs to the tradition of the "underground man," who was a "believing Christian" despite a "lifelong struggle against institutional Christendom." See Walter Kaufmann, *Existentialism from Dostoyevsky to Sartre* (Cleveland and New York: World, 1956) pp. 14–18; and William Barrett, *What Is Existentialism?* (New York: Grove, 1964), pp. 25, 42–47, 104–7.

32. These include Edmund Husserl's *The Phenomenology of Internal Time-Consciousness,* trans. James S. Churchill (Bloomington: Indiana University Press, 1964), and Martin Heidegger's *Being and Time,* trans. John Macquarrie and Edward Robinson (New York: Harper & Row, 1962).

33. For the term "doublethink," a fictional adaptation of the trope known as oxymoron, see George Orwell, *Nineteen Eighty-Four* (New York: Harcourt, Brace, and World, 1949), pp. 215–19. "*Doublethink* means the power of holding two contradictory beliefs in one's mind simultaneously, and accepting both of them" (p. 215).

34. As discussed in the preceding chapter, these include the perspectives of *in itself, for itself, for us,* the narrative voice of "immediate" transcription, and the omniscient narrative voice.

35. "Clatter, mill, clatter on and on . . . you clatter just for me" reflects Kafka's K. late in *The Castle* as he speaks with the bureaucrat Bürgel, continuing a movement begun in the *Either:* "They produce the same effect in life as the mill in the fairy story, about which it is said that whatever happened, the mill went klip klap, klip klap" (*E,* 233) (Franz Kafka, *The Castle,* trans. Willa Muir and Edwin Muir [New York: Schocken Books, 1974], p. 345). More significant than such a literal borrowing are the structures of reversal and interlocution that make Kafka's great story "Description of a Struggle" a veritable exercise in the ambiguities pervading *Repetition* and the "Diary."

36. The profound influence exerted by Kierkegaard over Ibsen has been amply documented in Theodore Jorgenson, *Henrik Ibsen* (Westport, Conn.: Greenwood Press, 1978), p. 127, and Halvdan Koht, *Life of Ibsen* (New York: Benjamin Blom, 1971), pp. 187, 230, 315.

FOUR

The Subject of the Nerves: Philosophy and Freud

1. All English citations of Freud refer to the *Standard Edition of the Complete Psychological Works of Sigmund Freud* (London: Hogarth Press, 1953–74). Both in my text and in the footnotes, I abbreviate *Standard Edition* as *S.E.* German terms, where I have supplied them, derive from *Sigmund Freud: Studienausgabe* (Frankfort: S. Fischer, 1969–75).

2. See Ferdinand de Saussure, *Course in General Linguistics,* trans. Wade Baskin (New York: McGraw Hill, 1966), pp. 120–22. For a highly suggestive discussion of the interaction between Freud and Saussure, see Jean-Michel Rey, *Parcours de Freud* (Paris: Galilée, 1974), pp. 57–110.

3. See Paul Roazen, *Freud and His Followers* (New York: Meridian, 1976), pp. 315–20.

4. For a fascinating account of this episode, see Samuel Rosenberg, *Why Freud Fainted* (Indianapolis: Bobbs-Merrill, 1978). Also see Ernest Jones, *The Life and Work of Sigmund Freud,* ed. Lionel Trilling and Steven Marcus (New York: Basic Books, 1961), pp. 206–7, 323.

5. See Roazen, *Freud and His Followers,* pp. 310, 322–23.

6. For a superb discussion of the Nietzschean convulsion, and the widest theoretical issues surrounding it, see Carol Jacobs, "The Stammering Text: The Fragmentary Studies Preliminary to The Birth of Tragedy," in *The Dissimulating Harmony* (Baltimore: Johns Hopkins University Press, 1978), pp. 1–22.

7. Walter Benjamin, "On Some Motifs in Baudelaire," in *Illuminations,* ed. Hannah Arendt (New York: Schocken Books, 1969), pp. 157, 159, 169, 176–77, 179, 185, 191.

8. See, for example, the passage from *The Interpretation of Dreams* where Freud describes "the dream's navel, the spot where it reaches down into the unknown. The dream-thoughts to which we are led by interpretation cannot, from the nature of things, have any definite endings; they are bound to branch out in every direction into the intricate network of our world of thought" (*S.E.,* V, 525).

9. See Jones, *Life and Work of Sigmund Freud,* pp. 145, 149–50, 155, 159, 167–68, 173, 175.

10. Here and throughout this chapter, I rely heavily on work on Freud that Samuel Weber has published in a variety of books and journals over the past decade. Weber may well be the most productive translator of the technical Freudian concerns and arguments into the decisive issues facing literary interpretation today. I refer here to his "The Divaricator: Remarks on Freud's 'Witz,'" in *Glyph 1: Johns Hopkins Textual Studies* (Baltimore: Johns Hopkins University Press, 1977), pp. 1–27.

11. See, for example, *S.E.,* II (1955), 87, 192, 229; IV (1958), 78, 142, 283, 287; V (1958), 483; VIII (1960), 121, 127; XII (1958), 70.

12. See *S.E.,* XVII (1955), 29–47.

13. In his writings, Jacques Lacan has done more than anyone else to survey the border between philosophy and psychoanalysis. The developmental and conceptual moment that he designates "the mirror stage" is an intricate study in Hegelian reciprocity. Lacan's tendency has been to sever psychoanalysis, with its imaginary and prerational domains, from Hegelian systematization. I am more prepared at this time to question the rigidity of this divide than Lacan's disfigurations and adaptations of Freud. The imaginary arises in Hegel in the form of an impaction of forces reaching no resolution without the intervention of Appearance. It returns in the excluded alterna-

tives for action that come to haunt Creon. The repudiation of Hegel is obviously a useful device on pedagogical and polemical grounds, and no one is less vulnerable to accusations of simplification than Lacan. For his attitude toward Hegel, see Jacques Lacan, *Écrits: A Selection*, trans. Alan Sheridan (New York: Norton, 1977), pp. 219–21, 254–55.

14. See, for example, *S.E.*, XVII, 105–6; XIX (1961), 14, 216–17.

15. See Franz Kafka, *The Trial*, trans. Willa Muir and Edwin Muir (New York: Schocken Books, 1968), pp. 168–79, 189–96.

16. Hoffmann's story "The Sandman" appears in *Tales of E.T.A. Hoffmann*, ed. and trans. Leonard J. Kent and Elizabeth C. Knight (Chicago: University of Chicago Press, 1969), pp. 93–125.

17. I refer to the momentous passage, located at the beginning of *Le Temps Retrouvé* in the Pléiade edition, where Gilberte Saint-Loup reveals the confluence of the Guermantes and Méséglise ways to "Marcel." See Marcel Proust, *Remembrance of Things Past*, vol. II, trans. C. K. Scott Moncrieff and Andreas Mayor (New York: Random House, 1930), pp. 864–66, or *A la recherche du temps perdu*, ed. Pierre Clarac and André Ferré, 3 vols. (Paris: Pléiade, 1954), III, 692–94.

18. Later in the work, Freud formulates this dualism quite explicitly: "I can therefore make the quite general assertion that *a hysterical symptom develops only where the fulfilments of two opposing wishes, arising each from a different psychical system, are able to converge in a single expression*" (*S.E.*, V, 569).

19. Here, largely at the suggestion of Weber's article on the *Witz*, "The Divaricator," I question the equations that Roman Jakobson makes between, on the one hand, displacement and metonomy and, on the other hand, condensation and synecdoche. The implicit metaphysical machinery of censorship is too pronounced to allow Freudian displacement merely to form and reform the contiguous bonds of metonymy. The Freudian *Mischwort* is so random in its combinations that it eludes the totalization of synecdoche. See Roman Jakobson and Morris Halle, *Fundamentals of Language* (The Hague: Mouton, 1956), pp. 76–82.

20. For a wider discussion of the notion of blockage as it both informs and is applied to Romantic literature, see Neil Hertz, "The Notion of Blockage in the Literature of the Sublime," in *Psychoanalysis and the Question of the Text: Selected Papers from the English Institute, 1976–77*, ed. Geoffrey H. Hartman (Baltimore: Johns Hopkins University Press, 1978), pp. 62–85.

21. Cf. Saussure, *Course in General Linguistics*, pp. 77–78, 113–17.

22. Not limited to a metaphysical role, the censor, or "critical agency," fulfills a mechanical function as well: "it stands like a screen (*Schirm*) between the latter [the agency criticized] and consciousness" (*S.E.*, V, 540). This is an instance of the manner in which the Freudian mechanics is at the service of a spiritual system.

23. See Saussure, *Course in General Linguistics*, pp. 13–17.

24. English citations refer to Johann Wolfgang von Goethe, *Faust*, Norton Critical Edition, trans. Walter Arndt (New York: Norton, 1976). German phrases derive from the *Hamburger Ausgabe: Goethes Faust* (Hamburg: Christian Wegner, 1963). The two editions correspond to one another in their line numeration.

25. I think especially of the passage entitled ". . . That Dangerous Supplement . . ." in Jacques Derrida, *Of Grammatology*, trans. Gayatri C. Spivak (Baltimore: Johns Hopkins University Press, 1976), pp. 141–64; also see pp. 6–26.

26. For a seminal discussion of the centrality of the figure of the sun both in classical metaphysics and in the conventions surrounding metaphor, see Jacques Derrida, "La Mythologie blanche: La Métaphore dans le texte philosophique," in *Marges de la philosophie* (Paris: Minuit, 1972), pp. 274–92, 298–99, 303–4, 311, 320–24.

27. See Goethe, *Faust,* pp. 53, 67–68 (ll. 2211–18, 2759–82).

28. I am not asserting that according to Freud children are immune from disease; merely that childhood, by virtue of its limited duration and its retrospective relation to adulthood, is an exemplary model for subjectivity.

29. One crucial element of Michel Foucault's account of the changing limits of knowledge from the Renaissance to modernity is his assertion that knowledge, during the "classical" period (roughly corresponding to the seventeenth and eighteenth centuries), could be tabulated, that is, represented on a continuous, all-encompassing table. See Michel Foucault, *The Order of Things* (New York: Random House, 1970), pp. 71–77, 145–65.

30. See *S.E.,* XVIII (1955), 57–61. This passage becomes a focal point in Samuel Weber's illuminating discussion and critique of the Platonic system of gendrification, which Freud draws upon and modifies in *Beyond the Pleasure Principle.* See Samuel Weber, *Freud Legende* (Olten and Fribourg, Switzerland: Walter-Verlag, 1979), pp. 179–211. This book is an excellent introduction to the interplay between Freud's writing and the agenda of contemporary critical theory.

31. See *S.E.,* XII, 68.

32. See George Wilhelm Friedrich Hegel, *Phenomenology of Spirit,* trans. A. V. Miller (Oxford: Oxford University Press, 1978), p. 97.

33. The popularity of the panther, which in Kafka's "Hunger Artist" deals fasting a *coup de grâce* as a spectator amusement, is described in terms very close to the Freudian attraction of narcissism. See "A Hunger Artist" in Franz Kafka, *The Complete Stories,* ed. Nahum N. Glatzer (New York: Schocken Books, 1976), p. 277.

34. See *S.E.,* VII (1953), 16–17.

35. For a post-Freudian instance of reciprocity, one assuming the form of mathematical inversion, see Harry Stack Sullivan, *The Interpersonal Theory of Psychiatry,* ed. Helen Swick Perry and Mary Ladd Gawel (New York: W. W. Norton, 1953), p. 35: "Now, it is a peculiarity of life that the level of euphoria and the level of tension are in reciprocal relation; that is, the level of euphoria varies inversely with the level of tension. And now I am going to make—partly, I suppose, for my own amusement—a frank and wholehearted reference to mathematics. This reciprocal relation may be expressed by saying that y is a function of x, and the relationship is $y = 1/x$."

36. See *S.E.,* III (1962), 169.

37. See *S.E.,* X (1955), 232, 236.

38. See *S.E.,* X, 233–34; XIV (1957), 76.

39. See *S.E.,* VII, 34, 54–55; XII, 65.

40. See Samuel Weber, "The Sideshow, or: Remarks on a Canny Moment," *MLN,* 88 (1973), 1102–33.

41. It is no accident that Stephen Dedalus's first narrated monologue in *Ulysses,* whose subjects number Lessing's *nebeneinander* and *nacheinander,* itself self-consciously elaborates its own spatio-temporal conditions (and those of the entire "interior" mode). As I have suggested elsewhere, among Kafka's many spatio-temporal experiments in *The Castle* is his gradual attenuation of all progress in the novel, to the point where its very possibility disappears (see Henry Sussman, *Franz Kafka: Geometrician of Metaphor* [Madison: Coda Press, 1979], pp. 113–19, 128–43). While remaining faithful to the more conventional novelistic scheme, in which the pace of events gradually accelerates, even such a text as Mann's *Magic Mountain* tests the spatio-temporal implications of isolation, withdrawal, and attenuation.

42. See Walter Benjamin, *Illuminations,* p. 186.

43. See Jorge Luis Borges, *Ficciones,* ed. Anthony Kerrigan (New York: Grove Press, 1962), pp. 17–20.

44. Ibid., p. 83.

45. Ibid., pp. 131–32.

46. See *S.E.*, XVIII, 53.

47. Samuel Weber details this revision with great specificity in *Freud Legende.*

FIVE

The Contours of Modernism

1. Carl E. Schorske, *Fin-de-Siècle Vienna: Politics and Culture* (New York: Random House, 1981), pp. xvii–xviii.

2. Fredric Jameson, *Fables of Aggression: Wyndham Lewis, the Modernist as Fascist* (Berkeley and Los Angeles: University of California Press, 1979), p. 2.

3. Hugh Kenner, *The Pound Era* (Berkeley and Los Angeles: University of California Press, 1971), p. 155.

4. Ibid., p. 42.

5. Ibid., pp. 99–100.

6. Ibid., p. 146.

7. Both Pound and Kenner were considerably influenced by the transposition from stasis and substantiality to dynamic process that Fenollosa ascribed to the Chinese ideogram. Interestingly, the grammar of the southern hemisphere of Jorge Luis Borges's counterworld of "Tlön" operates by Fenollosan principles. See Ernest Fenollosa, *The Chinese Written Character as a Medium for Poetry*, ed. Ezra Pound (San Francisco: City Lights Books, 1964). Also see Jorge Luis Borges, "Tlön, Uqbar, Orbis Tertius," in *Ficciones*, ed. Anthony Kerrigan (New York: Grove Press, 1962), p. 23.

8. For some major instances of this rhetoric, one so prevalent as to be hardly implicit, see Martin Heidegger, "The Origin of the Work of Art," in *Poetry, Language, Thought,* trans. Albert Hofstadter (New York: Harper and Row, 1971), pp. 42, 44–46, 55, 69–71.

9. Walter Benjamin, "The Image of Proust," in *Illuminations*, ed. Hannah Arendt (New York: Schocken Books, 1969), p. 201. For an excellent reading of this essay, as well as a groundbreaking application of critical theory to Benjamin, see Carol Jacobs, "Walter Benjamin: Image of Proust," in *The Dissimulating Harmony* (Baltimore: Johns Hopkins University Press, 1978), pp. 87–110.

10. Citations refer to Marcel Proust, *Remembrance of Things Past*, vol. I (1934), trans. C. K. Moncrieff, and vol. II (1930), trans. C. K. Scott Montcrieff and Andreas Mayor (New York: Random House).

11. Nothing can be more indicative of the existence of a homosexual genealogy in the novel than the fact that Charlus's grand passion is named Charlie. Charlus and Charlie, corresponding respectively to the forms of the nominative and genitive cases, begin a succession following the order of a Latin declension. The declension of homosexuality in the novel is the grammatical counterpart to the genealogical reproduction determined by the heterosexual domain.

12. No one has been more incisive with regard to the semiological implications of the tokens and expressions of love in Proust than Gilles Deleuze. See his *Proust and Signs,* trans. Richard Howard (New York: Braziller, 1972), p. 9: "Love's signs are not like the signs of worldliness: they are not empty signs, standing for thought and action. They are deceptive signs which can be addressed to us only by concealing what they express. . . . They do not excite a superficial, nervous excitation, but the suffering of a deeper exploration. The beloved's lies are the hieroglyphics of love."

13. Samuel Weber has exemplified the fluidity of the Proustian metaphor with passages from the *Recherche* (such as the one from I, 620, cited above) in which submarine imagery is prominent and where there is a confluence of liquid and solid, organic and inorganic, states. For his excellent discussion of this metaphoric condition in Proust, see "The Madrepore," *MLN*, 87 (1972), 915–61.

14. It is Gérard Genette who has most forcefully elucidated the process of superimposition in Proust's style and perspective. See "Proust Palimpseste," in his *Figures I* (Paris: Seuil, 1966), pp. 46–57. Another of Genette's major contributions to the Proust literature is his ingenious exposition of the manner in which metonymic substitution invades and dominates the Proustian metaphor. See "Métonymie chez Proust," in his *Figures III* (Paris: Seuil, 1972), pp. 50–61.

15. Paul de Man provides the broadest current overview of metaphor in the *Recherche* and its implications for reading. For de Man, the figure of Albertine combines both a suspicion and an elusiveness that inform textual process. See Paul de Man, *Allegories of Reading* (New Haven: Yale University Press, 1979), pp. 58, 71. De Man's formulation of Albertine's textual status runs as follows: "The resulting pathos is an anxiety . . . of ignorance, not an anxiety of reference—as becomes thematically in Proust's novel when reading is dramatized, in the relationship between Marcel and Albertine, not as an emotive reaction to what language does, but as an emotive reaction to the impossibility of knowing what it might be up to" (p. 19).

16. In a paper presented at a conference on "Models in Literary Criticism and Theory," sponsored by the Melodia Jones chair at the State University of New York at Buffalo in October 1979, Luzius Keller, of the University of Zurich, first made me aware of the connection between the architectural settings in Proust and the problematic of homosexuality. Work related to other aspects of Proust by Keller has recently appeared.

17. For Derrida's scenario of the marginal and suspicious supplement that infiltrates and usurps the place of the origin, see *Of Grammatology*, trans. Gayatri C. Spivak (Baltimore: Johns Hopkins University Press, 1976), pp. 61–63, 70–71, 156–57.

18. Citations refer to Henry James, *The Turn of the Screw*, ed. Robert Kimbrough, Norton Critical Edition (New York: Norton, 1966).

19. The first edition of Breuer and Freud's *Studies on Hysteria* appeared in 1895. *The Turn of the Screw* was published both whole and as a serial in England and the United States in 1898.

20. For a fine discussion of "reading in" as it is dramatized and examined by the story, see Walter Benn Michaels, "Writers Reading: James and Eliot," *MLN*, 91 (1976), 834–37. Michaels also elaborates the "political" implications of the various choices that the story imposes upon the reader.

21. By far the most comprehensive treatment of *The Turn of the Screw* and its ramifications in terms of psychoanalytical and critical theory to date is Shoshana Felman's "Turning the Screw of Interpretation," *Yale French Studies*, 55–56 (1977), 94–207. Felman anticipates many of the key concerns of my reading, including the application of Freudian theory to the story (Felman, pp. 103–11, 115–18) and the displacements within the narrative framework (p. 144). It is indicative of the critical controversy posed by the story that Felman and I would diverge at the point of placement. Having attempted to isolate a moment of irreparable stress in Hegel, I inscribe James's story back within a continuous Hegelian-Freudian tropological tradition. Felman finds in the text and its interpretations an occasion for delineating the systematic limits of precisely that tradition.

22. Cf. Henry James, *Daisy Miller*, in *The Bodley Head Henry James* (London: Bodley Head, 1972–), XI (1974), 45: "He [Winterbourne] had perhaps not definitely flattered

himself that he had made an ineffaceable impression upon her heart, but he was annoyed at hearing of a state of affairs so little in harmony with an image that had lately flitted in and out of his own meditations; the image of a very pretty girl looking out of an old Roman window and asking herself urgently when Mr Winterbourne would arrive."

23. It is in this regard that despite all superficial contrasts, the governess is a close relative of the frenetic subterranean rodent in Franz Kafka's story "The Burrow." For a close reading of this text, see Henry Sussman, "The All-Embracing Metaphor: Reflections on 'The Burrow,'" in *Franz Kafka: Geometrician of Metaphor* (Madison: Coda Press, 1979), pp. 147–81.

24. The works in question are *La Voix et le phénomène* (Paris: Presses Universitaires de France, 1967); *De la Grammatologie* (Paris: Minuit, 1967); and *L'Écriture et la différence* (Paris: Seuil, 1967).

INDEX

THE JOHNS HOPKINS UNIVERSITY PRESS

The Hegelian Aftermath

This book was composed in Baskerville text and display
type by the Composing Room of Michigan. It was printed
on S. D. Warren's 50-lb. Sebago Eggshell paper and bound
by Universal Lithographers.